ALL THE
WORDS
YOU'LL EVER
NEED

ALL THE
WORDS
YOU'LL EVER
NEED

A Comprehensive Christian Guide
to Writing Graceful Letters
and E-Mail

CrossAmerica
Books

CrossAmerica Books
Crossings Book Club, Garden City, New York

Contributors

INTRODUCTIONS
Julie Ackerman Link

LETTERS

Robyn Andraszczyk
Diane Bloem
Kate Convissor
Lorna Dobson
Dennis Hillman
Paul Hillman
Nathan Hillman

Rachel Hillman
Margaret Johnson
Julie Ackerman Link
Sue Ripley
Anne Severance
Gerard Terpstra

SIDEBARS

Myrel Allison
Fred Bauer
Ellyn Baumann
Gina Bridgman
Mary Lou Carney
Mary Jane Clark
B. J. Connor
Faye Field
Arthur Gordon
Rick Hamlin
Walter Harter
Marilyn Morgan Helleberg
Phyllis Hobe
Marjorie Holmes
Lisa Isenhower
William Jenks
Sam Justice
Kathie Kania
Carol Knapp

Carol Kuykendall
Aletha Jane Lindstrom
Patricia Lorenz
Bonnie Lukes
Linda Neukrug
Norman Vincent Peale
Ruth Stafford Peale
Faye Roberts
Vicki Schad
Daniel Schantz
Teresa Schantz
Penney Schwab
Linda Ching Sledge
Toni Sortor
Dolphus Weary
Marion Bond West
Bonnie Wheeler
Susan Williams
Isabel Champ Wolseley

CONTENTS

INTRODUCTION
Reasons for Writing **15**

1. *Keeping in Touch* **25**

Missing dear friend 27
Why I haven't written 27
Why haven't you written 29
Friend coming to town 29
Inviting friend to visit 30
Word of encouragement to
   daughter 32
Word of encouragement to son 34
To homesick daughter 34
Love letter to husband 35
Love letter to wife 35
Get well 35
Christmas letters 36
To pen pal 41
Appreciation for pen pal 42
Secret pal 42

2. *Letters to God* **45**

Gratitude 47
Praise 48
When I need to repent 49
When I lose my spouse 50
When I feel depressed 53
When I am lonely 54
When I am afraid 56
When I lose my job 56

3. *Announcements and
Congratulations* **57**

Announcing an engagement 58
Announcing a new baby 59
Announcing a new career 59
Announcing a new business 60
Announcing a divorce 61
Congratulations on graduation 62
Congratulations on engage-
   ment 62
Congratulations on wedding 62

Congratulations on eightieth
   birthday 64

4. *Thank You and
Appreciation* **65**

For companionship 67
For friendship 67
For birthday gift 68
For financial support 69
Thanks, but we're not inter-
   ested 70
For providing information 70
For giving advice 70
For recommendation 70
For dinner invitation 71
For recognition 71
For going away party 71
For loving care during illness 71
For job well done 72
For referral 72
For attending a meeting 72
For visiting our group 73
To a family 73
For an evening out 74
For an anonymous act of
   kindness 75
To favorite author 76
To spouse 77
WHEN A THANK YOU IS NOT
   RECEIVED **78**
Inquiring about gift not ac-
   knowledged 78

5. *Letters of Welcome* **79**

To new resident 80
To new neighbor 80
To church visitor 82
To new member 84

6. *Letters of
Encouragement* **85**

ENCOURAGING WORDS IN
   DIFFICULT TIMES **88**

When emotions are at the
  breaking point 88
When life doesn't make sense 89
When God seems distant 90
When a relationship ends 91
When making the grade
  seems impossible 91
**AFFIRMING WORDS IN GOOD
  TIMES** **92**
Taking on a new job 92
Moving into a new house 92
Bringing home a new baby 92
Finishing a job well 93
Meeting high expectations 94
Going the extra mile 94

7. *Letters of Blessing* **95**

How to do it 97
Baby's birth—record of deliv-
  ery 98
Baby's dedication or bap-
  tism—to parents 101
Baby's dedication or bap-
  tism—to child 101
Birthday letter to a two-year-
  old 102
Birthday letter to a ten-year-
  old 103
On entering adolescence 104
On graduation from high
  school 105
On engagement 106
On wedding day 106
On a holiday 108
Blessing to mother 109
Blessing to parents 111
Spiritual heritage—
  Grandfather to grandchild
  Why I became a Christian 113
To work through grief 114

8. *Letters of Invitation* **117**

Inviting a friend for dinner 119
Inviting a speaker to address
  your group 120
Inviting a friend to join a club 121

Inviting neighbors to a
  church dinner 122
Inviting employees to a bar-
  becue 122
Inviting the boss to dinner 124
Inviting college classmates
  to a reunion 124
Memo regarding business
  meeting 125
DECLINING AN INVITATION **125**
Close with encouragement 126
Philosophical differences 127
Scheduling conflicts 128
Will be out of town 128

**9. *Letters of Sympathy
  and Condolence*** **129**

Death of spouse 133
Death of relative 133
Death of child 133
Death of neighbor 134
Death of business associate 134
Condolence from a business
  firm 136
Death by suicide 136
Belated condolences 138
Sentences expressing sympa-
  thy 138
Thank you for sympathy 140
Sentences of gratitude for ex-
  pressions of sympathy 142
**SITUATIONS OTHER THAN
  DEATH** **142**
Marriage separation 143
Divorce 143
Personal reverses 143
Misfortune 144
Hospitalization 144
Illness 145
Birth defect 145
Unnamed tragedy 146
Sudden resignation 146

10. *Letters of Apology* **149**

Careless remark 151

Delayed thank you 152
Bad behavior 152
A written apology to follow a verbal one 152
Delayed return of borrowed item 154
Unable to attend 155
Delayed answer 156
Postponed dinner 156
Indiscretion 156
Incomplete project 158
Missed our date 158
Late report 158
Wrong information 159
Project failure 159

11. Dealing with Neighbors 161

Before sitting down to write ... 162
As you write ... 163
Thanks to conscientious pet owner 163
Request to careless pet owner 164
Commending parents for their honest child 164
Complaining about rowdy child 166
Noisy children in an apartment building 168
Snooping 168
Warning on a zoning violation 169
Requesting neighbors' cooperation 169
Asking a favor 170
Good fences and good neighbors 170
When leaves blow your way 171
Appreciating good neighbors 171
Thanks for help while hospitalized 172
Thanks for bringing dinner 172
Thanks for Christmas exhibit 172

12. Letters Expressing Anger 173

A problem with the Post Office 175
Poor package design 178
Delivery never made 178
Hurtful remarks 179
Incompetent repairman 179
Unsafe cab/bus driver 180
Discourteous bus driver 182
Unpleasant restaurant experience 182
Incompetent tour guide 183
Tired of working for those who won't 183
Corporate arm-twisting not appreciated 183
Inconsiderate retail clerk 184
Intentional overcharge 185
A sticky rebate problem 185
Seeking help from consumer action column 185
Letter to editor 186

13. Letters to Clergy 187

Notes on criticism 188
Notes on encouragement 189
Regarding titles 190
Disruptive children 191
Why so much old music? 192
Why so much new music? 192
Music appreciation 193
Let's not forget the older folks 194
Paying a compliment 195
Great job with youth 196
Need to hire additional staff member 196
Recommending candidate for youth pastor 197
Requesting participation at event 197
Assurance of prayer 198
Requesting help in handling church problem 198
Appreciation 200
Thanks for spiritual sensitivity 200
Appreciation to pastor's wife 201

Thanks for special assistance 201
Requesting advice 202
MATTERS OF BUSINESS **202**
From search committee 202
Letter of call 204
Welcome to our congregation 204

14. *Requesting Donations* 205

LETTERS TO ACCOMPANY DONA-
TION **208**
Thanks for good work 208
Offering to give time as well
  as money 209
Suggesting other ways to
  raise money 209
REASONS FOR NOT GIVING **209**
Budget limitation 209
Disagree with project 210
Annoyed by too-frequent re-
  quests 210
FUNDRAISING—LIBRARY **210**
Need for new books 210
Need volunteers 212
Need additional staff 212
Need additional equipment 213
FUNDRAISING—CHURCHES **213**
Campaign for specific project 213
Budget can be met 214
Delinquent pledge 216
Appeal to faith 216
Sponsor a kid who can't af-
  ford camp 217
Short-term mission trip 218
Missions project 220
FUNDRAISING—SCHOOLS **220**
Give more than last year 220
Funding for extracurricular
  activities 221
Library needs 221
Alumni association 222
Haven't given yet 222
Minorities program 223
Building fund 223
Student union building 224
Religious appeal 225

Financially disadvantaged
  student 225
Pledge not received 226
Personal letter requesting
  one-time donation 226
Thank you for bequest 227
Worthy project 227

15. *Letters about Children* 229

IN SCHOOL **231**
Requesting information
  about preschool 231
Checking on enrollment 231
Day care 232
Parent/teacher follow-up 232
Appreciation to teacher 234
Working out conflict be-
  tween child and teacher 234
Proposal to principal for af-
  ter-school club 235
Need to control rowdyism 235
To teacher about unwise han-
  dling of situation 236
To principal about teacher's
  unwise decision 236
To teacher about need to en-
  courage students 237
To principal about problems
  on buses 237
Field trip suggestion 238
Need for more supervision 238
Abusive patrol person 239
Concern about textbooks 239
Request for building improve-
  ments 242
Request for policy change 242
Need to update equipment 243
Request to use classroom 243
Notifying school bus driver
  of change 243
Notifying preschool of
  change 244
Requesting early dismissal 244
Absence due to illness 244
Absence due to injury 244

Advance notification of absence 245

Thanks for pointing out problem 245

Thanks for patience 245

Request for college information 246

Choosing another college 246

IN OTHER ACTIVITIES **248**

Appreciation for coach 248

Appreciation for sports coordinator 248

Incompetent coach 248

Incompetent umpires 249

Appreciation for Little League volunteer 249

Need to break down prejudice 249

Appreciation for scout leader 250

Too much pressure 250

16. *Making Requests* *251*

Requesting information, asking questions 254

Requesting additional information 255

Responding to a request for additional information 255

Response to inquiry 258

Procedural change 258

Time extension 259

Shorten deadline 260

Meeting deadline 260

Rescheduling order 262

Share experience 262

Business guidance 263

Permission to reprint article 263

Obtaining an interview 264

To speak 264

Getting speakers 265

Entertaining a friend 265

Alleviating fear, a request 266

Alleviating fear, a response 267

Board a relative 267

Job for a relative 268

Child care 268

Feed the cats 269

Watch the house 269

Closing a request with confidence 270

17. *Letters about Vacations* *271*

Invitation to bed and breakfast 273

Requesting general information 273

Offering to exchange houses 273

Requesting resort brochures and rate information 274

Requesting information from chamber of commerce 274

Inquiring about overseas accommodations 276

Confirming reservation 276

Thanking host for thoughtfulness 276

Thanking resort owner for service 278

Requesting information about national park 278

Requesting road maps from state tourism office 280

Checking on item lost in hotel—a follow-up letter 280

Requesting compensation for lost luggage 280

Lost luggage settlement unacceptable 281

Requesting compensation after being bumped from flight 281

Seeking refund from hotel 282

When illness forces a cancellation 282

Canceling flight and requesting refund 283

Telling friend of illness and canceling vacation plans 283

Complaint about tour package 283

Inquiry about tour operator 284

9

Requesting information
  about insurance 285
Requesting help from con-
  sumer action group 285
Complaint about unsanitary
  restroom 286

18. *Credit Matters*   *287*

Slow pay 289
Credit report 289
Cancel 289
Need more information 292
New in area 292
Lack of work record 292

19. *Letters of Complaint*   *295*

MAKING COMPLAINTS   **297**
Transit damage 297
Cost of purchases 298
Inadequate explanation 298
Messy area 299
Manufacturing error 299
Manufacturing problem 300
Billing error 300
Catalog order 302
Computer error 302
Misrepresentation 303
Parking in driveway 304
Meetings out of control 304
Newspaper not delivered 306
Delivery person 308
No stop light 308
ANSWERING COMPLAINTS   **309**
Accountability 309
Disturbed retail customer 310
Our mistake 310
Misunderstanding 312

20. *Special Situations*   *313*

CAR PROBLEMS   **317**
To manager of dealership 317
To manufacturer's district of-
  fice 317
Certified letter to officer at
  corporate headquarters 318

Requesting arbitration
  through Better Business Bu-
  reau 318
Premature rusting and ex-
  tended warranty 320
Certified letter to used car
  salesperson 320
Greedy dealer blows a sale 321
Reporting fraudulent sales
  tactics 321
A safety-related inquiry 322
Can design flaw be cor-
  rected? 322
Good job spoiled by greasy
  fingers 322
Service station complaint 323
Complaint to president of
  motor club 323
MEDICAL PROBLEMS   **324**
Request for insurance infor-
  mation 324
Request for more informa-
  tion on insurance form 324
Reminder that insurance
  form is long overdue 325
To doctor at home when all
  else fails 325
A way around that "pay
  now" sign 325
Why I'm changing doctors 326
Explanation of partial pay-
  ment 326
Complaints and compliments 326
Complaint about rude nurse 327
Compliments to hospital staff 327
Thanks to surgeon 327
Gratitude to staff of rehabili-
  tation center 328
Thanks to nursing home 328
Refusing to pay bills 328
Complaint about bad doctor
  to state licensing agency 329
MOVING TO A NEW AREA,
  HOUSE, OR APARTMENT   **329**
Requesting information prior
  to move 329

Missing item claim after
  move 330
Damage claim 330
Inconvenience or delay claim 330
Seeking clarification of bill-
  ing dispute 331
Dealing with unethical mover 331
See you in court 332
Status report to regulatory
  agency 332
Engaging real estate agent 332
Thanks to real estate agent 333
Notifying utility company of
  move 333
Notifying garbage collector
  of move 333
School records and transfers 334
APARTMENT LIVING (from land-
  lord) **334**
Please pay rent on time 334
APARTMENT LIVING (from ten-
  ant) **334**
Getting back security deposit 334
Need an exterminator 335
Trying to get things fixed 335
Noisy tenants 335
Noisy dog 336
Emergency in rented house 336
A way out of a lease 336
HOME OWNERSHIP **337**
Prodding a slow contractor
  into action 337
Delays and poor workman-
  ship 337
No more money until job is
  done right 338
Pickets will get a builder's at-
  tention 338
CONDOMINIUM LIVING **338**
Working with the board 338
Clarification of rules and
  regulations 339
Monthly maintenance fee
  must be paid 339
Payment will be delayed 339
INSURANCE COMPANIES **340**

New car 340
Finding out options for
  changes in policy 340
Furnishing agent with claim
  information 340
Substantiating a claim with
  photographic evidence 341
Inquiry to company request-
  ing statement 341
Name change notification 341
Requesting payment on life
  insurance policy 342
Changing beneficiary 342
Notification to company of in-
  tent to cash in policy 342
Requesting change of agent 342
When more than one insurer
  pays on a claim 343
Appealing nonrenewal notice 343
Asking insurance commis-
  sion to help speed up settle-
  ment 344
Threatening suit if liability
  denied 344
Requesting arbitration from
  state 344
Will cancel if not treated
  fairly 345
MISCELLANEOUS **345**
Requesting deposit refund
  from store manager 345
Never got my rebate check 346
Asking newpaper's con-
  sumer column for help 346
Canceling door-to-door sales
  contract 346
Home demonstration fiasco 347
Poor landscaping job 347
Protesting high utility rates 348
Dissatisfied with carpet-
  cleaning firm 348
Billing error on bank charge 348
Dealing with Medicare 349
Charge account error 349
Refusal to send payment on
  disputed invoice 349

Package never delivered—
    delete charge   350

21. *The Caring Citizen*   *351*

GOVERNMENT   **354**
Contacting House committee
    on pending bill   354
An appeal to U.S. senator to
    change a law   355
Protesting fund cutbacks to
    state representative   355
Complaint to mayor of neigh-
    boring city   356
Proposing new ordinance for
    village   356
Alerting city hall to danger-
    ous street conditions   358
Complaint to alderman clear-
    ing tree damage   358
Requesting absentee ballot   358
Asking U.S. representative
    for help   360
Asking U.S. senator for help
    in securing a job   360
Requesting U.S. senator's in-
    tervention with VA   360
Requesting scholarship infor-
    mation from state senator   361
Requesting home re-ap-
    praisal   361
Assessed value of home is
    too high   362
Social Security—notice of re-
    tirement   362
Requesting education aid
    from the Veterans Admini-
    stration   362
Requesting deferral from
    jury duty   363
POLICE AND FIRE DEPARTMENTS **363**
Requesting a stop sign   363
Offering to be a crossing
    guard   364
Request a crossing guard for
    busy corner   365

When help doesn't come in
    time   366
Thanks to paramedics   366
Officer was great   367
Officer was rude   367
My side of the story   368
Anonymous tip   369
Identifying suspect by name   369
Witnessed hit-and-run acci-
    dent   369
RADIO, TELEVISION, NEWSPA-
PER   **370**
Thanks for good music   370
Suggestion for talk show
    guest   370
When your favorite DJ gets
    fired   371
Criticism of listener-sup-
    ported station   371
TV soap opera is in poor
    taste   371
Protesting poor taste in TV
    show   372
Criticizing children's TV pro-
    gram   372
Complimenting children's TV
    program   373
Request for rebuttal time   373
To the sponsoring advertiser 374
TV commercial compliment   374
TV commercial complaint   374
Reporting fraudulent adver-
    tising tactics   375

22. *Letters of Employment*   **377**

LETTERS OF RECOMMENDATION **379**
How to give one   379
How to get one   380
Character references   381
APPLYING FOR A JOB   **382**
Cover letter for a résumé   382
Applying after being relo-
    cated   382
Applying after being out of
    work   382
Answering ad for a teacher   384

Answering ad for a computer
    programmer   384
Answering ad for a buyer
    trainee   385
Cold call application for a
    secretary   385
Cold call application for a re-
    tail manager   385
Cover letters for job applica-
    tions   386
Interested in job suggested
    by a present employee   386
Accepting offer to be inter-
    viewed   386
Thank you for recommenda-
    tion   388
Thank you for interview   388
Accepting job offer   388
Rejecting job offer   389
Resignation   389
GETTING A BETTER JOB   **389**
Cover letter accompanying
    résumé   389
Letter of application for
    sales position   390
Homemaker's return to job
    market   390
Follow-up letter to employer   390
Follow-up letter to inter-
    viewer   391
Using network of fraternity
    brothers   391
Using network of profes-
    sional associates   392
Using network of industry
    colleagues   392
Using network of former
    classmates   394
Special situations   394
Thanks for help getting a job   395
Congratulations on promo-
    tion   395
Congratulations on retire-
    ment   395
LETTERS WRITTEN BY
EMPLOYERS   **396**

Requesting data from refer-
    ences   396
Requesting data from appli-
    cants   396
Tentatively accepting appli-
    cant   396
Invitation to interview   397
Rejecting tentatively ac-
    cepted applicant   397
Rejecting applicant who re-
    sponded to newspaper ad   397
Rejecting applicant, position
    filled   397
Rejecting unqualified appli-
    cant   398
Accepting applicant   398
Welcome to new employee   398
Preparation of performance
    evaluation   400
Job performance review   400
Recommendation for promo-
    tion   401
Congratulations on promo-
    tion   401
Notice of promotion   401
Reprimand   402
Termination warning   402
Termination   402
Accepting resignation   403
Notice of employee leaving   403
Retirement congratulations   403
LETTERS WRITTEN BY
A THIRD PARTY   **404**
Recommending an applicant   404
Rejecting an applicant recom-
    mended by a third party   404
Acknowledging a recommen-
    dation   404

Appendix
The Nuts and Bolts of
Writing and Sending
Letters   *405*
THE FORM OF LETTERS   **405**
Formal letters   405

Punctuation, salutation, and
  closing   407
Informal letters   410
FORMS OF ADDRESS   **410**
ENVELOPES   **416**
State abbreviations   417
Zip codes   417
Postage   419

Index   *421*

Introduction

Reasons for Writing

**An envelope is one of the few things in the modern world
we seal, thus creating a private space for expression.**
—Thomas Moore

**A letter always feels to me like immortality because it is
the mind alone without a corporeal friend.**
—Emily Dickinson

What causes the pleasure you feel when you see your name and
address written by hand on an envelope, or when the name of a
friend appears in your E-mail inbox? What is it about personal letters
and E-mail that sets them apart from other forms of communication?
And why do they have such universal appeal?

Once you understand what it is that makes you enjoy receiving letters and E-mail, you'll have a better idea of why it's important to write
them. Here are some of them.

A letter says you are special. "Letters take time to write, usually more time than talk. They require a certain level of artfulness and thoughtfulness in expression. They remain, to be reread, perhaps to be stored away for another day of reading," wrote Thomas Moore in his book *SoulMates.* Like everyone else, you like to know that other people are thinking about you. A letter or an E-mail is evidence not only that someone had you in mind but also that you were important enough to merit the time it took to pick out a card, write a letter, or compose an E-mail.

A letter invites you to see inside someone else's life. Human beings love getting a glimpse into other people's private lives. That's why novels, movies, and soap operas are popular. They all provide an illusion of intimacy. By watching them you don't really get to know anyone, but you're made to feel as if you do. Letters and E-mail, on the other hand, are the real thing. They allow you to get to know real people, and to grow closer to the people you care about the most. The type of things people write about reveals a great deal about them.

A letter gives you a record of your life and thoughts. When you write a letter or an E-mail, you have something to show for your time. You can even print-out an E-mail and save it with your nonelectronic correspondence. Writing letters gives you tangible proof that you've accomplished something.

Whether you are writing to a friend, a family member, yourself, or to God, keep a copy or a rough draft of your letter in a special notebook or in a blank book, or store it in a special file on your computer.

A letter enables you to say what needs to be said. Even when you know in general what needs to be said, it is still difficult to find "just the right words" to say. A letter or E-mail, because you can write more than one draft, allows you the luxury of "trying out" different words until you find just the right ones. Whether what needs to be said are words of encouragement, apology, explanation, or sympathy, a letter is an effective forum. "Much unhappiness has come into the world because of bewilderment and things left unsaid," wrote Fyodor Dostoevsky. Rather than leaving important things unsaid because you're not sure how to say them, write down the possibilities until you are happy with the result.

We often assume that letters and E-mail are only useful for keeping in touch with people who are far away, just a substitute for conversation, a way to let people know what we're doing. But letters, and especially E-mail, are also useful for keeping in touch with people who live in the same house. In fact, when we write a letter to a spouse, child, or parent we create a space where honesty and objectivity can grow and mature.

One of the more famous cases of such communication, where letters sustained and nourished an intense but often difficult relationship, was that of British leader Winston Churchill and his wife, Clementine. Throughout their fifty-six-year marriage, they wrote letters to each other daily, sometimes more than once a day. Their letters, which survived and were collected by their daughter, show clearly that letter writing was their private time away from the decisions of war or the pressures of public life. Their correspondence was at the heart of their marriage, whether they were together or apart.

It's not only the letter itself that has value; the act of letter writing also has many benefits. Here are a few . . .

Letter writing gives you time to contemplate your thoughts, feelings, and attitudes. Thomas Moore wrote that "letters offer the opportunity to express our feelings, especially when the soul is undergoing a particularly disturbing attack." Through our letters we find out what we believe and value.

Letter writing helps you think clearly. "Precision of communication is important, more important than ever, in our era of hair-trigger balances, when a false or misunderstood word may create as much disaster as a sudden thoughtless act," wrote James Thurber. You are more likely to say what you mean when you write than when you speak because you can reread and revise a letter or E-mail until you get it just right. Through our letters we make our thoughts and ideas concrete.

Letter writing encourages self-disclosure, which prompts self-

discovery. Stan Mooneyham, former president of World Vision, wrote, "No person, I think, can come to know himself truly except through the process of disclosing himself to others." Through our letters we reveal ourselves and by so doing we find out who we are.

Considering all these benefits, it's sad that letter writing has diminished in popularity. Writing E-mail, however, has done much to restore letter writing to the prominence it once had in people's lives. The only significant difference is the material you use. With E-mail, your thoughts can flow faster because you can see them in front of you on the computer screen, and it's harder to put off keeping in touch when you don't have to buy stationery.

Sometimes people think letters have to be more formal than E-mail, and this keeps them from putting pen to paper. They have trouble writing down things they find they can express easily on the screen. It's not that one medium is more formal than the other, but that some letters need to be more formal than others, and those tend to be the ones it's more important to send by mail rather than electronically. While you wouldn't make requests to a government official or send a card of sympathy via E-mail, writing to friends and family is no different when writing E-mail than when writing a letter. You can be as formal or as chatty with the recipient of your E-mail as you are when you're face to face. This is as true with interoffice E-mail as it is with E-mail between friends and family. You should decide what's appropriate based on your relationship with the recipient of your letter, not based on which medium you're using.

There are, however, two kinds of letters that you should be careful with when you're sending them as E-mail. They are requests for charitable donations and letters of complaint.

One E-mail can be sent to many recipients at once. Even when written with the best intentions, fundraising letters can quickly become spam. Your intended readers may delete solicitations like that before they even open them, in the same way they might throw away junk mail unread. The best approach is still to individually write each person you are soliciting.

INTRODUCTION

Because words flow more freely when they're typed into a computer than when they're written by hand, letters of complaint can take a mean turn in an E-mail's first draft. And because it's so easy to hit "send," before you know what's happened you may have sent someone hurtful words you never intended them to see. It's easy to vent in an E-mail, and it's healthy to get down what you feel so you can get it out of your system. Sending your harsh, unedited feelings is another matter entirely. The best course to follow may be to wait a day before you send an E-mail of complaint. Wait twenty-four hours and read it again. Then decide whether you should send it.

Technological innovations like E-mail are taking us back to a time when a letter was the best way to communicate over long distances. In recent years letters have continued to be the least expensive way to communicate, but for many years they were the only way to get in touch with others. The difference is that today a letter can be written, sent, and received instantaneously.

For several decades phone calls replaced letters as the communication medium of choice. Although they were more expensive than sending a letter, the immediacy they offered made the additional cost inconsequential to most people. But immediacy is no longer an issue. A letter sent via the Internet reaches its destination within seconds and waits in the receiver's inbox until it's picked up. And unlike a call on a cellular phone, its arrival never bothers anyone in a church or a movie theater.

The advantage of this type of communication is especially apparent when communicating with someone in another time zone or overseas. No more figuring out what time it is there before you make a call. No more waiting until you think the person you'd like to call might be home or awake.

These developments are contributing to a revival of letter writing. It's now easier, more efficient, and more economical to sit down at your computer, type a letter, and send it electronically than it is to make a phone call. When your friends, loved ones, or colleagues are overseas, using E-mail instead of the phone can save you money by allowing you to keep in touch without the financial burden of long-distance phone calls.

With so many different ways to write letters today, letter writing is more convenient than ever. But sometimes it's still hard to know exactly what to say or how to say it. We've all had the feeling when sitting down to write a letter or E-mail of not quite knowing where to begin. *All the Words You'll Ever Need* will answer that question for any type of letter you can imagine.

A Symbol of Love

Toni Sortor

Therefore I write these things being absent. . . .

— 2 CORINTHIANS 13:10 KJV

NOBODY writes letters anymore. Sure, it's nice to get a phone call, but it's not the same. Five minutes after you hang up, it's gone and forgotten. You can't reread a phone call to be sure you didn't miss something written between the lines or to relish the turn of a phrase. There's no commitment in a phone call, either—Americans call perfect strangers every day, but they write only to people they really care for. At least they used to.

People are afraid to write. Their spelling's not good, their handwriting's a scrawl. Yet all over America, other people are riffling through the day's mail, hoping for just one letter amid the junk and bills, one sign that another human is willing to invest a half hour in them, even if there is no news to tell. A world without letters is a shallow, uncaring, lonely world.

Aunt Jessie doesn't care about my spelling. She cares very much about me. My father-in-law hates to read, unless it's about his grandchildren. We're all willing to invest in one another, to proudly sign our names right under the word *love*. If you're willing to do that, believe me, no one will ever notice or care about your spelling!

Father, help me find time today to write to one person I care about.

ALL THE WORDS YOU'LL EVER NEED

1
Keeping in Touch

I keep my friends as misers do their treasure, because, of all things granted us by wisdom, none is greater or better than friendship. **PIETRO ARETINO**

A companion loves some agreeable qualities which a man may possess, but a friend loves the man himself. **JAMES BOSWELL**

A friend loves at all times, and a brother is born for adversity . . . but there is a friend who sticks closer than a brother. **PROVERBS 17:17; 18:24** NIV

*G*ood intentions are among the few things that most people have in abundance. What they never seem to have enough of, however, is the ability to convert those good intentions into good deeds.

This may be especially true of your good intentions to keep in touch with the people you love. Miles (to say nothing of the years) separate you from many of them. But there was a time when you were close, when you agonized together over lost loves, when you laughed your-selves sick at some silly joke or prank, when you encouraged one another in moments of sadness, and when you gave courage to one another in moments of weakness. You would do the same today if you were close. But ask yourself this: Why do you let distance disrupt your friendships? It's not as if you're living in the era of the Pony Express. Letters sent across the country can arrive the next day. E-mail sent around the world can arrive the next minute. What excuse is there for failing to keep in touch?

None. At least none that is good enough.

The one you may fall back on is "too busy; not enough time."

But of course you manage to find time to shop even when there is nothing you need to buy, watch the news even though there's seldom anything new to find out, and read magazines even though this month's issue is hardly any different from last month's. What your mother used to say is indeed true: "You find time to do what you want to do."

Does that mean you don't want to write, don't want to keep in touch?

Not necessarily. It may simply mean that you consider letter writing more work than pleasure.

So then the challenge is this: How can you put enjoyment into your letter writing? Here are some suggestions.

Make letters personal. Instead of simply recounting what you've been doing, also include what you've been thinking and feeling. This not only helps you keep in touch with your friends, it helps you keep in touch with yourself as well.

Tell more by saying less. In other words, choose one event and tell it like a story. If you pretend you are sitting across the table from a friend telling about your latest crisis or success, revelation or stupid mistake, your letters will be more interesting. It is often better to give all the pertinent details about one event than to simply list many events. Think of it this way: Would you rather read a list or a story?

Make letter writing an adventure. If you let your letters lead you, you may be pleasantly surprised to find out where you end up. Start with one idea and write until you've exhausted your thoughts on the subject.

Keep it simple. One of the biggest hindrances to frequent and good letter writing is the feeling that you need to do all your catching up in one letter. Short and frequent is better than long and infrequent.

So for those of you who have good intentions that far outweigh your good deeds, we offer this sample of "Keeping in Touch" letters. Notes like these can be written in a few minutes, but they'll be remembered for a long time. And they'll help you start a good habit—one that you won't have to worry about trying to break.

Missing dear friend

Dear Chris,

So many little thoughts, sights, or sounds trigger memories of our many years of friendship. Just the other day I used a recipe you gave me long ago and I recalled our meal together and the honest conversations we often shared. I miss you, dear friend, and regret that our busy lives and the distance between us keep us from sharing more time. Let's get together as often as possible—by letter if not in person—and nurture the special gift of our friendship.

Affectionately,

Why I haven't written

Dear Arlene,

You must be wondering why you haven't heard from me for so long. Let me assure you that the lack of written letters is no indication of the absence of loving thoughts or a lack of concern for you.

Busyness is my honest but unacceptable excuse for not writing to you more often. This may seem to you to suggest that maintaining our friendship is not high on my priority list but this is not true. The truth is that a quick note is never satisfying when I have so much to share

Why I Haven't Written

Gina Bridgeman

I have not stopped giving thanks for you, remembering you in my prayers.
— EPHESIANS 1:16 NIV

WHEN my brother and his family went to San Diego for a week's vacation, I took care of their poodle D'artagnian. When they returned, my five-year-old niece Meredith came with her mother to pick up their dog.

Meredith was so happy to see Dart, and Dart was ecstatic. He danced on his hind legs, wagged his tail, and reached for her with his front paws as if to give her a hug.

"Did you miss Dart while you were gone?" I asked.

"Oh, yes," Meredith said. "But as soon as we got to San Diego, I forgot all about him!"

I laughed at her honesty, but as I thought about it later, I asked myself: Are there people in my life I've forgotten about simply because I don't see them often? I immediately thought about my good college friends. We shared many great joys and sorrows, yet now that we live in different cities and are busy with our lives, we've lost touch.

Right away I made a list of their names and promised myself to write each a short note, just to say I was thinking about them.

Are there people in your life who need to know you haven't forgotten them? Would hearing from you brighten their day? Why not send them a short "hello" today?

Father, remind me to keep in touch with those I love, especially when we cannot be together.

with you. So, I promise myself a large block of time for writing a heart-to-heart epistle and the days go by one after the other and none allows me that large block of time. Now I have become more realistic and have resolved to write brief notes more often so that we will not lose contact. I am beginning today by writing about just two things that I am working on at this time . . .

Affectionately,

Why haven't you written

Dear Norma,

You must have some very good reason for being unable to write to me for such a long time. I know that our relationship is as important to you as it is to me so I am concerned that something is troubling you.

Could it be that a misunderstanding has come between us? Are you waiting for me to write to you? Is there some problem in your life that I am unaware of and could help you with? You are important to me so I want to hear from you. Please write to me soon—even a brief note will be welcome. In the meantime I will continue to pray for you, asking the Lord to meet all your needs.

Sincerely,

Friend coming to town

Dear Thelma,

Good news! Connie will be in town for two weeks this month. She has told me that one of her wishes is to meet with you and me and as many of our high school group as we can manage to pull together. Don't you agree that it would be great fun for us all to meet and hear about her recent travels and to share pictures and news of our families and careers?

I hope you are free sometime in those two weeks and are willing to help me plan this get-together. We need to set a date, find a place, and contact the others. I'm looking forward to seeing you and Connie and the others to rejuvenate our friendships. Please call me within the next few days.

Sincerely,

Inviting friend to visit

Dear Shirley,

Your friendship is dear to me. I often wish that we could spend more time together but the days and weeks go by so quickly and we don't seem to find time. It seems to me that the only way we are going to

Welcome to My Heart

Marion Bond West

Nevertheless let every one of you in particular so love his wife. . . .
— EPHESIANS 5:33 KJV

WHEN my husband became interim minister of a church, we'd only been married two years. On our first Sunday in Perry, Oklahoma, the woman seated next to me showed me how to fill out an attendance card. I wasn't accustomed to doing this, but I did as she instructed. Then I forgot about the incident. Until Tuesday, that is. On that day I received a letter from the pastor, my husband, Gene. At the bottom of the form letter, in his familiar handwriting, he'd scribbled, "Hey there. You need to attend our church more regularly. I'm so glad to look out and see you. God loves you and so do I, sweetheart."

What a creative way to remind me of his love! I immediately mailed a card to him at his office and addressed it, "To My Pastor." I also accomplish this is to schedule an appointment. This may seem like a formal approach, but we know it is just realistic and practical.

So I invite you to come for a light supper and an evening of conversation on June 6. Are you able to be here by seven o'clock? Please let me know as soon as possible. If this plan does not work for you, please offer an alternative and I will do my best to make my plans mesh with yours.

Just writing this to you makes our prospective visit seem like a real possibility. I am looking forward to it already!

Sincerely,

scribbled a note: "I sure like your preaching. Could you come for Sunday dinner—fried chicken. Sister Marion."

The next Sunday another woman sitting by me insisted that I fill out an attendance card, and I did so without hesitation. Sure enough, my letter from the pastor came on Tuesday. He'd written: "What an encouragement you are! Let me take you out to dinner Sunday. My, but I love you!" I almost did somersaults right in the post office. His note took less than five minutes to write and had cost only cents to mail, but it made me feel like a million dollars.

So whether married a few months or a half century, write your wife or husband a little note, even if there's no special occasion. It'll make your spouse feel like one in a million!

Father God, encourage spouses to risk feeling vulnerable and put their feelings of affection on paper. And help the recipient to respond to such declarations of love with your creativity and joy. Amen.

We seldom write letters to people we see every day or talk to regularly by phone. However, when we have something particularly difficult or important to say, a letter may be the best way to do it. A letter gives us time to think about our words, choose them carefully, and express them clearly yet gently. First, list clearly what you want to say, then set it on paper. It isn't that difficult. Write as if you were speaking. Use words and phrases that are common to you. If you do this, the person reading the letter will be able to hear you speaking as he or she reads. Letters of this type can strengthen a relationship because they speak from one heart to another. They also become heirlooms that are treasured for generations.

Word of encouragement to daughter

Dear Melissa,

    Sometimes I see a tired look in your eyes and my heart aches for you. I know the high goals you have set for yourself and I know some of the disappointments that have left you discouraged and drained.

    Most children want to please their parents and make them proud of them. As your mother, I want you to know that I am proud of the way you cope with adversity and that I admire your idealism. I know from experience, however, that we are human beings with limitations. I am often comforted by Psalm 103:13–14, which tells us that God, our Father, has compassion on us and remembers and understands our human weaknesses.

    If God evaluates our lives with such kindness and understanding, we should extend these same graces to ourselves and others. I encourage you to allow yourself to rest, to trust God's love and strength to carry you through each day, and to believe that God has great and wonderful joys prepared for you. God does this for me and I know he will for you as well. As always, I hold you up before him in loving, confident prayer.

Love,

A Symbol of Love

Rick Hamlin

He sent his word, and healed them. . . . — PSALM 107:20 KJV

CAROL put her typewriter back in its case. "I guess we should give it to the church to sell at the bazaar," she suggested.

"I guess so," I said wistfully. The venerable portable had been replaced by a speedy word processor. We hated to see it go. Not only had Carol used it to type term papers, short stories, articles, and recipes, she had used it to write me innumerable letters.

There was a time, before we were married, when Carol and I lived two thousand miles apart. We wrote newsy letters and chatty notes in which we sometimes philosophized about life. We kept in touch, at first occasionally, then once a week, and then in a torrent of several letters a week. Neither of us could afford many long distance telephone calls or frequent transcontinental flights. We fell in love through the mail.

Now we're husband and wife, living under one roof, joined by the bond of marriage. In a way, that typewriter symbolizes the beginning of our union, which makes it hard to see it go. But as I think about what has taken its place—daily face-to-face communication—I have to smile. I thank God for the power of words. They brought us together, and with his help they are also keeping us together.

O Word made flesh, help me transform my words into deeds worthy of your glory.

Word of encouragement to son

Dear Kevin,

I am so proud of you! Are you surprised? I hope you know that I see how devoted you are as a husband and father—how concerned you are to provide the best experiences and opportunities and material blessings for your family. I admire your resolve to offer loving, Christian leadership in your home.

And yet I am touched by the stress you experience as the pressures of your business demand so much of your time and energy. I can't solve these conflicts for you, but I can assure you that not only I, your mother, appreciate your efforts, but your Heavenly Father reads your heart and will bless you as you faithfully work for your family and invest yourself in them. I always pray for you.

Love,

To homesick daughter

Dear Lisa,

Where is home these days? I know it seems as if home is far away and you miss us as we miss you. Yet just as I look around and see evidences of your life all around us, I encourage you to look through your things and see evidences of us and of your home. Look at your clothes and remember the shopping experiences we shared. Look at our pictures and remember how we always love you and pray for you. Arrange your area in as cozy a way as possible with little mementos of home in visible places. Eat a favorite homelike food. These things will help you discover that you didn't leave home behind—you took part of it with you! No one can ever take home out of your heart.

I encourage you to go a step farther as you try to cope with pangs of homesickness. Look around for some way to help or cheer someone else. If you look up to God and out to others, you will find comfort for your inner aches.

We continue to support you with our love and prayers. Keep in contact with us, and know that each day will be better than the last.

Love,

Love letter to husband

Dear Robert,

Sometimes I pause and just wonder at God's goodness and his great plan for our lives. I think how I grew up not knowing you and you grew up not knowing me. We wondered if God had someone planned for us. Who would that person be?

And then, on that magical day your life touched mine and God ignited the spark of love that has warmed us and comforted and energized us ever since that day.

I am so thankful for each growing experience we have shared and I look forward to each moment with you.

Your loving wife,

Love letter to wife

Dear Diane,

You have made my life interesting and exciting. I cannot imagine how lonely I would be without you. I thank God that he has blessed our resolve to bring out the best in each other. I know you bring out the best in me and I want to spend the rest of my life caring for you and encouraging you.

I love you. I appreciate you. I pray for you.

Your loving husband,

Get well

Although the abundance of get-well cards on the market today has pretty much eliminated the need for get-well letters, there are times when signing your name to a card doesn't quite seem like enough. You'd like to write a note inside the card but you aren't quite sure what to say. You want it to be meaningful but not preachy. You can do this in just a few sentences. Think of something positive to say and follow it with a few words of hope and encouragement.

Dear Donna,

    We are happy to hear that your surgery went well and that you are starting to recover. It is our hope and prayer that your strength will increase each day. Though you are weak now and face many challenges, we are confident that God will be with you and will heal you with his love.

                                       Sincerely,

Dear Harry,

    We can't visit you in person today so we are sending you this note to tell you that we are praying for your complete recovery. Knowing how you love to work, we have a small idea of the patience it must take for you to rest and lie still while healing takes place. In addition to our regular prayers for you, we hope to help your recovery by sending you interesting articles or ideas to think about once a week for the next six weeks. We look forward to visiting you in person when you have more strength for conversation.

                                       Sincerely,

Christmas letters

People either love them or hate them. They either criticize them for being too impersonal or too phony or they commend them for being interesting and newsy. What is this item that causes such conflicting opinions? Just a simple Christmas letter.

    It is hard to say why there is such diverse opinion about something as innocent and well-intended as a family Christmas letter, but perhaps we can learn a few tricks to counter the criticism.Here are a few guidelines to follow.

Be truthful. *The temptation when writing a Christmas letter is to try to make your family sound perfect. This is where the "too phony" criticism comes from. A Christmas letter is not the place to dwell on downers, but it's not the place to deny them either. Being honest about struggles and difficulties bonds people because struggles and difficulties are what all of us have in common. Making a good impression is not as important as making an honest attempt to connect emotionally and spiritually with the people we love and care about.*

Use humor when you can. *You may want to write about one funny incident that happened in your family or you may just want to let your sense of humor weave in and out of the entire letter. You can be lighthearted without sounding silly or frivolous.*

Write things that you want to remember. *This is the surest way to guarantee that your letters will be interesting. It's also the surest way to guarantee that your letters will be treasured by family members who will want to keep them as part of their family biography.*

Feel free to experiment with different formats. *The most common format for a Christmas letter is to highlight the accomplishments of each person in the family. Another kind of format would be to highlight different types of events. For example: the most humorous event; the saddest event; the happiest event; the most significant spiritual event; the event that taught us the most.*

Christmas letters are a wonderful way of keeping in touch with distant friends and relatives, and they can also be a place to store valuable pieces of our family histories. Let's not let a few grumblers rob us of the pleasure.

Dear Friends,

What is it about Christmas that prompts us to want to make contact with people we care about? It has to be love. Christmas is more about love than Valentine's Day is. We think about family and friends because they are the fabric of life that supports us and gives us encouragement.

We remember the good times we shared as neighbors and how you were always there when we needed you. We appreciate all those precious memories. Now as we share just a few of the events of our lives

In Praise of Christmas Letters

Marjorie Holmes

May the God of hope fill you with all joy and peace as you trust in him,
so that you may overflow with hope by the power of the Holy Spirit.

— ROMANS 15:13 NIV

ADVENTURES in living—that's what Christmas letters are all about. Most of them are joyful. I can't remember ever reading one that was filled with self-pity, doleful doings or complaints. Not because we're being brave, or just reluctant to admit our failures, pain, and problems, but because at this season such things somehow dwindle in significance, lose their sting. Even the times when we must include important news such as divorce or a death in the family, these are related in terms of tenderness, faith, and hope for the bright new year.

No, at Christmas it isn't the burdens we long to express; it's the glow within us, the bounties and blessings. The achievements, the pleasures. And if some people are offended by reading of other people's happiness, in what they may consider "brag sheets," I'm not. I applaud. They are not meant to make me envious or affronted; they are paying me the compliment of believing that their news will be welcome. And as a friend I will rejoice.

But quite apart from other people's reactions to your Christmas letter, the truth is, you're not writing them for other people, you are writing them for yourself. You are harvesting these memories for the sheer joy of hugging them to your heart again, fixing them in time, setting them down. And if you keep them, they will be a rich harvest of memories for your family as well. Your Christmas letters can become their history. One-sided, yes, leaving out most of the troubles, but important in their statement that no matter what else may have happened during those difficult years, our life together was good.

I realized this recently when, in a box of old files, I found copies of some of our Christmas letters, many of them written long ago. Fascinated, I sat on the floor, reading all afternoon.

The year I was rushed to the hospital the week before Christmas to deliver our baby girl (described in loving detail): "We brought her home on Christmas Eve. The kids had helped their dad trim an enormous tree in the window; its colored lights were shining on the snow. Everybody gathered around, eyes sparkling, as we unwrapped the precious bundle (her eyes were sparkling too, we're sure). But I'm afraid the boys were just as excited over the TV set Santa had brought early (our first) as they were over their new baby sister. . . ."

Again: "Mark, 13, is busting his buttons. His picture made the Washington *Evening Star* with his 100-pound marlin, the biggest caught so far this year. . . ."

Paper routes and Scouting, dancing lessons, cheerleading, the year Mickie was prom queen, the graduations from high school or college. Moves, promotions, trips, remodeling a house, the thrill of a book or story sold.

On and on I read—events large or small, things I'd almost forgotten and which at the time probably meant little to anybody else. But oh, how important they were to us!

Many of those letters are missing. How I wish I had saved them all. But there are enough to gather together, every one I can find, and bind into booklets for my children. To refresh their memories, to read and laugh about and cherish, perhaps to pass along.

That first Christmas, while the heavenly chorus sang, the angel proclaimed the birth of Jesus, saying, "I bring you good tidings of great joy, which shall be to all people!" Our Christmas letters are our hearts' carols proclaiming, "Joy to the world! We've made it through another year, and life is good!"

Sure this is a beautiful thing.

After Christmas Letters

Sam Justice

Love is patient, love is kind. It does not envy, it does not boast, it is not proud. It is not rude, it is not self-seeking, it is not easily angered. . . .
— 1 CORINTHIANS 13:4–5 NIV

IN Christmases past I often found myself embarrassed by late-arriving Christmas cards. Sometimes they came from old friends with whom I had lost contact, or sometimes from new friends who decided they wanted to send a special greeting. These late arrivals always upset me because I didn't have time to reciprocate before Christmas.

Last year my wife, Ginny, saw my reaction and asked, "Why get upset? This isn't a contest, you know. Just send them a Happy New Year card."

"Hey, that's not bad!" I exclaimed. When the bustle of Christmas passed, I wrote nice, leisurely notes. I followed up some of the cards with phone calls to make them even more personal, and I recall the warm chats that resulted.

This year, instead of being annoyed, I was grateful for those stray cards. They reminded me of why we exchange Christmas cards in the first place—as a way to remember special people and to share our friendship and happiness over Christ's birth.

Maybe you'd like to join me in renewing forgotten or neglected friendships. I'm writing a few notes this month. Is there someone whose new year would be brightened by hearing from you?

Lord, keep me from being concerned that the goodness of others may make me look bad and concentrate instead on doing good myself.

this past year, we hope you will also share with us so that we can keep our friendship alive and strong.

May God's gift of love and salvation be yours and give you hope and peace for the coming year.

Sincerely,

Dear Friends,

Your friendship and the memories we share are gifts we treasure at Christmas. Because of this we hope to hear how your family is faring and how your work is progressing.

We want to tell you that we have appreciated God's goodness to us in the past year as he provided a job for Kelly who graduated in June. Kristin is fifteen and looking forward to having a driver's license. Kurt has baseball on the brain most of the time.

We, the parents, are trying to keep up with a world invaded by computers. Susan has some ongoing health problems that we would like you to pray about. Please ask God to heal her and provide work she can do as she recovers.

As we thank God for the gift of the Christ Child, we also thank him for his love shown to us by providing friends like you. We pray you may experience his love and guidance as you look forward to the new year.

Sincerely,

To pen pal

Everyone benefits when people try to view the world from more than their own limited perspective, and a good way to do this is by corresponding with someone in another part of the world. Many people want very much to learn English and would love to write to someone in the English-speaking world so they can practice the language. Also, people often reveal more about themselves in letters than in everyday conversation, so a pen pal may become one of your best friends.

Dear Hans,

As I read the newspapers and wonder about the changes and struggles in our world today, I am thankful to have you for a pen pal so that I can get your perspective on current events. I always appreciate your candidness as you comment on the impact of American culture and economics on your daily life. We can learn much from one another about the long-range effects of seemingly small decisions.

Please share with me your thoughts about the violence you see in American movies and hear about in the news. Do you perceive the United States as a violent nation? I would like to assure you that it is not. Our daily lives are mostly concerned with family and work and church. . . .

Sincerely,

Appreciation for pen pal

Dear Katie,

As our families grow up and the children become independent, I reflect on how much I look forward to your letters. We have been corresponding for many years now and I appreciate your thoughts and suggestions as we have discussed various changes going on in our world. It always helps me to take the time to visit with you on paper because as I write, I examine my thoughts and get a better understanding of myself as I communicate with you.

I hope you too have experienced this bonus of our friendship.

Sincerely,

Secret pal

Dear Millie,

I am your secret pal for this year and while my identity must be kept secret for now, what isn't a secret is that I appreciate the way you use your gift of listening to comfort many people.

Perhaps you think this is a silent gift and therefore not very valuable, but I know that it has lifted the spirits of many people who have learned that you care about their joys and sorrows.

Secret Angels

Marilyn Morgan Helleberg

"Do not let your left hand know what your right hand is doing, so that your giving may be in secret."   — MATTHEW 6:3 NIV

WHEN our son, Paul, was critically injured in a car accident, I received a card that read: "You don't know me, but I just want to tell you that someone who cares is praying for Paul every day." It was signed, "A friend in Jesus." After Paul was home from the hospital, another card came: "I was reading Romans 8 today, and verses 18, 28, and 31 seemed to be meant just for you." When our son was fully recovered, a third card came, with only five words on it: "Praise God for answered prayer!"

I'll probably never know who sent those cards, but of this I'm sure: It was a person of humility who wanted to give comfort and didn't care about receiving credit for it. Since then, I've kept a packet of cards handy, and when I'm moved to pray for someone, I follow the example of my anonymous "friend in Jesus." I know that those prayers are specially blessed, because part of the blessing spills on me.

How about letting an anonymous card carry your message of loving concern? Send it on the wings of prayer, and it will bless two—the one prayed for and you.

Lord, let me be content today to let you get the credit for any good that I may do.

Next month I plan to tell you of another gift you have that I appreciate, so stay tuned! And watch for surprises!

Your secret friend,

2

Letters to God

Today any successful and competent businessman will employ the latest and best-tested methods in production, distribution, and administration, and many are discovering that one of the greatest of all efficiency methods is prayer power.   **NORMAN VINCENT PEALE**

Do not pray for easy lives. Pray to be stronger men.
                                                        JOHN F. KENNEDY

*G*od put a lot of time and energy into writing a letter to us, so it seems reasonable to assume that he would enjoy receiving letters from us. In fact, the best example we have of someone who wrote letters to God is David, the Old Testament Jewish king, and God called him "a man after my own heart" (Acts 13:22 NIV). Many of the Psalms are David's letters to God. For example: Psalm 17, a plea for vindication; 38, a plea for relief; 51, a plea for mercy; 70, a plea for help; 86, a plea for assurance; and 103–106, 111–113, prayers of praise.

David was not shy about telling God exactly what was on his mind: "I *cry aloud to the LORD; I lift up my voice to the LORD for mercy. I pour out my complaint before him; before him I tell my trouble" (Psalm 142:1–2 NIV). According to this verse, four things characterized David's letters to God.*

Boldness. *David didn't whisper or whimper; he cried aloud. He did not try to appease God with pious-sounding phrases; he simply told God what was wrong and made bold suggestions as to what God might want to do about it.*

Humility. *David knew that some of his problems were of his own making, and he took full responsibility. At such times he pleaded for mercy rather than justice.*

Fearlessness. *David wasn't afraid to complain because he knew the right way to do it and he had the right reason for doing it. His complaints were not useless grumbling. He didn't just tell God how bad off he was; he invited God to tell him how he could make things better.*

Forthrightness. *David didn't go around telling his problems to anyone who would listen; he told God. And he didn't go whining to his friends about the injustices of the world; he went directly to God, and "before him" he told his troubles.*

Putting your prayers on paper as letters to God will quickly reveal whether you are following this healthy pattern of prayer or some unhealthy one, such as telling God what you want him to do but never asking him what he wants you to do.

Politicians are notorious for saying what they want people to hear regardless of what question they have been asked. Election years are filled with frustration because voters want to yell into their television sets, "Just answer the question!" But the candidates seldom do. Despite the pleas of their constituents, they continue to expound on what they want voters to know rather than on what voters want and need to know.

Sometimes when people pray they become like politicians. They pay no attention to what God is asking them. Prayer for them is a speech to inform God of their desires, plans, and needs. Using all their persuasive skills and human logic, they try to sell God their ideas of what needs to be done to make the world (at least their piece of it) a better place.

But that is not the purpose of prayer. The purpose of prayer is to tune your heart to God's perfect pitch. To do that, of course, you must first listen—listen to what God has in his heart.

When we do so we may find out that God has been as frustrated with us as we are with our legislators. While we rattle off our list of requests and complaints, and try to impress him with our plans and strategies, he's quietly trying to ask one question. "Do you love me?"

Prayers of gratitude, praise, and repentance are always appropriate. And they don't require any special skill or know-how. They are simple expressions from your heart to God's. "Be joyful always; pray continually; give thanks in all circumstances, for this is God's will for you in Christ Jesus" (1 Thessalonians 5:16–18 NIV).

Gratitude

Dear Father God,

You have told us in your Word that we are to enter your presence with praise and thanksgiving. I come now, gladly acknowledging your sovereignty, your majesty, your awesome omnipotence. But I am equally aware that you are a God of love and grace, of mercy and peace. And I bask in the warmth of our friendship.

Today I have no agenda but to worship you and to thank you for who you are and what you have already done for me. It is enough that you sent your Son to die in my place. It is enough to know that you—mighty God—are also my loving and forgiving Father.

Devotedly,

Praise

Dear Father,

"I will praise you, O Lord, with all my heart; I will sing praise to your name, O Most High . . . . My lips will shout for joy when I sing praise to you—I will praise you as long as I live, and in your name I will lift up my hands" (Psalm 9:1–2; 71:23; 63:4 NIV).

King David knew how to praise you, Lord. Sometimes I, too, feel like singing, shouting, lifting my hands—telling you in body language how

Prayer Letters

Myrel Allison

In the same way, the Spirit helps us in our weakness. We do not know what we ought to pray for, but the Spirit himself intercedes for us. . . .
— ROMANS 8:26 NIV

JOAN and I were sitting on the glider on her screened-in porch. Both of us had been going through painful times. She was suffering in the aftermath of a child's death, and I was torn up by the dissolution of a thirty-five-year marriage.

I'd been talking about the ups and downs of faith, how sometimes when you need God most, you feel most distant from him. "Lately, I can't seem to concentrate on my prayers," I confessed. "I'm too scared and sorry for myself. I get caught up in feelings of unworthiness!"

A few minutes later Joan excused herself to get iced tea for us. She came back with two tall glasses and a piece of paper with some closely written lines on it.

much I adore you. At other times, stunned by the wonder of your majesty, I am simply still, knowing that you alone are God.

Whether exulting in your presence or awed to silence, I worship you, my Lord and my God.

With all my heart,

When I need to repent

Dear Lord,

I've blown it already, and it isn't even noon! That ugly comment I

"Maybe you'll think I'm silly when you read this," she said, handing the sheet to me, "but I just started writing . . . and so much came out!"

"Dear God," I read, "Things have been so unbearable in my life lately that sometimes I wonder if I'll ever feel like laughing again. . . ."

What had begun as a letter of hurt and complaint to God ended as a beautiful prose-poem praising him.

"You have no idea how helpful writing that letter has been to me," she told me.

"Yes, I think I do," I replied. "And I think I know why you showed it to me."

Sure enough, when I began writing to God my feeling of intimacy with him was strengthened.

Now as I read my notebooks filled with prayer-letters to God, I can see how I've grown and how the Lord has been working in my life. Writing to him helps me pull my thoughts together and keeps my mind from wandering.

Prayer letters. They're a literal way to worship God!

made to my husband when he criticized the eggs. The little tidbit of gossip I passed on in a telephone conversation with a friend. My reluctance to act on a nudge from your Spirit to say a word about you to the mailman.

But I'm so glad you've given me a way back from failure. I found it in 1 John 1:9. It says that if I confess my sins you are faithful and just and will forgive my sins and purify me from all unrighteousness.

I am sorry, Lord, and I accept your gracious offer of forgiveness. Thanks for the clean slate.

Gratefully,

When I lose my spouse

Times of grief and sadness pull our hearts toward God as we look to him for comfort and relief. Sometimes our thoughts and feelings become so jumbled that we seem like strangers to ourselves. We cannot make sense out of anything that is happening, and we are even caught off guard by the way we are responding to it. Talking to other people helps some, but they're not always around. But God is, and he's always ready to listen. And to take prayer one step further—to keep a written copy of our prayers—is to hold in our hands proof that we have indeed placed ourselves and our circumstances in God's hands. Whenever we put into words our fears and frustrations, we move them from our consciousness into God's. As we do this time and time again, their power over us decreases and God's power in us increases.

O my dear God,

There has never been a pain so blinding, so breathtaking. Never a loss like this. My companion. My lover. My best friend. The empty years yawn before me like a great dark chasm. All the memories of our life together flood my senses and send me reeling. If I could only lie down beside him and sleep forever. . . .

But even now—even in my numbness—I can feel your loving arms around me. In answer to my unspoken prayer, you have sent the Com-

My Thank-you Note to God

Bonnie Wheeler

Be joyful always; pray continually; give thanks in all circumstances, for
this is God's will for you in Christ Jesus. — 1 THESSALONIANS 5:16–18 NIV

I'VE been doing battle all month with a very large kidney stone, and
so far, it is winning. I have had discomfort, pain, and numerous
uncomfortable medical tests. The first week that I managed to work
an eight-hour day, I had to go back into the hospital.

In my daily devotions, I'm reading Paul's admonition to rejoice and
give thanks. I'm definitely not rejoicing over my current situation, and
my depression deepens. As I reread the verses, I notice "Give thanks
in all circumstances."

"How can I start giving thanks in all circumstances?" I ask myself.
Then I decide to make a list of all the things I have to be thankful for.

I'm thankful for the speed my doctors used to save my kidney. For
my friend Pat, who drove me to the out-of-town hospital and stayed
with me all day. For family, friends, and coworkers who prayed for
me. For my husband, Dennis, who has done all the extra work without
complaining.

Suddenly I see that I have almost filled up a page, and most impor-
tantly, my attitude has changed.

If your situation seems bleak, try a thanks list. You may be surprised!

Lord, I'm so grateful for your patience in showing me that no
matter what situation I find myself in, you are there. Therefore I
can give thanks and rejoice.

forter, the One who will grieve with me, the One who knows how it feels to be human.

And it helps to know that the one I love is seeing you at last, face to face. He always said he'd like to spend the first hundred years of eternity asking all the questions he'd never found answers for. Then he wanted to meet Moses and Abraham and the other greats. After that, he had a "bone to pick" with Adam.

Teach me to live again, Lord. Then take me home so we can both enjoy you forever.

Until then,

The Best Thing to Be Is Me

Carol Knapp

Only, let every one lead the life which the Lord has assigned to him, and in which God has called him. — 1 CORINTHIANS 7:17 RSV

NEAR our home is a quiet lake where a beaver family has built a lodge on a secluded cove. I can lean over from my canoe and scoop into my hand freshly peeled sticks floating in the water. God has created a fascinating design for these shy, industrious creatures. Behind a beaver's large front teeth are two flaps of skin that close, enabling it to gnaw wood and carry branches while swimming and yet not swallow splinters or take in water. Its transparent eyelids close underwater, allowing unobstructed vision while keeping debris away from sensitive eyes.

A familiar display I delight in watching is tail-slapping. The beaver, signaling others of potential danger, lifts its wide flat tail and smacks it

When I feel depressed

Dear Lord,

Is this your correct address? Are you still there? I haven't heard from you in so long that I was wondering if you had taken a leave of absence or a lengthy vacation. I wouldn't blame you. Why should you—Lightbearer and Lifegiver—take the time to communicate with someone who sees only darkness and dead ends? Lately the only kind of party I've known how to give is a pity party!

But when I picked up my Bible this morning (for the first time in months, I must admit), your message came through: "Don't worry about anything, but pray about everything. With thankful hearts offer

down hard on the water, making a sharp cracking sound. Then it dives for safety beneath a flurry of spray.

As the beaver paddles toward shore, I ponder nature's precisely laid pattern. Each animal is at home in its own setting. The beaver doesn't frustrate itself trying to fly like an eagle or scramble over peaks like a mountain goat. It doesn't strain to develop the strength of a bear or grow the coat of a musk ox. A beaver's instinct says, "Be a beaver."

There are some things I will never be: a soloist (even my "Amen" is flat); an artist (a salesman thought I had young children after glancing at my clumsy holiday drawings taped in the window); a skydiver (my hands go clammy at the top of a ladder). So I will applaud those who possess abilities I do not have, and proceed to do the things I can. My instinct tells me, "Be yourself!"

Father God, who formed us after your likeness, thank you for the unique expression that is myself.

up your prayers and requests to God. Then, because you belong to Christ Jesus, God will bless you with peace that no one can completely understand. And this peace will control the way you think and feel" (Philippians 4:6–7 CEV).

I understand now, Lord. Your letter, addressed to me, has been right here all along! I just hadn't picked up my mail.

Thankfully yours,

When I am lonely

Dear Friend Jesus,

What would I do without you? Still, you must get tired of hearing my

Practicing the Power of Prayer

Carol Knapp

And you show that you are a letter from Christ delivered by us, written not with ink but with the Spirit of the living God. . . .

— 2 CORINTHIANS 3:3 RSV

I'VE started something new recently: I write prayer letters. They are fun and nonthreatening; they can be read without embarrassment; and everyone loves to receive them. Here's one I wrote to surprise my friend Cathy Johnson in Missoula, Montana:

> Dear God,
>
> You sure gave me a solid-gold friend when you brought Cathy and me together. You know, God, I really miss her now that I moved north to Alaska and she headed east to Montana. It is so wonderful that we both have you to keep us together.

litany of loneliness day after day. Even with cluster housing, neighbors are not "close" anymore. Everyone is in a hurry. No one drops by for coffee or a leisurely conversation. And my friends stay busy with their own families.

But you always have time to listen. You encourage me when no one else seems to care. You whisper my name in the night and tell me that all is well. You remind me that in your sight I am precious and beloved and that my name is written on your heart.

Having you as my Friend, I will never be alone.

With love,

I am praying right now that you will refresh her and brighten her day with the light of your presence. Lord, thank you for all Cathy's work with her church's teens, and for her generous spirit. Remind her today of her own thoughtful ways, just as I am reminded of thoughtfulness whenever I think of her.

Love, Carol

Is there someone who needs a word of comfort or cheer? Perhaps you have friends or family members whom you want to bring nearer to God? Write a prayer letter to him about them and your feelings for them. These letters can stay private between you and God, or you can send your friends copies of your prayer letters to lift their spirits and let them know they are cared for. Let your prayer letters pray blessings into another's day.

God, teach me creative ways to pray for others that will draw them closer to you. Amen.

When I am afraid

Oh, God!

I'm terrified! All I can do is gasp out a few weak cries for help. Waiting for the results of the biopsy is sheer torture. All that comes to mind is the latest cancer statistics for people in my age bracket.

There is comfort, though, in the number of times your Word encourages me not to be afraid. Fifty times? One hundred and fifty? Surely you would not be so insistent on this issue if you did not intend to help me achieve it. Even the Christmas angels prefaced the divine birth announcement with the words, "Fear not!" Maybe my news, too, will be "good tidings of great joy." But, if not, I will trust you for the outcome.

Faithfully yours,

When I lose my job

Dear Father,

At a time like this, you are the first person I thought of, knowing you would understand my shock and devastation upon finding a pink slip waiting for me when I got to work this morning! With John gone and the children to care for, we'll be leaning on you more than ever.

I must confess a feeling of rejection and betrayal, though. Was my work not good enough? Did I fail to measure up to someone's expectations? Or am I merely another victim of a downturn in the economy? But you know all about rejection, don't you? You know how it feels to be a victim of society. And when I think how you suffered—for me—my own problems don't loom so large.

Still, the children and I need your help. And you promised to be a father to the fatherless, a husband to the widow, and a faithful provider. So you'll work out something, I know. I'll leave the details to you. As for me, I'm going to end this letter and go to sleep.

Expectantly,

3

Announcements and Congratulations

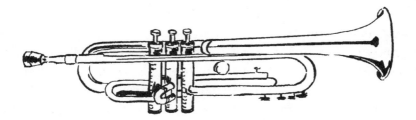

This communicating of a man's self to his friend works two contrary effects; for it redoubleth joys, and cutteth griefs in half. FRANCIS BACON

Through loyalty to the past, our mind refuses to realize that tomorrow's joy is possible only if today's makes way for it; that each wave owes the beauty of its line only to the withdrawal of the preceding one. ANDRÉ GIDE

*L*ife is a series of crossroads and turning points, and each one is an occasion for a letter of announcement or congratulation. A letter of announcement tells friends and acquaintances what is new in your life. It invites them to participate in your joy or sorrow. It is a way of saying, "You are a part of my life, and I want you to know what is happening to me." An announcement is not an intimate form of communication, but *letting other people know what is going on in your life is part of an intimate relationship.*

When writing a letter of announcement, it's the facts that are important, so remember the five W's: Who? What? When? Where? Why? In other words, "Who did what?" "When and where did it happen?" "Why did it happen?" or "Why did he or she do it?" If you answer these questions clearly and concisely, you can be quite sure you have written an effective letter of announcement.

Letters of announcement are among the few types of correspondence that can be mass produced. Their purpose is to convey one piece of information to as many people as necessary, and they require little, if any, personalization. E-mail is also a possibility here.

These letters can be handwritten notes (if your announcement is going to only a handful of people) or they can be computer generated or photocopied letters (if your news needs to be more widely distributed).

Office supply stores and copy centers have a wide variety of specialty papers and envelopes available for use in customizing correspondence. Many also have computers you can rent and design specialists with whom you can consult to find ways to give your mailing a unique look.

The technology available today makes mass mailing a possibility for everyone. And it also makes it easy to keep friends and loved ones up to date on every change in your life, even the seemingly small ones. Ironically, it is when you tell people about the small, seemingly unimportant things in your life that you are telling them how important they really are to you.

Announcing an engagement

Dear Sandy,

    I am excited to inform you that as of last weekend I am officially engaged to Matt Langdon! He is the wonderful, handsome guy I've been dating since last fall.

Matt and I were at our favorite restaurant when he presented me with an unexpected gift: a beautiful diamond ring! I said "yes" as fast as I could get the words out of my mouth! We've not yet set a wedding date, but we will let you know as soon as we do.

Thank you for praying,

Announcing a new baby

Dear Family and Friends,

We are privileged to announce the arrival of our first baby girl: Nicole Suzanne. She made her appearance on Thursday, July 12, at 11:20 A.M. She's tiny—weighing in at 7 pounds, 6 ounces and measuring 20 inches long—but she's a beautiful bundle of joy. She possesses all ten fingers and ten toes and is, in every way we can perceive, PERFECT! She's definitely a miracle sent from God!

Please join us in praising him for her.

Celebrating God's miracle of life,

Announcing a new career

Dear Greg,

I'm writing to let you know of my upcoming career change. Effective November 15 I will be joining Abraham Construction, Incorporated in Detroit. I am looking forward to this move to a new city as it will allow my wife and me to spend more time with our parents, who are reaching the age when they need more of our attention. I am also looking forward to working for a company that is so highly regarded in our industry.

I will be replaced at Keegstra Lumber by Steve Smith. He's been with Wick Lumber for ten years so he knows the business, and I'm sure he will service your account well.

It's been a pleasure doing business with you.

Sincerely,

Announcing a new business

Dear Cynthia,

I've recently started a new business that really excites me, and I think it's something that might interest you as well. I've enclosed an invitation for a brunch I'm having at my home to familiarize people with more of the details. I will be contacting you in a week or so to find out if you are able to come.

If you know of anyone else who would be interested, you're welcome to invite her also.

Looking forward to seeing you,

Celebrating Success—Even Someone Else's

Carol Knapp

"Out of the mouth of babes . . . thou hast brought perfect praise."
— MATTHEW 21:16 RSV

As I waited backstage with my twelve-year-old daughter, Kelly, a contestant in Alaska National Pre-Teen Competition, I overheard a young girl in the "Petite" competition talking to her mother. The little one had just won in the sportswear category, and her nervous older sister was now competing. "I wonder which one she'll get!" the little champion exclaimed excitedly.

Her mother gently replied that her sister probably would not receive a trophy.

Bewildered, the little girl's voice fell, and she asked sorrowfully, "Then why did I win, Mommy?"

Here was a child who didn't think it was right for her to win if her

Announcing a divorce

Dear Darla,

I'm sorry to have to tell you that John and I are now divorced. We signed the papers Thursday. I know you will be disappointed and hurt because you always remained so hopeful that we could work out our differences. I do appreciate your support through many difficult years, and I hope we will be able to maintain our friendship. I need your support now as much as ever.

Please try to understand,

sister could not win too. I wondered if I still carried that childlike sense of goodwill toward others. How many times do I cheer for others, sincerely desiring their success? How often—and here I really had to wince—do I cheer for those who do the same things I do, and do them well, or even better?

Whether it is job performance, athletic ability, academics, talent, or ideas, I want to outdo the competition. When I lose in a game of Scrabble, I am gritting my teeth beneath the smile I flash my opponent. I can't outdistance my running partner, but I've strained calf muscles trying. If I'm unable to afford something new or I fail to meet a personal goal—such as weight loss—I'm often secretly pleased when my friends can't seem to do it either.

Boy, do I have a long way to travel—backward, to the undiluted wisdom of my childhood, where I don't lose if somebody else wins.

Lord, it's me . . . all grown up . . . needing to rediscover childhood's boundless capacity for admiring without envying.

A letter of congratulation differs from an announcement in that it is more personal. It is appropriate for one person on one specific occasion. A letter of congratulation is a way to "rejoice with those who rejoice" (Romans 12:15 NIV), and it is always an appropriate response to another person's positive turning point.

Whether the occasion is a new baby, a new job, a new house, a new mate, or a personal accomplishment, it calls for a card, note, or letter of congratulation.

Greeting cards are available for most of these occasions, but sometimes a store-bought card just doesn't seem quite personal enough. And other times you'd like to personalize a greeting card with a brief note inside. The following letters can be adapted for either situation.

Congratulations on graduation

Dear Scott,

I am proud of you for accomplishing your goal at Aquinas College. I trust that you will continue to look at each day as a learning experience. And always remember the most important ingredient for achieving true success is integrity.

Congratulations!

Congratulations on engagement

Dear Ellen,

Congratulations on your engagement! How thrilled we are for you and Matt. If half of what you've said about him is true I'm sure the two of you will be very happy together. We look forward to meeting him soon!

Best wishes,

Congratulations on wedding

Dear Chad and Annette,

Congratulations to both of you on your wedding day! Your Uncle

Celebrating Age

Marilyn Morgan Helleberg

To every thing there is a season, and a time to every purpose under the heaven.
— ECCLESIASTES 3:1 NIV

ON November 1, I'll become, officially, a senior citizen. When I told a friend I planned to write about being sixty-two, she said, "Don't tell me you're going to admit that publicly . . . before God and everybody!" I laughed, because it reminded me of a speaker I'd heard at a retreat last spring, a man in his eighties who said, "My wife is always telling me I should act my age, but I tell her, 'Why in the world would I want to do that?'"

Aging does have its rewards. At last, I have an excuse for my lifelong absentmindedness! I can now get by with being a bit silly. I've dropped many of the unnecessary "shoulds," and I can say what I think, letting the raised-eyebrow people whisper, "Tsk, tsk, senior citizen, you know!" I've also been playing more than I have since age twelve. Second childhood? Well, yes! I think I'll claim that! The first one was much too short.

Each age brings its own gifts, so I'd like to propose, right here before God and everybody, that we celebrate our aging—whether we're thirty, fifty, sixty-two, or older—by making a thank-you list of the special blessings that come with the stage of life we're in. Then write A+ at the top of the page and offer your list, with thanks, to God. (Bonus for seniors: When your list is done, reward yourself by hugging a grandchild!)

Thank you, Creator God, for the special gifts of this wonderful time of life.

Tim and I trust and pray that the Lord will do for you what he has done for us during our twenty-five years of marriage. Every year we are amazed at how he has continued to make our "love increase and overflow for each other" (1 Thessalonians 5:28 NIV). And there is no reason why your marriage has to be any different. Love *can* last a lifetime if you nurture it and treat it as your most valued treasure.

With love,

Congratulations on eightieth birthday

Dear Grandma,

How pleased we are to be able to celebrate with you on your eightieth birthday. But more than that, we are pleased to celebrate your life. You've always been thoughtful and considerate of your family and friends. You're good-natured even with all the teasing from your many grandsons. You are a good listener and easy to listen to. We've enjoyed your many sweet delights for our tummies over the years as well as all the nourishment you've provided for our hearts and minds through stories about our family heritage and about God's faithfulness to you. Thank you for providing us with a legacy of love, honesty, and faithfulness. We are blessed to have you with us!

We love you,

4

Thank You and

Appreciation

**Wise men appreciate all men, for they see the good in each
and know how hard it is to make anything good.**
BALTASAR GRACIÁN, *The Art of Worldly Wisdom*

*M*any acts of kindness go unrecognized. Others are acknowledged
by a quick word of thanks. And some, though few, are acknowledged by a note of appreciation.

Words of appreciation are certainly nice, but a note of appreciation is
even nicer. Words of thanks mean that a person noticed your contribution, but a note of thanks means that a person not only noticed it but was
moved to action by it.

And what does a note of thanks do for you when you receive it? It
motivates you to do even more kind deeds, doesn't it? Surely that is the
type of behavior the writer of Hebrews was trying to inspire when he
instructed us to "spur one another on toward love and good deeds"

(Hebrews 10:24 NIV). Expressing appreciation is a simple way to follow that admonition.

A letter of appreciation is appropriate for any occasion or for no occasion at all. It can express gratitude for something in particular or anything in general. For example, you may have been particularly grateful when someone in your church or community started a ministry for unwed mothers. Perhaps you cannot help them financially, but you can encourage them in their well-doing with a letter of appreciation like the one the apostle Paul wrote to the first-century church in Corinth.

> *The rendering of this service not only supplies the wants of the saints, but also overflows in many thanksgivings to God (2 Corinthians 9:12 RSV).*

Or maybe you were impressed with someone's faith and positive attitude during a long period of unemployment. Sometimes the most meaningful letters are those written in recognition of a person's character. If so, you could write a letter like the one Paul wrote to the church at Ephesus.

> *Ever since I heard about your faith in the Lord Jesus and your love for all the saints, I have not stopped giving thanks for you, remembering you in my prayers (Ephesians 1:15–16 NIV).*

Letters of thanks and appreciation generally have two parts. First, they acknowledge the person's action or attitude that was meaningful, and, second, they tell why it was so meaningful. For example . . .

- *It made me want to do better in my own life.*
- *It showed me how I could be a better wife/husband/parent/ friend.*
- *It helped me see how much good there is in the world.*
- *It helped me understand God better.*
- *It showed me how God is working in my life.*

- *It made me realize how blessed I am.*
- *It helped me through a difficult time.*
- *It made me realize that God really does care about me.*

Never hesitate to be grateful, for genuine gratefulness has no bad side effects. In fact, it has such powerfully positive effects that it can keep our hearts soft toward God and goodness.

> Encourage one another daily, as long as it is called Today, so that none of you may be hardened by sin's deceitfulness (Hebrews 3:13 NIV).

For companionship

Dear January,

Thank you for the time you've spent with me since Dad died. Going out for breakfast on Tuesdays and playing Scrabble in the afternoons has helped keep me from being overwhelmed with loneliness. Your thoughtfulness is one of the traits you inherited from your father, and I am truly blessed to have been the beneficiary of it twice: first of his and now of yours.

Your loving mother,

For friendship

Dear Ellen,

Having a friend like you makes life so enjoyable! I appreciate your listening ear and your willingness to give your opinion when I ask. Thanks for sticking with me through hard times and good! Whenever I hear people say how difficult it is to make good friends these days, I think of you and know how fortunate I am..

Love,

For birthday gift

Dear Mom,

Your package arrived today, and Benjamin loved the puzzle you sent for his birthday. When he opened it he announced, "Just what I always wanted!" He's been playing with it all day, and I had to do some fast talking to explain why he shouldn't sleep with it. He knows it came from you, and I'm sure that's why he doesn't want to be separated from it.

Thank you so much.

With love,

Appreciation Never Depreciates

Norman Vincent Peale

A soft answer turneth away wrath. . . .   — PROVERBS 15:1 KJV

THEIR marriage had been going badly. Quarrels and recriminations. Criticisms and complaints. Then one evening when he came home, the husband sat down near his wife. With pad and pencil in hand, he began to write.

"What are you doing?" she finally asked him.

"Writing a list of your good qualities," he said.

"Good qualities?" she echoed incredulously. "I didn't know you thought I had any!"

"Well, you do," he said, and went on writing.

Pretty soon she asked to see his list. She read what he had written with amazement and pleasure. "Why," she said, "I had no idea that anything about me pleased you any more."

For financial support

Dear Teresa,

Thank you for your generous gift in support of our short-term mission trip to Albania. We appreciate your enthusiasm for the task we have before us to accomplish, and we hope you will pray for us as we go. I'll give you a full report when I return.

Thank you,

"Lots of things do," he said cheerfully. "A few don't."

"Well," she said, "maybe you'd better list those, too."

"I will," he said, "if you'll do the same for me."

The result was that both got their grievances out in the open in such a calm and amicable way that they were able to resolve quite a few of them.

How do I know about this? Because I was the one who had reminded the husband that the desire for appreciation is one of the deepest of all human cravings. If he would make a deliberate effort, I told him, to satisfy that craving in his wife, things might improve dramatically in their marriage. And they did.

The method he used was all his own, but it's not a bad technique, is it? Wouldn't it help almost any marriage? Even yours?

Father, give us the insight to see the good qualities in other people—and the wisdom to tell them.

Thanks, but we're not interested

Dear Doug and Dave,

Thank you for spending time with us at the open house yesterday. Even though we were very impressed with the quality of your homes, we have decided to look at existing homes rather than build a new one at this time.

Sincerely,

For providing information

Dear Linda,

I really appreciate all the information you shared with me about putting together a photo album that won't yellow and deteriorate with age. Once I have gathered and organized the pictures for my dad's album I will contact you so I can attend one of your workshops.

Thanks for your time,

For giving advice

Dear Tammie,

You have such a gift with plants! Thanks so much for your time and advice regarding my anemic ferns and ivies. You probably saved their lives!

I appreciate you,

For recommendation

Dear Barb,

Thank you for recommending my services to your neighbor. She was very enthusiastic about getting started. I'm looking forward to helping her. It's been a pleasure doing business with you.

Sincerely,

For dinner invitation

Dear Kirk and Chris,

We were delighted to receive the dinner invitation for Thursday, February 16. We will plan to be there at six o'clock, and we look forward to spending an evening with you. I would be happy to bring a salad or dessert if that would ease some of the pressure of preparation and allow you to enjoy the evening a bit more. Just let me know a day or so ahead of time. Thanks for thinking of us.

Sincerely,

For recognition

Dear Carol,

Thank you for the special recognition in your newsletter for our accomplishments here in our community. It meant a lot to our team here in Michigan to know that someone recognized the effort we put forth to make a difference in the lives of troubled teens. We appreciate your support!

Sincerely,

For going away party

Dear Class,

We were absolutely overwhelmed with the party you gave us last Sunday! The gifts (especially the photo album), the song, and the presence of so many of you who came to wish us well was very meaningful to us. You'll always have a special place in our hearts.

We'll miss you,

For loving care during illness

Dear Calvary Church Family,

We wish to express our appreciation for your loving care during our son's illness. The meals, calls, and prayers helped us not only get through this difficult time but be uplifted spiritually as well.

Thank you and bless you all,

For job well done

Dear Mr. Schneider,

Thank you for going the extra mile when you installed our carpet. The seams are nearly invisible, and we especially appreciated that you cleaned up before you left.

Everything looks great!

A very satisfied customer,

For referral

Dear Kelly,

Thank you for referring us to Dr. Quiroz. It's very difficult to find a physician that the whole family can be comfortable with, but I think we will all like him. Now I can be confident that we will have quality medical care when we need it.

With much relief,

For attending a meeting

Dear Sheryl,

Thank you for attending our training meeting last weekend. I hope you found that it was worth giving up a Saturday. I learn something new each time I attend, and I hope you did too. Your tip about the Starter Kit was great!

Enjoyed having you there,

For visiting our group

Dear Denise,

Thank you for visiting our women's Bible study last Tuesday. We hope you will make it a regular date on your weekly calendar. You have rich insights to offer and we felt privileged to have you share them with us. Be assured that we will continue to pray about your husband's job situation. We hope to see you again next week.

Sincerely,

To a family

When you express appreciation, take the time to think of and mention specific characteristics that you admire in the person. Not only will you encourage people to develop their positive qualities, but you might also help them recognize gifts—both natural and spiritual—that they are not able to see in themselves.

Such a letter is a nice thing to write for a family. By mentioning positive characteristics of each family member, you not only express your appreciation, you also help them see each other with a renewed sense of appreciation. (All too often people living under the same roof see only the negative characteristics of the other family members.)

The following letter is longer than most you will write in order to show the scope and variety of qualities to admire.

Dear Bill and Mary, Elizabeth, Andrew, and Joel,

If I had planned for weeks, I couldn't have come up with a more perfect Sunday than the one we spent with your family. Everything about it—from the church service to the meal to the feeding of the goats—was meaningful and delightful. Thank you for inviting us to be part of your family. Each one of you added your own special touch to make the day special.

Elizabeth, I want to thank you for helping me find my way around church and for helping with Olivia and Kristiana as well. You were generous in finding toys for them to play with and you showed great kindness and maturity in the way you steered them away from things they could break and toward things that were appropriate for their age.

Andrew, thank you for being so patient, gentle, and understanding with the girls. Those are three wonderful qualities that I seldom see in boys your age, and their scarcity makes them even more valuable. Your willingness to take the time to teach Kristiana how to feed the chickens without getting her fingers pecked by hungry hens revealed your kind and caring nature.

Joel, thank you for being so creative and fun-loving. Your quick-wittedness and spontaneity make you a joy to be around. Thank you for entertaining Kristiana, and for using your intuition to respond in such a clever way when she was crying on her daddy's shoulder. That was a moment we all will remember.

Bill and Mary, your family is truly a treasure of immeasurable value. The investment you are making in your children will pay important dividends not only in their lives and yours, but in the lives of all the people they interact with in the years to come. Thank you for making them a priority. The world owes a big debt to parents like you who are raising their children to be confident, moral, and loving people.

Your graciousness and generosity are beyond measure, and Jay and I consider ourselves privileged to have been on the receiving end of it.

Thanks again for a truly great day.

With warm regards,

For an evening out

Dear Jim and Marge,

Thank you for your generosity in buying our tickets for *Annie*. We had a great time with the two of you at the show and at dinner. Jay and I have been the recipients of your thoughtfulness for so many years now that we are no longer surprised by it. But we certainly don't want you ever to think that we take it for granted. Being kind and generous comes so naturally to you that you probably have no idea how rare those qualities are.

And I want to say an extra special thank you for being the kind of people we can invite in for coffee even when we have several loads of laundry piled in the middle of the living room floor. Life doesn't get much better than when you have friends who know you so well (and love you anyway) that you don't have to pretend to be something you're not.

Only God knows the number of people who are living godly lives today because of your Christlike example of unconditional love, and Jay and I continually thank God for allowing our lives to intersect with yours.

We love you both,

For an anonymous act of kindness
(for local newspaper or church newsletter)

Dear Kind Person,

Last Sunday while helping a friend deal with an emergency in our church parking lot, I unknowingly dropped my airline tickets, which were in my jacket pocket. Two hours later, while driving to the airport, I realized they were missing. By then, however, I had been several other places, so I had no idea where I'd lost them, nor did I have time to check all the places I'd been. In desperation, I called the airline to ask what to do. Somehow, after speaking to several people, I got through to a ticket agent at our local airport. "What is your name, sir?" the clerk asked.

I told her.

"I have your tickets in front of me," she said. "Someone found them in a church parking lot and dropped them off here."

By the time I got there to claim my tickets, it seemed as if everyone in the terminal had heard the heartwarming story of the uncommonly thoughtful person who had made a special trip to the airport on a Sunday afternoon to deliver a stranger's lost airline tickets.

Since I don't know who you are, I can't thank you personally; however, I hope you see this note because I want you to know that your act of kindness not only blessed me, it also furthered God's kingdom by demonstrating to people working at the airport that Christians are different in a positive sense. And that's something they might never have learned if not for your example.

With gratitude,

To favorite author

You may be among the people who assume that a note of appreciation would be insignificant and meaningless to your favorite author because he or she receives so many. That is seldom the case. Most authors receive few letters and, except for family and friends and people inside their publishing house, never know what people think of what they write. Sales figures show whether or not people are buying their book, but they don't tell why. A note of appreciation not only encourages authors, it can also help them determine what they have said that is significant to people. If a particular book has had a strong impact on your life, try to put into words what made it so meaningful to you—for example, its honesty, insights, perceptions, treatment of the subject, unusual point of view; the author's vulnerability, willingness to take a risk, ability to make complicated truths understandable or, perhaps, to create believable characters. Address your letter to the author in care of the publishing house that released the book. The publisher will forward your letter to the author.

Dear Philip,

If you could see my copy of *Disappointment with God* you would probably think that I have little appreciation for books and that I treat them carelessly. The dust jacket is dirty and dog-eared, and the pages are crinkled and smudged. It looks as if it has suffered years of abuse.

But the truth is, it has simply suffered years of use. I have read it straight through several times and so has my husband. I also go back to it frequently and reread portions to refresh my memory as to what you said about certain subjects. Every Christmas I read the parts about Christ's incarnation and every Easter I read the parts about his passion. I confess that I do mark up the book, but only with pencil. And I loaned it to quite a few people before I realized what a loss it would be if the copy with all my markings and comments never came back. So now whenever I want someone to read it I buy him or her a copy.

I believe that through your writing you are, as John the Baptist urged, preparing the way for the Lord. Your ability to make complex truths seem like simple ideas is a modern-day equivalent of making "crooked roads . . . straight, the rough ways smooth" (Luke 3:5).

The only other author whose writing affects me this way is C. S. Lewis, and I believe that your books, like his, will endure because you both write about timeless issues in a way that makes them timely for all generations.

Thank you for your commitment to truth as well as to good writing. And thank you for recognizing that clear thinking is as important as clear writing. For without those two things, all that I (or any reader) would understand is your opinion of God. What makes your books different is that they make me understand God's opinion of me.

May God bless you and your work for his kingdom.

With deep appreciation,

To spouse

In times of corporate down-sizing (or "right-sizing," as some call it), people find very little security in the workplace. This is considered by most people to be quite unfortunate, but there's another way to look at it. When things are insecure at work, it's a perfect time for working on the security of home. A note of appreciation to a spouse who doesn't know whether he or she will have a job tomorrow can be a real boost to a sagging ego. Think of some of the qualities you admire about your mate that people at work don't recognize or don't appreciate. Then write a note saying how important those qualities are to you.

Dear Doug,

I don't tell you often enough how much I appreciate it when you spend time with the children. Reading stories to them and playing games with them are wonderful ways of letting them know how much you love and enjoy them. I'm sure you will reap lifelong benefits from your investment in their lives.

I love you,

WHEN A THANK YOU IS NOT RECEIVED

Inquiring about gift not acknowledged

Dear Karen,

I'm wondering if you received the Christmas gifts I sent in early October. I realize you may have been too busy to respond yet, but I'm beginning to wonder if I have put too much faith in the delivery service I used. Please let me know if you received the gifts or if this is a matter I need to check into.

Looking forward to your response,

5

Letters of Welcome

All changes, even the most longed for, have their melancholy; for what we leave behind us is a part of ourselves; we must die to one life before we can enter into another!
                                                            ANATOLE FRANCE

Do not forget to entertain strangers, for by so doing some people have entertained angels without knowing it.
                                                            HEBREWS 13:2 NIV

*C*hange is traumatic for most people. We all tend to be creatures of habit, and anything that disrupts our routines takes some getting used to. One of the most traumatic changes is moving. Whether the move is to a different state or just a different neighborhood, it requires lots of adjustment. New neighbors, new grocery stores, new schools, a new church, new friends, new coworkers, a new job, a new doctor. Where does the list end?

You can help newcomers adjust to their unfamiliar surroundings quickly and easily by giving them a warm welcome and offering to *answer their questions or listen to their tales of frustration and loneliness. Some people find the changes exhilarating and adjust quickly. Others are nearly traumatized by so much that is unfamiliar, and it may take months or years before they feel at home in their new surroundings.*

You can help ease the trauma by not placing your own set of expectations on their struggle to adjust. The best things you can do are listen, encourage, and be patient. And every now and then send them a note saying how glad you are for the opportunity to get to know them.

To new resident

Dear Mrs. Smith,

Meeting you yesterday was my pleasure. It will be nice to have someone else in the complex who shares my love of Shakespeare. What an impressive collection of his works you have! Now that winter has set in, perhaps we can pass some time together reading. I look forward to it.

Sincerely,

To new neighbor

Dear neighbor,

I have seen you out walking your beautiful dog and have wanted to run outside and welcome you to our neighborhood, but that dog of yours keeps up quite a pace and I've not yet been quick enough to catch the two of you. I'll keep trying, but in case I continue to miss you I'll introduce myself by letter.

My name is Marla Smith, and my husband, Ed, and I have lived in the house two doors east of yours for twenty-two years. We're pretty familiar with everything around here, so if there is anything we can do to help you adjust to your new surroundings don't hesitate to call.

The Circle Is Unbroken

Linda Ching Sledge

There is a friend who sticks closer than a brother.
— PROVERBS 18:24 NIV

MY dear friend Gwen was gone. Room 530, her old office, was empty, the door locked tight. Every day for years, I had come to the door of that office for advice, gossip, companionship.

My thoughts were broken by the sound of high-heeled shoes tapping down the hall. The footsteps halted outside room 530. Then I heard the jingle of keys and a heavy book bag dropping as the English department's newest teacher arrived.

On my way to the water fountain, I peeked in at the doorway of 530. A woman looked up from the desk as I passed; her face was terribly young and terribly unsure. Had I once looked that way to Gwen? Quickly, I walked on.

It seemed a long way to the water fountain, even longer going back. When I looked in at the doorway of 530 this time, I saw bare walls and empty bookshelves: a familiar space with a scared young teacher sitting alone.

"Want to go to lunch with an old-timer?" I ventured in my best big-sister fashion. "There's a place down the road that serves great macaroni and bean soup."

What better way to honor an old friend than by showing a new friend all the tender mercies that have been shown you.

Lord, in every lonely face, I see marks of your humanity.

We are looking forward to getting acquainted with you soon.

Sincerely,

To church visitor

People who fill out a vistor's card at church usually receive a form letter from the pastor sometime during the following week. This is about the best way churches know of welcoming new people to their congregation. A form letter is better than nothing, of course, but think how much better and more meaningful it would be if the visitor received a personal letter from the person seated next to him or her in the pew. Maybe you could make it your ministry to introduce yourself to newcomers in your church and write a personal note of welcome to them.

The Best Long-distance Service of All

Teresa Schantz

Because He has inclined His ear to me, Therefore I shall call upon Him as long as I live. — PSALM 116:2 NAS

HAVING recently relocated to St. Louis, I found my new job fulfilling, my apartment comfortable, and city life fascinating. But I hadn't had much opportunity to make friends, so I made a lot of phone calls home to ease a case of the "lonelies."

I kept waiting for my parents to chide me about wasting my money on expensive chats. Oddly enough, they never said a word. In fact, I began to get cards and notes from them that read, "We love you and enjoy your calls. You are always interesting. We're always happy to listen." I was grateful for their understanding and appreciated their patience.

Dear Mrs. Jones,

Thank you for visiting Calvary Church last Sunday. I was glad we had a few minutes after the service to get acquainted. As you probably noticed in the visitor's brochure, Calvary has two services in the morning (8:30 and 10:00) and one on Sunday evening at 6. A variety of Sunday school classes are offered for children and adults during both morning services.

I hope that you and your family found meaning and spiritual refreshment during your time of worship with us. If you have any questions about our church, I would be happy to chat with you about them.

My husband and I have been members for fifteen years, so we are familiar with most of the programs and doctrinal positions of the church. And if you have questions we cannot answer, we can probably

It occurs to me frequently, as I think back to that period, that my Father in Heaven is equally generous with his time and patience. His Word is a constant reminder of how he welcomes our conversations. He urges us to "give him a call" and chat about our frustrations, our fears, and our victories. With such a direct line, you'd think I'd talk often, but I frequently forget his willingness to listen.

Now when I come home to my little apartment at night and start to feel a case of the lonelies, I try to leave the receiver in its cradle and make another kind of long-distance call. Believe me, the bills are much easier on my budget.

God, one of the things that makes you most powerful to me is the instant access you offer. Remind me to take advantage of your availability always.

refer you to the people who can. I look forward to seeing you again soon.

In Christ's Name,

To new member

Dear Carla,

Welcome to our community and thank you for taking the time to attend our Mothers of Young Children meeting. Everyone enjoyed your participation. We believe that each member has something special to offer, and we all look forward to getting to know you better and discovering the treasure in you.

God Bless,

6

Letters of

Encouragement

The men . . . gathered the church together and delivered the letter. The people read it and were glad for its encouraging message. ACTS 15:30–31 NIV

Hope is necessary in every condition. The miseries of poverty, sickness, of captivity, would, without this comfort, be insupportable. SAMUEL JOHNSON

*T*he need for encouragement is universal. The pressures of life weigh down even the strongest of people at one time or another. *Generally it is easy to tell when people are discouraged. You can see it in their eyes, hear it in their voices, sense it in their behavior. They move slowly, smile infrequently and halfheartedly, and go through the motions of life with little joy or enthusiasm.*

With some people, however, discouragement is not as easy to detect.

They may cover their insecurity with an air of confidence. They may go into hiding. Or they may deny that anything is wrong even when you come right out and ask. So sometimes you need to be a detective to know when an encouraging word is called for.

Whenever you sense that it is, you can respond with an uplifting letter. Depending on the circumstances, your letter might . . .

- *Remind the person of the good he or she has done in the past.*
- *List some of the person's unique gifts and abilities.*
- *Assure the person of future accomplishments.*
- *Help the person see life's bigger picture rather than just the troubling circumstances of the moment.*
- *Confirm that doing the right thing is more important than getting the desired result.*
- *Remind the person that he or she is part of God's sovereign plan for the universe.*

The New Testament is full of encouraging words that you can use as patterns for your own letters of encouragement. Here are the basic tools that you will need.

When people are discouraged due to an emotional crisis, encourage them with . . .

> ***Love****—Your love has given me great joy and encouragement, because you . . . have refreshed the hearts of the saints (Philemon 1:7 NIV).*

When people are confused, encourage them with . . .

> ***Truth****—[An elder] must hold firmly to the trustworthy message as it has been taught, so that he can encourage others by sound doctrine and refute those who oppose it (Titus 1:9 NIV).*

When people are in a spiritual crisis, encourage them with . . .

> **Faith**—*I long to see you so that I may impart to you some spiritual gift to make you strong—that is, that you and I may be mutually encouraged by each other's faith (Romans 1:11–12 NIV).*

And when people are discouraged due to a relational crisis, offer them . . .

> **Fellowship**—*Let us not give up meeting together, as some are in the habit of doing, but let us encourage one another—and all the more as you see the Day approaching (Hebrews 10:25 NIV).*

Is there anyone who doesn't need encouragement? Is there anyone who wouldn't benefit from a kind word, a word of affirmation, a word of assurance? And is there ever any good reason for failing to offer a word of encouragement to those who need it?

No. No. No.

So we hope the following letters will not only show you how to write a note of encouragement, but will also help you think of people who might benefit from one. As you think of names, list them in the spaces below and check them off as you finish the letters.

☐ _____

☐ _____

☐ _____

ENCOURAGING WORDS IN DIFFICULT TIMES

When emotions are at the breaking point

Remind people of their good qualities and assure them of your love.

Dear Sandy,

    The disappointment you are feeling must seem overwhelming at times, and I know there is nothing I can say or do to make the hurt go away. I want you to know, however, that I am here to give you whatever emotional support I can. You are a kind and caring person, and many of us have been on the receiving end of your thoughtfulness. Now it is our turn to take care of you. Please let us do it.

More Than a Miracle

William Jenks

WHEN I was a freshman at Holy Cross College in Worcester, Massachusetts, Father Pat Cummings, a Jesuit priest, taught my English class. He seemed an ordinary man. The one unusual thing about Father Pat was his practice of devoting time and energy to counseling young men.

    The summer after my freshman year at Holy Cross I was stricken with polio and left paralyzed from the neck down. I asked my parents to alert Father Pat to my need for a miracle.

    Father Pat responded immediately, nct with a miracle but with the promise of prayers and letters. That first year he wrote me a letter every day. Then when I came home from the medical center, he agreed that his other friends had some claim on his attention and so

We love you and we want to help you through this exceedingly difficult time.

With love and concern,

When life doesn't make sense

Remind people that truth doesn't change when circumstances do.

Dear Sam,

If I were you, the question I would be asking right now is the same one the prophet Jeremiah asked many years ago: "Why does the way of the wicked prosper?" It certainly seems as if that is what has happened in your situation. You did the good and honest thing, and your employer used it against you.

he revised his schedule. He wrote only every other day—for the next seventeen years.

In more than 3300 letters Father Pat kept me posted on the events of campus life. He brought me out of the confines of my four-walled room into the life of my contemporaries.

What did Father Pat accomplish with those one million words he wrote to me? He helped one human being make an accommodation to a difficult fate. Through Father Pat my immobile body did not become the total prison I'd feared. I'm able to read and type by holding a stick in my mouth. With books from the library and directions from Father, I've furthered my education and have been able to tutor a dozen kids over the years. From my bed I've managed the family farm and served as a member of the church's parish council.

Father Pat quietly affirmed that useless does not mean worthless. He taught me that words can be deeds and that there are miracles of healing perceptible only to the heart.

The anger and confusion you are feeling right now are probably causing you to question the value of honesty and perhaps even to plot ways of getting even. That is certainly a natural response. And that is the part of evil that is so insidious. It tempts good people to make bad choices.

One thing I learned when I was in a situation not much different from yours is that you will ultimately feel much better about yourself if you take the high road. Unfortunately, it's not an easy one because it's all uphill. But you will be so much stronger when you reach the top that you'll look back with gratitude for this present trial.

I know it's hard to believe now, but trust me. I've been there.

Sincerely,

When God seems distant

Try to find a point of identification with the struggling person, but don't say you understand if you really don't.

Dear Leslie,

Recently I've been sensing that your spiritual life is lacking direction. You seem troubled by something. Even though I don't know what it is, I can assure you that you are not alone. I too know what it means to wander spiritually. I know what it means to chase after things that are bad for me. I know what it means to avoid relational pain. I know what it means to be afraid to get too close to God. And I know what it means to run from him.

If you identify with any of my experiences, I hope you'll give me a call when you're ready to talk because I'd like to tell you the story of how God's voice finally got through to me.

I would love to help you find your way out of this wilderness, Leslie. I would love to help you find your way back to the heart of God.

Many people love you very much, and I am one of them.

Sincerely,

When a relationship ends

If at all possible, make time to be personally available. But don't make promises you can't keep.

Dear Emily,

It's going to be difficult for you to trust anyone for a while because the one you trusted with your life and future proved to be untrustworthy. Although there is nothing I can do to replace your loss, maybe I can do something to help restore your trust. I promise that I will be here for you whenever you need to talk or cry or just sit in silence. You're welcome at our house whenever you need to get away from yours. And just in case you feel awkward about making your needs known, I will call you regularly to set up a time for the two of us to get together so I can find out how you're doing.

Right now you feel like you're alone, but you're not.

Your loving friend,

When making the grade seems impossible

Dear Ron,

I was pleased to get your letter yesterday. It's always good to hear from you—especially now that you've gone off to college.

Your concern about your grades is understandable. You have always worked hard to do your best, and I greatly admire you for that. Try to remember that doing your best is of far greater importance than getting the best grades. I'm convinced that your strength of character, honesty, integrity, and perseverance will mean more in the long haul—whether you work for yourself or for someone else—than getting top-notch grades now.

Stay with it and trust the Lord to guide you. I'm praying for you.

We love you and wish you the best,

AFFIRMING WORDS IN GOOD TIMES

Taking on a new job

Dear Eleanor,

I was not surprised when you called to say you had found a new job. Your previous position did not bring out your best, and I was happy to know you recognized that.

It's understandable that you are a bit fearful: Can you measure up to the boss's expectations? Will you be able to handle the work load? Will there be opportunity for advancement? Your courage to change jobs makes me confident that you will do well. You are the kind of person who welcomes challenges and thrives on meeting them, so I'm sure the answer to all the above questions is a clear and emphatic yes.

Ever your friend,

Moving into a new house

Dear Bob and Sandy,

What an exciting event! Moving into your own house at last. This is something you've dreamed about, saved for, and prayed about for many years. We wish you well.

Be sure (and we're speaking from experience—some happy, some sad) to make important decisions together. Put a lot of fun into the give-and-take of your discussions. If you recognize and respect one another's gifts and abilities, you will each find joy and satisfaction in your areas of expertise.

Do enjoy settling in, and let the Lord be the head of your home.

Cordially yours,

Bringing home a new baby

Dear Jeanne and Dave,

Congratulations! We were delighted to hear about the new member of your family—baby Camille. You were right when you said, "What a wonderful gift from God she is!"

And you were wise to admit that you feel "a little apprehensive about caring for such an awesome gift." I can assure you, however, that the two of you have access to the wisdom and knowledge necessary to raise your daughter "in the fear and admonition of the Lord." Both of you have a lot of love to give, and when you show your love in tender care every day, you will find that your responsibilities will naturally and easily expand to include social, intellectual, and spiritual nurture.

As you allow God to guide you, he will give you the wisdom to make good choices, and you will see your little girl develop in ways that will be exciting to watch. And you will find that as she grows, so will you.

Do enjoy parenting.

Sincerely,

Finishing a job well

Dear Greg,

When you offered to direct vacation Bible school this year, I must admit that I wasn't sure you could do the job. You are young and quiet, and I wondered if you could gain the respect of the teachers and leaders.

Well, you did! Long before opening day you had lined up teachers, assistants, and even people to teach crafts—and you had them all assigned to classes they were best suited for. Everyone was eager to start, and there was good cooperation all around. Everything went remarkably well.

I never expressed my misgivings to anyone, and I'd like to tell you it was good to be proved wrong. Now I will heartily recommend you to serve again—maybe as Sunday school superintendent next year?

Gratefully yours,

Meeting high expectations

Dear Pastor Mike,

This has been a difficult year for you, I know. Following in the footsteps of a pastor the people all loved and admired was a tough assignment, but you have handled it well. Better than well, in fact. You have far exceeded everyone's expectations.

This has been a good year for our church. We have become a stronger, more unified body, and we have grown in our knowledge of the Bible. It has become clear to us that the Lord has called you here and that you are trying to please him first of all. And that is what has made us come to love and respect you so much in such a short time.

I pray that the Lord of the church will give you long and fruitful service with us.

Sincerely,

Going the extra mile

Dear Laura,

We wonder if you know how much our daughter Ellen is benefiting from your teaching this year. We didn't expect her to enjoy sixth grade, but she certainly does. And homework is a priority for her now. We can hardly believe it. She tells us that you take time to answer all class questions—even the dumb ones, she says—and you explain the lessons carefully. You always take time for her when she asks for help.

So you have touched our hearts too by the quality of your teaching and by your authentic Christian love.

With deep appreciation,

7

Letters of Blessing

For the soul of intimacy there is no better home than letters of intimate value saved over a lifetime.

THOMAS MOORE, *SoulMates*

Then all the people left, each for his own home, and David returned home to bless his family. . . . "Now you have been pleased to bless the house of your servant, that it may continue forever in your sight; for you, O LORD, have blessed it, and it will be blessed forever."

1 CHRONICLES 16:43; 17:27 NIV

*P*laces to go. Things to do. People to see. The pace we keep leaves little or no time for family storytelling, so today's children are growing up without a sense of their own history. Advances in technology that have solved one type of problem have left us with new ones. For example, improvements in transportation have given the business community access to world markets, but the community known as family has been pulled and stretched to the breaking point due to the resulting *travel requirements for employees and relocations to other states and countries.*

Grandmothers and grandfathers and aunts, uncles, and cousins—all once a part of the nurturing family environment—no longer live down the street or across town; they live in different parts of the state or across the nation. Children don't get to sit on Grandpa's knee and listen to him tell about the "olden days" because Grandpa lives two thousand miles away.

To compensate for the lack of an intimate family setting, you can create a "surrogate" setting for intimacy. Writing your stories as letters will help overcome the physical distance between you and your loved ones by creating an emotional closeness with them.

We call these written accounts "letters of blessing" because they are written documents that "speak well" of someone. There are two types of letters of blessing: those that speak well of the person to whom they are sent and those that speak well of God. Both types are important to write.

Letters of blessing that speak well of the person to whom they are sent are generally written by the older generation to the younger one (e.g., a parent, grandparent, or other significant adult to a child or young adult). But they can also be written by a younger person to an older one (e.g., to a parent, grandparent, or other significant adult).

When you write these letters focus on what you appreciate about the child. Why is he or she special to you? Think of your letter as a gift of love that will outlive you. If you ask yourself what kind of information will make a difference in the child's life, you will know what to say. You don't need to be a professional writer. Just be observant, honest, and loving.

Letters of blessing are appropriate for children of all ages. Young or old, children love to hear stories about themselves. You can write as many of them as you want and as often as you can find time. Some people write letters annually. Others write whenever a year is especially significant. Some who are unusually ambitious write them for holidays, special events (e.g., concerts, recitals, performances, sporting events), or special accomplishments (e.g., honor roll, dean's list, graduations, or other individual achievements).

As you write, try to imagine the child as an adult. What information do you want him or her to know? What has happened in the last year that will give the child self-understanding as an adult? Write as you would talk. Make it personal, but keep it simple.

How to do it

Make a list of things you want to include in the letter. *To come up with ideas you may want to review photos taken during the year, look at notes you made on the calendar, and reread your journal. Here are some topics to get you started:*

- *typical daily schedule*
- *Mom and Dad's ages, jobs*
- *child's personality traits, likes, dislikes, etc.*
- *cute things the child has said*
- *accomplishments made during the year*
- *special family memories*
- *favorite toys, playmates*
- *favorite phrases*
- *meaningful poems or verses*
- *best mess of the year*

Arrange the list in an outline.
Write a rough draft.
Polish the letter. *Check spelling and grammar and look for places where you can add interesting details or a bit of humor. Try to make the person reading it feel as if he or she is experiencing the action you are writing about. Write in a style that is similar to the way you speak. That way the person reading it will hear your voice when reading your words. Paint a picture by using descriptive words. Use precise details and strong, active verbs. Eliminate repetitive words (consult a thesaurus or synonym finder if necessary).*

Write the final draft. *If you use a pigma pen (a special pen with* *nonfading ink available at art or office supply stores) on acid-free paper, your letter will last for many years. Some people type their letters—even personal ones—but a handwritten letter is more valuable as a keepsake because your handwriting will be meaningful to future generations.*

Preserve the letter in a scrapbook or photo album. *Once you get started, you'll find it so meaningful that you'll wish someone had done this for you. You might even decide to write one for yourself by recording your own memories.*

The sample letters in this chapter are longer than the others in this book simply because details are more important than brevity in this type of letter.

Baby's birth—record of delivery

Write a rough draft of this letter while the details are still fresh in your mind. Try to write it before you leave the hospital or within the first week.

Dear Zachary Douglas,

In November, 1987, your sister Nicole asked God for a baby brother. Daddy and I were planning to wait a while longer before adding another child to our family, but God and Nicole had different plans. Three weeks after Nicole's request, you were conceived.

The first three months of my pregnancy I was much more nauseated than I had been with your sisters. I had several migraines too. After three months I felt better, but then the summer heat hit! July and August were miserable!

You weren't due to arrive until August 25, but on August 9 I told Grandma that I didn't think it would be long before you came. Sure enough! I woke up at 1:45 the next morning feeling as if I were in labor! I got up and did some laundry, but the contractions didn't stop. I called Daddy at work (he was working the night shift), but he had already left. Next I called the doctor, and then I called Grandma and Grandpa and asked them to come stay with Nicole and Jessica. I got dressed, put on some makeup, packed my bag, and sat down to wait. I got a little nervous wondering if I would have to deliver you all by myself.

When Daddy arrived at 3:30, I asked him to please hurry! We arrived at the hospital at 3:40, and the emergency room attendant took me up to maternity while Daddy parked the car.

The nurse checked me and said I was "almost complete," meaning that you weren't in the mood to wait for anyone, not even your Daddy. The nurses paged Daddy and told him to run! He came rushing up, followed by the doctor a few minutes later. They said I could push, so I did, and three contractions later you arrived. It was 4:20 A.M.! I pulled you up onto my tummy, and Daddy exclaimed, "We got our boy!" Then Daddy cut the cord.

Mommy held you for a while, and you were fussing. When Daddy took you, you quieted right down. The nurse cleaned you up while the doctor finished up with me. Then I breastfed you, and the nurse brought a snack to Daddy and me.

The nurse and Daddy took you to the admitting nursery to be weighed and measured. You weighed 7 pounds, 15 ounces (bigger than your sisters). I was glad you had come two and a half weeks before your due date! The nurse said you were strong because you pulled your head right up. The doctor agreed when he tried to straighten your legs out. That didn't surprise me since I was used to feeling you push your feet into my side before you were born.

Daddy picked Zachary for your first name, and I insisted on Douglas (after Daddy) for your middle name. When Grandma told Nicole and Jessica they had a new baby brother, Nicole exclaimed, "I prayed for a baby brother!" They came to see you in the evening and were so excited. They both kissed you and hugged you, and Nicole held you, sang to you, and called the little white spots on your nose "sparkles."

When we left for home, you screamed all the way from my room to

A Birthday Blessing

Faye Field

Behold, what manner of love the Father hath bestowed upon us. . . .
— 1 JOHN 3:1 KJV

WHEN my son Mike was born, I was overwhelmed by the miracle of this baby, red and wrinkled but beautiful beyond compare with anything I had ever seen. When I returned home from the hospital, one of the first things that I did was to write a letter of joyous welcome to this infant. I placed the letter in the filing cabinet, thinking, *Someday I will read this message to him.*

When Mike's first birthday came, I wrote another letter to him telling of the various happenings of this first amazing year. Year after year this became a habit. On each birthday I wrote another letter, dated it, and sealed it. There were thank-you notes for happy days spent together, records of illnesses and recoveries, descriptions of changes from babyhood to boyhood, from childhood to adolescence. On Mike's twenty-first birthday we opened each of these letters saved for more than two decades. What a happy parade of memories!

On that very day I thought of another type of letter to write. So since that time twenty years ago, I write a letter to Christ on his birthday. These Christmas letters also tell of thankfulness for joyful days, appreciation for recovery of an ailing body or a faltering spirit, and prayers of gratitude for strength needed to meet changing lifestyles during the year. Perhaps no one will ever read them. But I know what they say. And Jesus knows.

Dear God, I am so thankful for birthdays and for their reminder that you are ever-present and ever-working in my life.

the lobby (I think you wanted everyone to know you were leaving). When we got home Daddy showed you the whole house.

You are such a wonderful gift from God! We love you very much and promise to be the best parents we can be, with God's help. We pray that you will commit your life to the Lord while you are young. Living to please him will be your best hope for a full and meaningful life.

With lots and lots of love,

Baby's dedication or baptism—to parents

Dear Doug and Sue,

We rejoice with you on the occasion of Nicole's dedication, or, better stated, *your* dedication as her parents.

The following verses of Scripture speak for themselves and, though short, will give you a framework for every parenting decision you have to make.

Deuteronomy 6:5–7 NIV: "Love the Lord your God with all your heart and with all your soul and with all your strength. These commandments that I give you today are to be upon your hearts. Impress them on your children. Talk about them when you sit at home and when you walk along the road, when you lie down and when you get up."

Proverbs 22:6 NIV: "Train a child in the way he should go, and when he is old he will not turn from it."

What a privilege and awesome responsibility to be Nicole's parents. As part of your family, we will be honored to support you in any way we can.

We love you three,

Baby's dedication or baptism—to child

Dear Whitney,

Today your daddy and I went before the whole church and dedicated you to the Lord. That means that we have promised to do our best to be godly parents and to bring you up "in the training and instruction of the Lord" (Ephesians 6:4 NIV).

Being responsible for your care and upbringing is an awesome task and one that we would not dare to attempt without God's help. We are happy to be part of a church that has many examples of godly parents that we can use as role models.

When Pastor Dobson took you from Daddy's arms you didn't even whimper, but your eyes did get big and I could tell you were trying to figure out if you should trust him or not. Then, just before he started to pray, you reached out to touch his beard, your eyes still fixed on his unfamiliar face. I don't think you blinked the whole time he was holding you.

Pastor Dobson prayed that you would come to know Jesus at an early age and that you would grow up to be physically healthy, emotionally strong, mentally alert, and spiritually sensitive.

We consider it an honor and a blessing from God to be your parents, Whitney, and we promise you that we will keep our lives submitted to him so that he can show us how to be the best parents we can be.

We love you,

Birthday letter to a two-year-old

Dear Benjamin,

Are you my Buster Brown? Daddy calls you Goomer. Anyhow, you're the cutest little brown-haired two-year-old we've had the privilege of loving!

You've really come to life this last year, and we love to see your dimpled smile and hear your husky voice! You love to talk about airplanes and balloons (and "balloon pop," which is what keeps happening to your balloons). Your newest sentence is "I need it first." Every morning you wake me up by announcing, "Eat breakfast?" And for the rest of the day you continue to think about food. You search the refrigerator, climb up on the counter, and sneak anything and everything edible you can find (including leftover popcorn from a bag in the living room wastebasket).

Second only to food, you love cousin Christopher. You're always ready to go "bye-bye," especially to Christopher's house. You pretend you're talking to Christopher on the phone, and all the blond-haired boys in your story books are Christopher.

You're learning how to go potty on the toilet, and I keep telling myself it won't be too much longer before you're completely potty-trained. You have the flushing part down pat. You flushed your toothbrush down one toilet and a pencil down another. The plumber charged us fifty dollars to fix them.

Your birthday was fun for all of us! You love to blow out the candles. It got to the point that every time we said the words *birthday, cake,* or *candles,* you asked, "Blow fire?" You even blow out the candles Aunt Catherine lights at her house, and you tried your hardest to blow out the fire in Uncle Phil's fireplace. I made a balloon cake for your birthday, but while I was in the bathroom you pulled it down and stuffed a handful of it into your mouth. Lots of frosting fixed the gaping hole in the cake. Daddy got three big balloons for you, and they were your favorite present!

We love you lots!

Birthday letter to a ten-year-old

Dear Lynne,

Your Dad and I have both remarked on how you are beginning to blossom into a young woman! You're becoming very capable and self-confident and you love to read, cook, and bake. You are very special to us!

One conversation we've had repeatedly (and it amuses me) is about the things you and I have in common. We've come up with a list of eight things. We both . . .

- were the firstborn child
- were born on the twelfth of the month

- love to read books
- like babies
- are (or in my case, was) picky about food
- have uncommonly thick hair
- have soprano singing voices
- have one crooked tooth

I'm glad we recognize these similarities, and although we sometimes clash because of them, I will work to make sure that we find ways to enjoy being alike!

Our hope for you is that you will continue to claim as your life verse Job 23:11 NIV: "My feet have closely followed his steps; I have kept to his way without turning aside."

Daddy and I do not expect that you will never sin, but we pray that you will stay on God's path and never swerve from it. The only way to do this is to remember what Jesus said are the greatest commandments: to love God and to love others. Only God himself can help you to do that. And we pray every day that he will help all of us do that.

Much love,

On entering adolescence

Dear Elisa,

You are entering a new stage in your life which is very exciting but potentially turbulent. You're beginning to bloom into a young woman. The changes your body is undergoing are immense. At times you may feel awkward, but take it from one who knows: Everything will come into balance.

You probably will go through a period of fatigue and you may be frustrated when your body requires more rest. During this time it is more important than ever to eat foods that nourish you (don't forget those veggies!). I expect that you will experience emotional extremes, especially when your menstrual cycle starts. Although the next couple of years may be stressful, they are a time when you can add many positive characteristics to the personality you will have as an adult.

Over the next several years you will gain more freedom, but also more responsibility as you move toward becoming an independent adult.

I'm confident, Elisa, that you will grow into a beautiful young woman, but I pray that your true beauty will shine from the inside.

I love you,

On graduation from high school

Dear Linda,

Today is your high school graduation. Is it possible? You can't be that old already! But you are. My graying head gives it away, doesn't it?

Eighteen years ago God gave you to Mom and me. I clearly recall the morning you were born. Your mother and I were in our Wheaton apartment. In the early morning hours she alerted me to oncoming birth pains. I hurried to shave but was interrupted when she came to my side and grasped my hand. I helped her through an excruciating pain. My hand hurt as she squeezed it during those tense moments! We hastened to the car and then raced to the hospital. Within an hour you arrived. You were a beautiful baby girl, and I was a beaming father.

In succeeding months I found deep joy in holding you and looking into your innocent oval face. While you were still a tender child your mother and I took you to the mission field. It was in Bangladesh you grew up. In spite of what the world might call "disadvantages," you changed from a little child into a beautiful young woman. Your accomplishments in so many areas make us realize that God has had his hand on your life from the beginning. He has a rich and wonderful ministry for you.

When I look at you now I see so many of your mother's traits. I see also something of myself in you! Your determination and thriftiness are to be admired. Should I mention stubbornness too? Behind that attractive face is a strong will that will be a great advantage if you surrender it to God and use it in the service of your Lord and Savior. With the will and determination to do what is right you'll be a success in life no matter what you do. Always remember Proverbs 3:5–6 NIV: "Trust in the Lord with all your heart and lean not on your own understanding; in all your ways acknowledge him, and he will make you paths straight."

Mom and I love you more than ever, and we offer our sincere congratulations to you on this your special day.

With love and affection,

On engagement

Dear Brian,

Thank you for taking time to write to Linda's mother and me about such an important subject. We appreciate your thoughtfulness.

We tried to teach our daughters to have good judgment in everything, and you are proof that Linda learned the lesson well. Since she has fallen in love with you, and you with her, and since you both love the Lord and want to do his will, we are delighted to offer our blessings on your marriage.

Linda's mother and I both agree that you will make a fine husband for our daughter. The two of you have our pledge of support as you plan your wedding and as you pursue life together.

We're praying for both of you,

On wedding day

Dear Jessica,

My tears are overflowing from a heart bursting with joy for you on this lovely day of your wedding. Your Dad and I are so thrilled that you have chosen a man that not only loves you, but also loves our Lord.

My marriage prayer for you is this: That you will always remember the qualities that attracted you to each other when you first met and

Love Lives Forever

Gina Bridgeman

Hearken unto me: hold thy peace, and I shall teach thee wisdom.

— JOB 33:33 KJV

I NEVER met Pop (as everyone called my mother's father) because he died before I was born. But I know him through my parents' many stories. He was strong, quiet and wise, with tremendous patience.

Pop was a "do-it-yourselfer," and his basement workshop was a handyman's dream. Perched atop his workbench was his "treasure chest," a collection of at least two dozen little drawers neatly holding screws, nails, hooks, tacks, staples, nuts, bolts, and washers. One day my two-and-one-half-year-old brother, Joe, reached up to pull out one of the drawers. Instead he brought the whole chest tumbling down with a tremendous crash. A jumbled mess of hardware lay an inch deep at Pop's feet. He took one look and said, "Well, you know, I really had to straighten out those drawers anyway."

That lesson in patience and understanding has gotten our family through many aggravations. When a mishap occurs, we all try to be the first to find the hidden consolation. Yesterday I broke a bottle of liquid soap in the bathtub and said, "Well, I needed to clean the tub anyway, and now I even have the soap!"

Although I never had the chance to cuddle in Pop's lap for a bedtime story, his loving spirit touches my life. Through the stories about him, his gifts of wisdom and love are still alive.

Dear God, help me to pass on the love and wisdom of my grandparents and to make some blessed new memories for my children today.

how you felt as your feelings of attraction turned into respect, admiration, and finally love. That you will work hard to turn your feelings of love into acts of love so that nothing and no one can divide you. That you will always have kind and loving hearts that are quick to ask for forgiveness when you have been wrong as well as to forgive when your partner has been wrong. That your love might grow into one that "bears all things, believes all things, hopes all things, endures all things" (1 Corinthians 13:7 NIV).

I pray that you will place your marriage in God's hands and that he will make your love increase and overflow beyond anything you can yet imagine.

With love,

On a holiday

Write about incidents that are just a little bit out of the ordinary. They make interesting stories that are fun to remember. Little details can spice up the story and provide information about yourself and other family members as well as of the main person of the story.

Dear Kristy,

When your Daddy asked if he could bring you to our house to make Christmas cookies, I said, "Sure, I've got everything we need. Just come on over."

But when you arrived and I started looking for the cookie cutters, the stars and bells and trees and angels were nowhere to be found. The only cookie cutters I could dig up were two I had used in college when I made a treat for classmates to munch on while I presented a paper on the McCarthy era. The two cookie cutters represented our nation's two political parties: a donkey for the Democrats and an elephant for the Republicans. Not exactly common symbols for a Christmas celebration. Well, your dad and Uncle Jay and I racked our brains to try to think of a way to make an elephant fit into the Christmas story, but our imaginations failed us.

The donkey, of course, was a little easier. According to tradition, Mary rode into Bethlehem on a donkey the night she gave birth to Jesus; we decided therefore that the donkey was a valid, though uncommon, symbol of Christmas. And so it came to pass in the year you turned two that you made a whole batch of donkey cookies and decorated them with red and green sprinkles. You didn't mind that nobody else made red and green donkeys for Christmas. You were just happy to be working alongside your daddy.

When you get older and see the pictures of yourself decorating that platter full of cookies, you can laugh about your wacky aunt and uncle and their uncommon cookie cutters.

Maybe the pictures will also remind you to think about how often God has used uncommon things (such as donkeys and frightened young girls like Mary) to accomplish his purposes. And maybe you'll also stop to think about how God uses whatever things are available to him, even the ones that seem to be unlikely candidates for greatness.

My prayer for you this Christmas, Kristy, is that you will make every area of your life, no matter how small, and every aspect of your being, no matter how insignificant, available to God.

Love,

Blessing to mother

Dear Mom,

I really enjoyed having lunch with you the other day. Afterward I pondered what it is that makes me enjoy you so much, and I want you to know what I figured out.

I appreciate your zest for grabbing hold of all the life you can get! When Dad refused to travel with you, you saved your quarters and took your own trips. (I was happy to go with you to California.) Although your parents never encouraged you to go to college, you dreamed of it and kept the dream alive. Then, once all your children were in school, you went too—and stuck with it. Not many kids get to

Messages that Matter the Most

Carol Kuykendall

Let there be thanksgiving.   — EPHESIANS 5:4 RSV

I CAME across this clipping in my files," said the note from an old friend of my mother's. "And I wanted you to know how much it meant to your mother." Tucked inside was a folded, yellowing copy of a Mother's Day column I had written for our local newspaper.

The urge to do it had come from Hospice, the group that helps families cope with death and dying. "Take care of all unfinished business with the people you love," they advise. "Say what you need to say. Don't save your words for a tribute at a funeral." I had written:

> That's good advice for any relationship. . . . To me it means that I must tell my mother right now how many things she's done well in her life and how much I appreciate some of the qualities, characteristics, and indelible memories she's given me.

The column highlighted some of those memories and touched upon those parts of me that will always aim to be like her. At the bottom of the clipping, my mother had written: "This is the best message a mother could hear." She died of emphysema a couple of months later at age sixty-five.

I put the letter down and began thinking about other messages I could write—to my husband, our children, our friends, our minister. Later that day I bought a bunch of cards that I'm going to use to tell others what they mean to me. Now. Because those messages matter.

Father, remind me to take the time to pass on the messages that matter. Now.

attend college with their mom. Even now, with many health limitations, you live through the books you read.

I love the way you enjoy my children. Thank you for laughing at their cute little phrases and taking their stories seriously. I appreciate your encouragement for my own dreams and aspirations.

Even with much adversity in your life, you refuse to succumb to despair. I admire you and I'm glad you're my mom.

Love,

Blessing to parents

Dear Mom and Dad,

Recently I have begun to realize that the best gift you ever gave me is one that has no monetary value. When I was ten, I thought the best gift was a poodle skirt "just like Sue's" because I believed it would make me popular. When I was thirteen I thought the best gift was a new pair of roller skates because I believed they would make me skate better and then Billy Olson would love me. When I was eighteen, I thought the best gift was a college education because it would make me intellectually and socially superior to the bums who didn't even notice my new skirt or my new skates.

You could have lectured me about the futility of thinking that an item of clothing could make me popular (and you probably did), but you also gave me the freedom to discover it for myself. You could have preached about the dangers of believing that anything other than practice will make me perform better (and you probably did) and that trying to win male attention by performing well leads to a frustrating life of unrealistic expectations (and you probably did) but you also gave me the freedom to find it out for myself. You could have warned me that a college education was only a tool to enable me to achieve my potential—either for evil or for good—(and you probably did), but you also gave me the freedom to find out for myself that knowledge apart from wisdom and love leads to destruction. You let me learn for myself that it's not what I have in my head that matters but what is in my heart.

Where did you find the courage to give me the frightening gift of freedom? Did you realize when you were giving it that it is the most godly gift of all? Were you aware that the freedom to choose good or evil is the great risk God takes with all of his children? Did you know that your gift of freedom was the ultimate act of love?

I didn't—until just recently, and I can't imagine how scary that must have been. Thank you for resisiting the powerful temptation to try to control me when it was time for me to control myself.

I love you,

If you did not write a letter of blessing to your parents before they died but wish you had, you can still write one. Even though they will never see it, it will be of immense value to you. By putting into writing the qualities you admired in your parents, you will in effect be erecting a monument of words in their honor. It will be a reminder to you and to future generations of the goodness that is part of your family heritage. And perhaps it will motivate others to see the value of those qualities and develop them in their own lives.

The second type of letter of blessing is one that speaks well of God. These letters are your personal testimony of how he has worked in your life; they tell of God's faithfulness to you; they are your spiritual heritage.

Moses, after receiving from God the Ten Commandments, wrote,

> *When your son asks you, "What is the meaning of the stipulations, decrees and laws the LORD our God has commanded you?" tell him: "We were slaves of Pharaoh in Egypt, but the LORD brought us out of Egypt with a mighty hand. . . . The LORD commanded us to obey all these decrees and to fear the LORD our God, so that we might always prosper and be kept alive, as is the case today" (Deuteronomy 6:20–24 NIV).*

It is important for children and grandchildren to know their religious heritage as well as their biological heritage. Perhaps they will never ask you why you believe as you do, but you can leave a written answer for them as part of their spiritual heritage. The apostle Peter said that a ready answer is something all Christians are to have: "Always be prepared to give an answer to everyone who asks you to give the reason for the hope that you have" (1 Peter 3:15 NIV).

Here are some topics you could write about in letters of spiritual blessing to your children and grandchildren:

- *Why I became a Christian.*
- *How God has helped me through difficult times.*
- *What I have learned about being obedient to God.*
- *Things that have challenged my faith.*
- *Things that have made my faith grow.*

Spiritual heritage—
Grandfather to grandchild
Why I became a Christian

Dear Julie,

Your Aunt Ruth was only eighteen when she died of tuberculosis, and her death changed my whole life. Up until that time I had been pretty selfish. Times were tough during the Great Depression, but my restlessness made them even tougher for my family. I never liked any of the jobs I had so I kept hopping from one to another, always looking for something better. I know now that all the moving we did was really hard on your grandma and our five children, especially the two youngest ones, your mama and Uncle Jack. They were always having to make new friends because they never went to the same school two years in a row.

For a long time after Ruth died I blamed her husband. I had myself convinced that if he hadn't taken her away and gotten her pregnant, she wouldn't have died. But I know now that blaming him was just another way for me to avoid taking responsibility. I couldn't bring myself to admit that maybe my own selfish choices were involved—that maybe the reason Ruthie got married so young was because she needed some stability in her life that I never provided for her.

It took your Aunt Ruth's death to make me finally realize that a lot of things in life were more important than myself and that it was time for me to find out what they were. Your grandma and I started going to a little church in town, and it was there that we heard the gospel message for the first time. I realized that I was a sinner in need of forgiveness, and I understood that the only way to receive that forgiveness was to identify myself with Jesus Christ, who gave his life in place of mine so that I would inherit eternal life with him.

I would never say that God caused my Ruthie to die, but God did use her death to get my attention. When she was taken from me I realized that eternal things were much more important than anything in this life.

I am leaving this letter for you and all my grandchildren so that you will have a record of the journey that brought me to faith in Christ. And I am praying that you will trust him early in life so that you will have his wisdom to guide you and keep you from making some of the selfish choices I made.

With love,

To work through grief

Some feelings are so intense that the only way to deal with them is to put them into words. Emotions have been described as a flood, a torrent, a force that rips us from our moorings and pulls us along in a feeling of helplessness.

If indeed emotions are like rushing floodwaters that pull us helplessly along, words are like a kayak and an oar. They allow us to navigate the rapids with some degree of control; they help us keep our heads above water; they keep us from crashing into the rocks. By trying to describe how we feel, we can begin to understand our feelings; and when we understand our feelings, we can learn to live peaceably with them.

Love, one of the strongest of all emotions, is often poured out in letters. But grief, which is equally powerful, seldom is. The logical explanation is that the cause of grief is often the death of a loved one, and so we are left with no one to write to.

But the therapeutic value of writing is in the writing itself; it has nothing to do with the response of the person about whom or to whom you are writing. So writing a letter has value even if the one writing it is the only one who ever reads it. On the other hand, a letter written by someone working through grief can have immense value to other members of the family.

As mentioned before, the process of converting feelings into written words is a way to make your emotions tangible. And once they are tangible they are more easily managed.

The following letter was written by a father* to a daughter after her death. You can see how such a letter would be beneficial not only to the father but also to his wife and other children as they struggled to make sense of seemingly senseless suffering.

My Dear Bristol,

Before you were born I prayed for you. In my heart I knew that you would be a little angel. And so you were!

When you were born on my birthday it was evident to me that you were a special gift from the Lord. But how profound a gift you turned out to be! More than the beautiful bundle of gurgles and rosy cheeks, more than the first-born of my flesh, a joy unspeakable, you showed me God's love more than anything else in creation. Bristol, you taught me how to love.

I certainly loved you when you were cuddly and cute, when you rolled over and sat up and jabbered your first words. I loved you when the searing pain of realization took hold that something was wrong—that maybe you were not developing as quickly as your peers, and then when we understood it was more serious than that. I loved you when

*   Used by permission of Ralph Plumb, Spring Lake, Michigan.

we went from hospital to clinic to doctor looking for a medical diagnosis that would bring some hope. And, of course, we always prayed for you . . . and prayed . . . and prayed. I loved you when one of the tests resulted in too much spinal fluid being drawn from your body and you screamed. I loved you when you moaned and cried, when your mom and I and your sisters would drive for hours late at night to help you fall asleep. I loved you with tears in my eyes when, confused, you would bite your fingers or your lip by accident, and when your eyes crossed and then went blind.

I most certainly loved you when you could no longer speak, but how profoundly I missed your voice! I loved you when your scoliosis started wrenching your body like a pretzel, when we put a tube in your stomach so you could eat because you were choking on your food, which we fed you one spoonful at a time for up to two hours per meal. I managed to love you when your contorted limbs would not allow ease of changing your messy diapers . . . so many diapers . . . ten years of diapers.

Bristol, I even loved you when you could not say the one thing in life that I longed to hear back, "Daddy, I love you." Bristol, I loved you when I was close to God and when he seemed far away, when I was full of faith and also when I was angry with him.

And the reason I loved you, my Bristol, in spite of these difficulties, is that God put this love in my heart. This is the wondrous nature of God's love, that he loves us even when we are blind, or deaf, or twisted— in body or in spirit. God loves us even when we can't tell him that we love him back.

My dear Bristol, now you are free! I look forward to that day, according to God's promises, when we will be joined together with you and with the Lord, completely whole and full of joy. I'm so happy that you have your crown first. We will follow you someday—in his time.

Before you were born I prayed for you. In my heart I knew that you would be a little angel. And so you were!

Love, Daddy

8

Letters of Invitation

Share with God's people who are in need. Practice hospitality.
                                                            ROMANS 12:13 NIV

Happy the man who never puts on a face, but receives every visitor with that countenance he has on.
                                                            RALPH WALDO EMERSON

A house may draw visitors, but it is the possessor alone that can detain them.   **CHARLES CALEB COLTON**

*O*ne of the most selfless gifts we can give another person is our time, for it is a commodity that we can neither replace nor replenish. So when we invite someone to spend time with us, we are in a sense giving away a part of ourselves.

Whenever we write a letter of invitation, therefore, whether it is for business or pleasure, we are paying the person a compliment, for we are saying, "You are so important to me that I want to spend time with you."

There are some occasions for which letters of invitation are not necessary, but they are always appropriate. For example, you can use the phone to invite someone to dinner, but sending a note or letter of invitation will make the occasion seem more special.

Letters of invitation can be either formal or informal, depending on the occasion. Formal invitations are sent for formal occasions such as weddings, and as a rule are professionally typeset and printed. Informal invitations are sent to friends or acquaintances for social purposes like office parties, birthday celebrations, or reunions. In between these two types are those sent for business or professional purposes.

When writing a letter of invitation, keep in mind five questions. They are the questions journalists use when writing stories, and they are useful in any situation that involves communication. The five questions are Who? What? When? Where? and Why?

If you answer these questions in your letter you will have communicated all the necessary information.

Who? *The person(s) to whom the invitation is addressed. Be careful to make it clear, for example, whether or not you are inviting children.*

What? *The occasion for the get-together. Is it a birthday, reunion, business meeting? Is it for lunch, dinner, coffee, dessert?*

*Other important parts of the **What?** question to answer in your letter are . . .*

What type of response do you expect from people? *Do you expect them to call you if they are coming? If so, write R.S.V.P. (Répondez, s'il vous plaît) somewhere on the invitation and be sure to include your phone number and a date by which you need to know.*

Will you call to confirm? If you promise to call, make sure you have access to up-to-date phone numbers.

Is a response necessary? If you are inviting many people to an event such as an open house, you may not need to know every person who is coming. If that is the case, a simple "regrets only" on the invitation will tell recipients that only those who cannot come need to respond.

What, if anything, do you want people to bring? *If your get-together is a picnic, you may want people to bring their own table* service; if it's a large reunion, you may want them to supply some of the food.

When? The date and time you want to meet. Make sure you include both of these details. Leaving out either the time or the date could cause serious frustration or disappointment.

Where? The place where you will meet. Your home? A park? A restaurant? If you're meeting at a restaurant which has more than one location in your town, be sure to specify which one. You may also need to include directions to the location for people coming from out of town.

Why? The purpose of the meeting or occasion. Is it a social occasion to renew an aquaintance, a business meeting to discuss your company's five-year plan, or a professional meeting to address a specific topic?

Generosity, hospitality, and willing and cheerful service to others are three qualities that please God because they reflect his character and accomplish his work in the world.

You don't need to wait for a special event or occasion to invite people to your home. Just being invited will make it a special occasion.

Inviting a friend for dinner

Dear Jennifer,

It's been much too long since we had some time to talk. If you are free for dinner on Tuesday, August 3, we could make up for lost time. If you can be at my house by about 6:00, I'll plan to serve dinner at 6:30. I found a new recipe for Mexican lasagna I'd like to try, and I know you love Mexican food as much as I do.

I'll call you next week to make sure that date works for you. If it doesn't, maybe we can decide on some other time. I'm looking forward to seeing you.

Your friend,

Inviting a speaker to address your group

Dear Ms. Walker,

I heard you speak at the Women's Art Club last September and was very encouraged by your talk. My chapter is holding its annual dinner on May 3. We would be delighted if you would agree to be our keynote speaker. Please contact me at your earliest convenience to discuss this further. My phone number is ___-____.

Thank you for your consideration of this matter. I hope to hear from you soon.

Sincerely,

A Stranger in Need

Marion Bond West

I was a stranger, and you invited me in. . . .   — MATTHEW 25:35 NIV

JOY and Wayne Dawson lived only fifteen miles from me, and I was surprised to learn of their unusual lifestyle when they were featured on a television news broadcast. Joy spoke happily to the interviewer, "Anyone can come and live with us if they don't have a place to stay," she explained. "They can remain with us as long as they like. They're welcome to become a part of our family. The Lord has given us a ministry of sharing our home with strangers."

I phoned Joy in Loganville, Georgia, and we chatted like old friends. I asked if I could come and meet her. "Sure, stay as long as you like," she laughed warmly.

The large, old, wooden house was painted beige and trimmed in farm red. Joy came running out to meet me wearing an ankle-length,

Inviting a friend to join a club

Dear Susan,

As you know, I belong to the City Writer's Club, which hosts luncheons every month at which speakers discuss an aspect of writing. Since you are interested in writing, why not join our group? It would be wonderful to have you in the Club and we could see each other more often. Let me know as soon as you can. The next luncheon is on Tuesday, August 4. I'll call you next week to find out if you can attend. Maybe we can ride together.

Your friend,

full skirt and a knitted sweater over a blouse. Her long, auburn hair was piled casually on her head. I don't think she wore makeup, yet she possessed the unmistakable beauty that comes from deep contentment. I knew she wouldn't reject my outstretched arms. We hugged for a moment, then I asked point-blank, "Do you really take in anyone who knocks on your door?"

She nodded matter-of-factly. "It's our lifestyle. Our children understand and help. God has been so good to us, helped us when we desperately needed help, and we want to pass along his love to those in need."

Driving home after our visit, I suddenly remembered houseguests though the years whom I had resented. Had they known? Had they sensed my cold heart and reserved smile? I made up my mind to do better.

Come into my house, Lord Jesus, and teach me about hospitality and unselfishness. Amen.

Inviting neighbors to a church dinner

Dear Jim and Denise,

Every Wednesday night our church offers dinner to families before the service. It gives us a night out of the house with our children at a price most families can afford ($2.50 for adults and $1 for children under 12). Dick and I were wondering if you and your family like to join us next Wednesday night as our guests? We would enjoy the company and the opportunity to spend more time getting to know you. After dinner there are club programs for the children and sessions for adults that address such topics as business ethics, the difference between Christianity and other religions, and parent-teen relationship (a question-and-answer session for parents of teenagers). You can go to whichever one sounds the most interesting.

Dinner is served from 5 to 6:15, and the programs run from 6:30 to 8.

I'll call you the first part of next week to find out if you would like to go with us.

Sincerely,

Inviting employees to a barbecue

Dear John and Laren,

As you know, my husband and I spend as many weekends at our cottage on Lake Michigan as we can, once our kids are out of school for the summer. This year we've decided to host weekend barbecues for all the people who work for me in the editorial department. We are wondering if you and your two boys could join us on Saturday, July 15, at about noon, for a steak fry. The kids can swim if the weather is nice (and the waves aren't too high) or they can just play games on the beach. You don't need to bring anything except bathing suits and towels. We're inviting two other families to join us as well. It should be a fun time for everyone.

Please check your calendars and let us know by June 30 whether or

Making an Effort to Make Friends

Linda Neukrug

A man that hath friends must show himself friendly. . . .
— PROVERBS 18:24 KJV

WHEN I first moved to California, I had a very difficult time adjusting. I'd heard that people here were friendly, so I looked forward to daily morning strolls and having strangers say, "Hello!" But nothing like that happened. No one ever greeted me, and as I searched for friendly faces, I became more and more dejected.

When I complained about this to my new coworker Cal, His forehead wrinkled. "That's odd," he said. "I've gone jogging many times on that very same path and every single person I pass says 'Hello.' Would you like me to show you?" I nodded, agreeing to meet him at seven the next morning.

The next day as I walked fast and Cal jogged, I was startled to hear an enthusiastic "Hello!" as we passed the very first person on our route—but it had come from Cal! Right away the man returned a cheery "Hello!" Another person came along. "Hello!" Cal called. "Hello!" the woman replied with a big smile. "Hey," I said to Cal, "that's cheating! You said hello first."

But then I laughed when I saw how I had been cheating—cheating myself! In the end, saying hello first could only make me the real winner. Not only the winner of good moods, a positive outlook, and heightened confidence, but of cheerful people and potential friends.

Why not practice being a "winner" with every person you meet today?

Dear God, help me to be the one to make the first friendly move.

not that date will work for you. Our phone number at the lake is ___-
____.

    We'll look forward to hearing from you.
                                                        Sincerely,

Inviting the boss to dinner

Dear Mr. and Mrs. Johnson:
    My husband, Tom, and I have been thinking how nice it would be to
get to know you better. I have so enjoyed working for you, Sandra, that
I would like to express my gratitude to you for treating me so well and
teaching me so much.
    Tom and I were wondering if the two of you could come for dinner
on Friday evening, August 9, at 7 o'clock. If it's nice outdoors we will
eat on the deck and enjoy the lovely sounds of summer.
    We do hope you can come. Please call us at ___-____ to let us know
if that date is convenient for you.
                                                        Sincerely,

Inviting college classmates to a reunion

Dear former classmates:
    The Emerys have moved back to town, and we believe that's cause
for a celebration. Please set aside Saturday, August 10, to join us at
our home for a backyard barbecue (a map is enclosed) and lots of
catching up. You're welcome to come as early as 3:00. We'll eat about
5:00, and you can stay until your voice gives out (or until you get bored
hearing all our same old stories).
    Please let me know by August 1 whether or not you can come and
if you will be bringing your spouse or a guest. Jay and I will provide
all the food and beverages, so you don't need to bring anything except
all your good memories and maybe some old photographs.
    We're not home much, so just leave a message on the answering

machine. If you have any questions, I'll call you back. Our number is ___-____.

We can't wait to see you all.

With fond memories,

Memo regarding business meeting

TO   Board of Deacons
FROM   Bill A.
DATE   25 May 199_
SUBJ   All-day planning meeting

Please mark your calendars for Saturday, June 17, for our annual all-day planning meeting. We have reserved a conference room at the Holiday Inn on Cascade Road. We'll get started promptly at 8 A.M. and will try to finish by 4 P.M. I'll send out an agenda a week before the meeting so you can prepare. I'll also talk to you individually to see if you need my help on any of the reports you're working on. It should be a great day. We've got some really exciting projects to consider.

Call me anytime if you have questions between now and then.

DECLINING AN INVITATION

When you are the one receiving an invitation rather than sending it, there will be times when you are unable to accept. A gracious letter explaining your situation can ease the disappointment of the person who invited you.

Close with encouragement

Dear Mary,

How delighted I was to learn that you've been made the Director of Volunteer Services at the hospital! Your gift of administration will be a great boon to the hospital personnel.

I appreciate your asking me to join your staff. I'd love working with you, Mary, but I'm committed at the present time to volunteer at the church library. Next year I plan to relinquish my duties and will definitely consider your proposal if you can still use me then.

There are a few women within my acquaintance who might be willing to volunteer. If you're interested, I'll arrange a meeting for you.

"Simplicate and add lightness"

Daniel Schantz

To win the contest you must deny yourselves many things that would keep you from doing your best.   — 1 CORINTHIANS 9:25 TLB

I GUESS I'm a one-speed person in a ten-speed world.

All my friends ride bikes that have ten or even twelve speeds, but the gears always seem to be out of adjustment. "How many of those speeds do you really use?" I tease them.

"Oh, one or two," is the usual reply.

A friend of mine has a fancy computer that does everything except fix coffee and carry out the trash, but he needs a college degree to run it, and it seems to be "down" more than it is up and running. There's a deluxe copy machine in our faculty workroom at the college where I teach. It copies in two colors, reduces, enlarges, and collates, among

I'm confident that with your outstanding organizational skills you'll have an efficient volunteer staff in no time.

Best wishes,

Philosophical differences

Dear Mrs. Gordon:

Your gracious letter requesting that I lead a workshop at your "Looking Within" seminar arrived on my desk yesterday. I carefully read your material and find that I agree with much of your philosophy.

However, I found several statements, which I have underlined, that are in opposition to my own beliefs. Though they may seem insignifi-

other things. It also sounds like a pile of junk, and it jams at least ten times a day. Too many bells and whistles, if you ask me.

Could it be that technology has made life a little too complex for our own good? Maybe. I know it's too much for *my* good. I've been a one-speed person ever since I first belonged to the Experimental Aircraft Association, a group that helps pilots who want to build their own aircraft. They had a motto that I adopted for my life: If you want to make a plane that will fly well, you must "simplicate and add lightness."

Would you like to "fly"? Here's a suggestion. Make a list of everything you have to do today. Now, see if you can delegate some of those items or combine a couple of them into one task. Eliminate where you can, and postpone some of the items to a better day. Lower your ambitions to fit the time and energy God has given to you.

"Simplicate and add lightness." It's a great formula for a ten-speed world.

Lord, I have such big ambitions and plans. Keep me from reaching beyond myself and falling short of you.

cant at first glance, they could cause confusion or conflict if I were to participate with you.

Therefore, I must respectfully decline to take part in the weekend seminar. I do, however, thank you for your invitation.

Sincerely,

Scheduling conflicts

Dear Dr. Sawyer:

Thank you for inviting me to join the "Yes We Can" Seniors Group. I am fully aware that you carefully select your members, and I am honored to receive this prestigious invitation.

As you know, I am a strong advocate of the "Yes We Can" philosophy and understand that your meetings are most informative and productive. However, your guidelines state that members must attend each monthly meeting. In looking over my calendar for the year, I see that this would not be possible for me.

Please express my appreciation to the selection committee along with my sincere regrets that I must decline your invitation.

Best wishes,

Will be out of town

Dear Mrs. Crawford:

Thank you for your invitation to do a workshop at your women's winter retreat in February. I am deeply honored by your request to address the women of your church.

Unfortunately, I am unable to accept your invitation. My husband and I will be on vacation during most of the month of February. Therefore, I must decline.

Again, thank you for your kind invitation. Perhaps some other occasion will bring us together in the future.

Sincerely,

9

Letters of Sympathy and Condolence

It is better to go to a house of mourning than to go to a house of feasting, for death is the destiny of every man; the living should take this to heart.   ECCLESIASTES 7:2 NIV

There is nothing sweeter than to be sympathized with.
                                          GEORGE SANTAYANA

*E*ven people who are never at a loss for words find themselves *speechless when grief is the subject. Words suddenly seem hollow and every phrase sounds trite when death or disaster invade a person's life. Yet to allow such an event to pass without acknowledgment is unkind, uncaring, even rude.*

Sympathy cards serve a useful purpose when the people involved are acquaintances, but they hardly seem adequate when the loss involves

close friends or family members. On such occasions, we struggle to find words to convey thoughts that are, at best, confused.

The first response of most people when someone they care about is hurting is to try to relieve the pain. But when pain is caused by grief, there is no relief. Nothing you can say will make it better, and nothing you can say will make it go away.

Ironically, the very thing that we think will comfort people may instead intensify their suffering. For example, Christians may believe that Scripture verses about God's promise of a future resurrection will give hope and encouragement. But such verses may instead make a grieving person feel unspiritual for not caring about eternity while they are trapped alone in the here and now.

One woman, whose husband was killed in a car accident, wrote this . . .

> *After the fatal accident of my husband, a special friend wrote a note to me describing the grief he endured after the loss of someone he loved dearly. This personal note addressed my own secret pain when I was feeling alone, screaming and sobbing to near exhaustion, not wanting to live, being angry at God, feeling guilty for being angry at God, and coming to the horrible realization that my husband and I would never again see each other on this earth. Knowing that we would be reunited in eternity did not help at that time. What did help, however, was knowing that another person understood and had experienced the things I was going through.*

As this indicates, the only way to help those who grieve is to offer to share their suffering. As Scripture says . . .

Mourn with those who mourn (Romans 12:15 NIV).

One definition of the word sympathy *is "a relationship between persons or things wherein whatever affects one similarly affects the other." Martin Luther King, Jr. said it this way, "True sympathy is the personal concern which demands the giving of one's soul."*

To express meaningful sympathy or condolence, then, we must be so in touch with grieving people that we feel their grief, carry their sorrow. Jesus modeled this behavior for us.

> *He was . . . a man of sorrows, and familiar with suffering. . . .*
> *[H]e took up our infirmities and carried our sorrows. . . .*
> *(Isaiah 53:3–4 NIV).*

Grief is such a personal thing that we often feel as if we are trespassers when we step into the space of a grieving person or family. The reason for this may be due to the fact that we misunderstand sympathy and therefore try to do what is impossible: take away the person's grief. The purpose of a letter of sympathy or condolence is not to take away grief; it is to share it. And there is a way to "mourn with those who mourn" without invading their privacy. Here are some ideas.

Express your own grief. *In so doing you are not adding to their sorrow but validating it. For some inexplicable reason, people receive more comfort from someone who cries with them than from someone who tries to make them laugh.*

Briefly mention the good things you remember about the person who has died. *For example, "She was always so cheerful," "He never said an unkind word about anyone," "I never once doubted his love for you," "She made everyone feel like the most important person in the world." Again, this type of statement confirms that the bereaved person's feelings of loss are legitimate. Not only has he or she lost a loved one; the world has lost a good person, and there is a valid reason to be sad. "There is nothing sweeter than to be sympathized with," wrote George Santayana, and when someone is tasting the bitterness of death, words of true sympathy are indeed sweet.*

Offer to do something specific. *This is the "carry their sorrows" part. The reason we struggle so much over finding something meaningful to say is that truly "meaningful" words will likely involve sacrifice;*

they will require that we do more than simply sign our names at the bottom of a card. It is much easier to feel another person's sorrow than actually to carry their grief. Even though we cannot replace the person who has died, we may, at least temporarily, be able to perform some of the tasks the person did. An offer like this allows the grieving person to deal with the loss of the loved one before having to deal with all the day-to-day realities of life without that person. For example, your letter to a bereaved neighbor might promise to mow the lawn or shovel snow for a month. Your letter to a bereaved parent with small children might include an offer to take the kids to school or to care for them on days when there is no school. Your letter to a bereaved aunt or uncle might promise to call once a week or to take him or her out to dinner regularly.

With a little creativity, you will think of some meaningful action to take; and when you truly feel sympathy, you will find great joy and satisfaction in "carrying each other's burdens" (Galatians 6:2 NIV).

Additional things to keep in mind . . .

- *Acknowledge their pain; don't minimize it. Assure them that their hurt is legitimate.*
- *Don't expect to relieve their pain with a few words.*
- *Avoid comments or implications, no matter how "religiously correct," that might add to their pain. As the writer of Ecclesiastes said, "There is a time for everything," and when a person is grieving it is a time for encouragement, not exhortation.*
- *If you have never had to say a final, tearful good-bye to someone you deeply love, don't say, "I understand how you feel."*

> *Unto a broken heart*
> *No other one may go*
> *Without the high prerogative*
> *Itself hath suffered too.*
>
> **EMILY DICKINSON**

Death of spouse

Dear Bob,

How saddened we were to learn of your grievous loss. Charlene was loved by so many and she will be dearly missed. Please accept our heartfelt condolences and be assured that we will be here for you should you need us.

We hope you can find comfort in knowing that you gave Charlene a happy and joyful life. She often spoke of her great blessing in having you as her loving companion.

Our thoughts and prayers are with you through this difficult time of your fresh grief.

Warmest wishes,

Death of relative

Dear Sarah,

How shocked we were to learn of Uncle Hal's death! He'll be sorely missed as he was the bulwark of the family. Our comfort lies in remembering that he lived a full and good life.

Aunt Mary will be affected in a far deeper way. We'll help her all we can and we feel certain that the rest of the family shares our concern for her well-being.

We'll be in town next week and do hope we can visit Aunt Mary together.

Love,

Death of child

Dear Martha,

How sad we were to hear the tragic news of your daughter Sara's untimely death! All who had the joy of knowing her were blessed, and we feel doubly blessed because of her close friendship with our own daughter.

Please know that you are in our thoughts and prayers.

When you feel ready, please do call. I'd love to take you to lunch and share precious memories of your lovely daughter.

May the Lord sustain you during these pain-filled days of your fresh grief and shower you with grace upon grace.

Lovingly,

Death of neighbor

Dear Rosemary,

We were deeply saddened this morning when the news came of Don's heart attack and death during the night.

Our hearts are filled with sympathy for the shock and grief you are suffering today. We want you to know that our entire community has often spoken of Don as a man who could be counted on in every situation. If ever a man lived his faith it was your husband. He will live in our memories as a wonderful neighbor and friend, and will be dearly missed.

Jack and I offer our heartfelt condolence to you and the children. Please call on us for any type of help you need.

Warmest regards,

Death of business associate

Dear Polly:

When news reached me last night of Bruce's death, I was filled with a deep sadness. Not only was Bruce my longtime business partner but a dear friend as well. There are no words to express the personal and professional loss I feel.

It's hard to imagine how I will carry on without Bruce, but how much more difficult for you and the children. The time I've spent with your family clearly revealed the depth of love and respect you all held for him.

Mary and I offer our heartfelt condolences and want you to know we are here for you should you need any professional or personal advice.

Warmest wishes,

Executive Mansion
Washington, Nov. 21, 1864

To Mrs. Bixby, Boston, Mass.

Dear Madam,

I have been shown in the files of the War Department a statement of the Adjutant-General of Massachusetts that you are the mother of five sons who have died gloriously on the field of battle. I feel how weak and fruitless must be any word of mine which should attempt to beguile you from the grief of a loss so overwhelming. But I cannot refrain from tendering you the consolation that may be found in the thanks of the republic they died to save. I pray that our Heavenly Father may assuage the anguish of your bereavement, and leave you only the cherished memory of the loved and lost, and the solemn pride that must be yours to have laid so costly a sacrifice upon the altar of freedom.

Yours very sincerely and respectfully,

A. Lincoln

Condolence from a business firm

Dear Mrs. Fielding:

The entire staff of ABC Plumbing offers our condolences on the death of your husband. Ray was a kind and honest man and will be greatly missed by all of us who knew him and had the pleasure of working with him.

Those of us who knew Ray best have sent a donation to the American Cancer Society in his name as an expression of our admiration and respect for him.

Our deepest sympathy to you and all your family.

Sincerely,

Death by suicide

Surely the most tragic of all deaths is when a person takes his or her own life. Loved ones who are left to grieve in such situations not only have the loss to contend with but also the feelings of guilt for having been unable to prevent the tragedy. It is especially important in these circumstances to not say anything that would add to the family's grief or guilt. Suicide is not a rational act, and often cannot be prevented. Even when there has been some warning that a person is suicidal, attempts to dissuade it tend to prove futile. The best persuasive techniques and the most rational arguments are useless against irrationality. Here again, the only thing you have to offer is emotional understanding and day-to-day support.

Dear Helen and Bob:

Upon our return from Hawaii, we learned the sad news of Alec's death. We're grieved and shocked and cannot find adequate words to express our sympathy.

We wish, dear friends, that we could relieve your suffering, but we know that is impossible. We remember Alec as a kind and sensitive young man, and we believe that in time you too will be able to focus

Walking Alongside a Friend in Need

Rick Hamlin

But they constrained him, saying, Abide with us: for it is toward evening, and the day is far spent. And he went to tarry with them.

— LUKE 24:29 KJV

IT was a sunny early spring day several years ago and I was in a gray mood. I'd been turned down for a job I truly expected to get, and after several such disappointments I was frustrated and discouraged. I called my old friend Jim to discuss the situation. He would understand.

We met outside his apartment and started walking. We walked through the park, kicking stones, tossing a Frisbee, watching a baseball game. We walked over to the museum and saw a mime perform for the crowds waiting outside on the steps. We bought some hot dogs, sat on a bench, and watched kids sail their model boats. We talked about the movies, his girlfriend, the weather, his job, some mutual friends, and a bit about my disappointment, but not much. Still, when the day was over, my spirits were lifted and I could look at life with a more hopeful attitude. Just being with Jim had done that for me.

On Easter Day, on the road to Emmaus, two of the disciples were walking when a stranger joined them. They were grieving over what they believed was Christ's end and told the stranger all that had happened. He walked with them and he talked to them, but only when he took bread and broke it did they recognize him as their Savior. In their grief, he stayed with them. Like him (and like Jim), some people stick with us in times of sorrow. Lord, let me be one of them.

Lord, let me walk with those in distress, as you walked with your disciples on the road to Emmaus.

on the joy and happiness your son brought to you for so many years. May the memory of this tragedy soon give way to all the good memories you have stored up, and may the goodness Alec lavished on his friends and loved ones be multiplied in the lives of those he's left behind.

Even though we cannot comprehend the depth of your sorrow, we want to assure you of our continued love and support as you work through your grief and sadness. If ever you need a "sounding board" for your expressions of anger, confusion, or frustration, we are available and we promise confidentiality.

Our prayers are with you and you have our deepest sympathy in this tragic loss.

With love,

Belated condolences

Dear Jackie,

I hope you'll forgive me for this belated expression of condolence for the sudden death of your beloved Wayne. I'm sincerely sorry I allowed a month to pass without calling or writing. It wasn't for lack of caring, Jackie, I simply couldn't find adequate words to express my sympathy for your grievous loss. I still can't find words, but before any more time passes I want you to know that my thoughts and prayers have been with you ever since I heard the news.

Could we arrange to have lunch together? I'll call next week and hopefully we can find a date convenient for you.

Lovingly,

Sentences expressing sympathy

- How inadequate are words to express my feelings of sadness over Sam's death!
- I'm simply without adequate words of comfort.
- Sam held a special place in our hearts.

Bearing One Another's Burdens

B. J. Connor

They shall bear the burden of the people with thee, that thou bear it not thyself alone.
                                                            — NUMBERS 11:17 KJV

I ONCE heard the mother of a teenage boy who was paralyzed in an accident explain how she kept from having a breakdown: "Our church friends formed a circle around us so tightly there was no room to fall."

I love her description. Can't you just picture people holding hands, surrounding that devastated huddle of a family like children playing "Farmer in the Dell"? Of course, they didn't literally encompass them. But they surrounded them with love. They sent cards and letters of encouragement, brought meals, built a wheelchair ramp, chipped in money for expenses, helped modify the house, visited with jokes and news, offered tutoring and prayers, and showered them with other unnamed kindnesses, all of which helped pull the family through a difficult time.

What a privilege to be fellow participants in this game called "Bearing one another's burdens." Because sometimes we're one of the strong ones forming the circle. And sometimes we're one of the broken ones inside.

Lord, motivate me to keep supportive arms so close that "there is no room to fall."

- Our many years of friendship will always be a cherished memory.
- Please take comfort from knowing how much love and happiness you offered Sam during his lifetime.
- Our thoughts and prayers are with your family during this tragic time.
- I'd like you to know how sorry we are; and how deeply we sympathize with you in your recent bereavement.
- All my thoughts are with you and your children today.
- I've just heard the sad news about Sam and offer you my heartfelt condolences.
- How impossible it is to express my feelings of sadness over Sam's death!
- I'm thinking of you, Sally, and hope you'll find a small measure of comfort in knowing there are many people who loved Sam and who love you.

Thank you for sympathy

When you have been on the receiving end of all those letters of sympathy and condolence, there will come a time when you will feel the need to say thank you. Unfortunately, feeling the need to do it will not necessarily mean that you will feel like doing it. Nevertheless, because you know it is the right thing to do, you will sit down at your desk or dining room table with your pen and notecards and good intentions. Perhaps you will know exactly what to say to each person, but if not, here are some letters and phrases you can either use or modify to fit your particular circumstances.

Dear Carol and Ralph,

Your beautiful note expressing sympathy for the loss of our son Mike deeply touched our hearts. The poem "Finally Home" brought streams of tears. How comforting it is to be reminded that our loss is heaven's gain; Mike is home with his God.

How to Help Hurting Friends

Linda Ching Sledge

He heals the brokenhearted, and binds up their wounds.
— PSALM 147:3 RSV

WHEN I first started teaching college in New York City, I admired a veteran professor named Jim. He was a happy-go-lucky person, until he lost a valued promotion. Then I watched him slide into depression. I wanted to make Jim feel better, but I didn't know what to say. Though I sympathized with his pain, I had never gone through what he was experiencing. So I did nothing for some time. But finally, out of cowardice, I wrote Jim a note. I avoided the issue of his promotion and focused on his fine teaching. Then I slipped the note into his mailbox, hoping I hadn't done the wrong thing.

The next day, as I was tiptoeing past Jim's office, his door opened. I looked up to see Jim's face beaming at me. "Thanks," he said. "That note was just the comfort I needed. You did exactly the right thing."

It's hard to know what is the "right thing" to do when friends are depressed or grieving, but here is what I learned from my experience with Jim.

Don't give in to your own indecision.

Do something as soon as possible.

Don't give advice unless asked.

Do listen with patience and sympathy.

Don't tell your friend that you know exactly how he or she feels. You don't.

Do something practical and tangible. Treat him or her to a meal, give a small gift, write an upbeat note.

Lord, where there is hurt, let me be brave enough to try to heal.

We treasure your gift of friendship and thank you so much for your care and compassion during this agonizing and painful time.

With deepest gratitude,

Sentences of gratitude for expressions of sympathy

- Your presence at Fred's funeral yesterday meant more to our family than I can express. Thank you for caring.
- What a good friend you are! Your loving presence at Fred's funeral was a great comfort to our family.
- It is during times like these that one understands the true meaning of friendship.
- Thank you, June, for your loving expression of sympathy at Fred's funeral. I know you understand what I'm going through since you also experienced the sudden death of your dear Ralph.
- It is because of friends like you that we can gather strength to carry on without Fred.
- From you we have learned what it truly means to be comforted, and because of this we will know how to comfort others in the future.
- Thank you for demonstrating the love and compassion of Jesus during our time of grief.
- What a dear friend you are! Your presence was a gift of love as you quietly listened to my expressions of grief and dried my tears.

SITUATIONS OTHER THAN DEATH

A letter of condolence or sympathy is appropriate for situations other than death. Although death is the ultimate and final separation, the breakup of a marriage can be equally painful due to the numerous other factors involved, such as rejection, betrayal, ongoing yet stressful interaction with the ex-spouse, and guilt.

Marriage separation

Dear Barbara,

How sad I was to hear that you and Larry agreed to a trial separation. It's a painful process and I pray that your first love will be rekindled and that the flame soon will burn more brightly than ever.

If that's not possible, your friends will understand and stand by your decision. Keep thinking positive thoughts, Barbara. You and Larry are in our prayers.

Your friend,

Divorce

Dear Barbara,

How profoundly sorry I am that Larry has filed for divorce. You must be suffering now and I hope you're not blaming yourself or thinking sad thoughts of failure.

Although I have not personally experienced divorce, I saw firsthand the pain it cost my daughter and grandsons.

If I can offer any words of comfort, if I can listen to your heart's cry, if I can say anything to ease your suffering, don't hesitate to call.

Joe and I offer you and your children our heartfelt prayers and loving support.

Lovingly,

Financial, economic, or employment crises are like death in that they too bring to an end a familiar way of life.

Personal reverses

Dear Bob and Helen:

We just heard the news of your financial problems. As you know, the stock market crash of 1987 toppled our finances, so we really do understand the bitter blow of financial reverses. During that difficult time we found comfort in knowing that the darkest night would pass and the bright light of morning would shine through. I hope that thought brings comfort to you too.

If there's anything we can do to help, please let us know. We cherish your friendship and hold you close in our thoughts and prayers.

Love,

Misfortune

Dear Marilyn and Jerry,

We were so sorry to hear of the catastrophic loss you endured during the recent California fires. To lose your beautiful home and all your personal possessions is heartbreaking and there are no words to comfort you adequately.

Natural disasters are a part of this life, but to think an arsonist deliberately caused such a devastating misfortune is a double blow.

We've enclosed a check that we hope will help with some of your immediate needs. We are also collecting some cooking utensils, dishes, linens, and towels that you can use until you are able to get reestablished.

We wish we lived close to you so we could help you emotionally as well, but we will ask God to do that for us as we continue to pray for your physical, emotional, and spiritual well-being.

Love,

Hospitalization

Dear Ruth,

I've been thinking of you today with the hope that you're feeling stronger. We all miss you and are diligently praying for your speedy recovery. A few of us from the class will visit as soon as you're feeling better. Be assured that our thoughts and prayers are continually with you.

Should you need any help at home, Ruth, please have your husband call us. We'll be happy to assist in any way we can while you're hospitalized and during your recuperation at home.

May God bless you with restored health, and may he daily fill your room with the joy of his peace and presence.

Love,

Illness

Shirley dear,

How sorry I am that you're suffering a serious setback after your surgery! John called Ralph and assured him that we're available to help in whatever way he might need us.

How well aware I am that none of us can walk through another's pain. Please know however that God is continually bringing thoughts of you to our minds and whenever he does we are praying that he will grant you his grace and that soon you may enjoy complete recovery.

Lovingly,

Birth defect

Dear Jeannie and Gil,

Dear friends, we just heard that the birth of your baby girl brought you a 'special needs' child. How hard it is to understand why these things happen, but we pray that your love for God, his love for you, and your love for each other will all work together in such a powerful way that you eventually will find meaning and purpose in what now seems like a senseless tragedy.

Many years ago I read Dale Evans's book *Angel Unaware*, which beautifully relates the story of their Down Syndrome child, Robin, and the joy and blessing she was in her brief lifetime. I was able to locate a copy of it and am sending it along with the hope that it will comfort you in a way that I cannot do.

You are in our prayers as is your baby daughter. We're praying that

God will grant you his peace, which surpasses all human understanding.

Lovingly,

Unnamed tragedy

Sometimes you know that a person needs your prayers, but you're not sure why. A letter expressing your sympathy will lift up the individual and show that, because you are a true friend, you respect his or her privacy.

Dear Donna,

Your mother called to request prayer for you and your son Eric. I don't know, nor do I need to know, the extent of this unnamed tragedy that's causing you such pain. It's enough that God knows and that my prayers will reach you through him.

I've placed your names on my daily prayer list and trust God to turn this tragedy into a triumph, far exceeding anything you could have ever dreamed possible.

Lovingly,

Sudden resignation

Dear Bob and Sue,

When word came of Bob's sudden resignation from the church staff, John and I were distraught. We sat in silence on our living room couch for several hours, unable to put into words our thoughts and feelings. You have been such an important part of our lives that we are unable to comprehend what this will mean. One of these days I will be able to put into words all that you have meant to me, but between now and then I want you to know that you will be in our thoughts and prayers continually. Even though we do not know, and may never know, the nature of the circumstances, we will pray that our love for you and God's love for you will be enough to sustain you through this difficult time and that he will work in all of our lives to turn our sorrow into joy and our separation into a time of joyful reunion.

Please know that we love you and pledge to you our prayers and support.

Your friends,

10

Letters of Apology

The bitterest tears shed over graves are for words left unsaid and deeds left undone. **HARRIET BEECHER STOWE**

"The son said to him, 'Father, I have sinned against heaven and against you. I am no longer worthy to be called your son.' But the father said to his servants, '. . . Let's have a feast and celebrate. For this son of mine was dead and is alive again; he was lost and is found'. . . ." LUKE 15:21–24 NIV

*L*etters of apology may be the most often needed and least often sent of all types of correspondence. This is because admitting you are wrong is a difficult thing to do. But the truth is, everyone is wrong from time to time, and so everyone has occasions when a letter of apology is called for. Some people hesitate to apologize because they think of an apology as an admission of weakness. But a letter of apology is instead an act of great strength and courage. When you write a letter of apology you are saying to a friend or family member, "Your feelings are more important than my pride." You are saying, "I do not think of myself more *highly than I ought" (Romans 12:3). A letter of sincere apology is a way of considering others better than ourselves (see Philippians 2:3).*

A letter of sincere apology has the following characteristics:

It clears up a misunderstanding. *When you admit you were wrong, you establish a new starting point for your relationship. Both of you can forget what is past and move into the future without hard feelings or fearful expectations. An apology reestablishes trust.*

It recognizes the importance of the other person's feelings. *The person who receives your letter of apology will breathe a sigh of relief and think, "I guess I wasn't being overly sensitive after all." Your letter will affirm the person's ability to trust her instincts, which in turn will increase her willingness to trust other people without fear of being insulted or belittled.*

It helps you recognize the seriousness of unkind words or actions. *Having gone through the effort of putting your apology on paper, you will better understand the feelings of the person you hurt and be more likely to think twice before doing it again.*

It pleases God. *The Bible makes it pretty clear that God expects his followers to be right with one another if they expect to be right with him. Jesus himself said, "If you are offering your gift at the altar and there remember that your brother has something against you, leave your gift there in front of the altar. First go and be reconciled to your brother; then come and offer your gift" (Matthew 5:23–24 NIV).*

Remember, you are apologizing for what you said or did that was wrong, and that has nothing to do with how the other person responded. Therefore, do not let phrases like "if I offended you" creep into your writing. Simply admit that you behaved badly and take responsibility.

The variety of situations that require an apology are so numerous that it is impossible to mention them all here. What follows is a list of some common ones. They are followed by sample letters or suggested opening phrases that you can adapt to fit your situation.

Careless remark

Dear Susan,

I can't imagine what I was thinking when I made such an unkind comment, but I realized it was wrong as soon as I said it. It would have

Practicing a New Skill

Lisa Isenhower

No discipline seems pleasant at the time, but painful. Later . . . it produces a harvest of righteousness.   — HEBREWS 12:11 NIV

WHEN I was a child, I liked to watch my carpenter grandfather work with his tools. His hammer moved with sure, even taps that drove in nails straight and true. Grandpa let me try my hand at carpentry. But my nails never slipped easily into the wood. My nails hesitated, bending under the misplaced blows of my inexpert hammering. I would wrench the bent nails out and try again. It was ten years before I could drive a nail straight.

Not long ago, my husband Bob and I had an argument that was mostly my fault. I knew I needed to apologize, but it took me several hours before I could utter the simple words, "I'm sorry."

"Thanks," Bob said, "I know that was hard for you."

It was hard. Hard like learning a new skill. Like learning to hammer, I realized. But maybe with a little practice, apologies would become easier, too. It's worth a try.

God, help me practice the skills of love.

been better, I know, if the realization had come to me before the words were out of my mouth, but I can't undo what's been done. I can only ask your forgiveness and God's and pray that you will be willing to continue our friendship and that I will be more sensitive in the future.

Your contrite friend,

Delayed thank you

Dear Marilu,

I have been negligent for not thanking you much sooner for the lovely weekend we spent at your home. Your hospitality was extremely warm and generous, and I don't want to let another day pass without letting you know how deeply appreciative we are.

Love,

Bad behavior

Dear Donna,

It will come as no surprise to you to hear that I was thinking only of myself when I. . . . It may surprise you, however, that I am admitting my selfishness and asking your forgiveness. I hope you can believe that I really do value our friendship and that I do not want my bad behavior to come between us.

Sincerely,

A written apology to follow a verbal one

Dear John,

Thank you for being gracious to me yesterday when I offered my apology. I hope you believe that it was sincere and that so was my request for forgiveness. And above all I hope you will be able to trust me again soon.

Sincerely,

Happy Landing

Ruth Stafford Peale

He that is soon angry dealeth foolishly. . . . — PROVERBS 14:17 KJV

EVEN when he was more that ninety years old, Norman always tried to pick up our heavy suitcases when we were traveling. Once, just as we were about to enter a taxi he started to do it again. I stopped him with a vigorous, "Don't pick that up!" Then I turned to the seemingly unconcerned cab driver and shouted, "We need some help!" Reluctantly he got out, picked up the bag, and we drove out of the airport with the driver sitting ahead of us in sullen silence.

I didn't like that silence and I didn't like myself either. Whenever I lose my temper, even in what seems like a just cause, I try to remember something Will Rogers once said: "People who fly into a rage always make a bad landing."

By the time we came to a tollbooth, I had the two-dollar toll ready, as the sign posted in the cab said I should. As I leaned forward to hand it to the driver, I said, "My friend, I shouted at you a little while ago. I'm sorry and I hope you'll accept my apology."

The driver stared at me, then mumbled something that I didn't understand. We didn't hear anything else from him until we arrived at our apartment building where he bounded out of the cab, came around to open the door, and hauled out the heavy bag. When I handed him the fare (with a generous tip included), he touched his hat. "My friend," he said, "it's been a pleasure."

So you see, even Will Rogers could be wrong. If you can get to the controls soon enough, you can have a happy landing.

Lord Jesus, make me kind and forgiving to others, even as God has forgiven me, for your sake.

Delayed return of borrowed item

Dear Paul,

I have had your battery charger in my garage for so long that our neighbor, thinking it belonged to me, asked if he could borrow it. That was when I realized that I had kept it much too long. Please accept my apology for the inconvenience I have caused you. The enclosed gift certificate to Damon's is my way of showing you how sincere my apology is. I hope you enjoy eating out.

Sincerely,

The Ninth Step

Bonnie Lukes

And he shall make amends for the harm that he hath done. . . .

— LEVITICUS 5:16 KJV

I WAS surprised when Jennie (not her real name), who'd been friends with my youngest daughter Sandi through elementary school, came to see me. I hadn't seen her for several years. When Jennie got into drugs in high school, she and my daughter had drifted apart. Now Jennie explained that she was a member of AA (Alcoholics Anonymous), and had been "clean" almost a year. "Do you remember the time after I'd graduated from high school that you loaned me some money?" she asked.

"Yes," I said.

"Well, I told you I'd hurt my back and needed to see a doctor. But I have to tell now that I lied. I used the money to buy drugs. See, I'm up to my ninth step in AA, which is to make amends to people I've harmed. You're my ninth step."

Unable to attend

Dear Robyn,

I must apologize for mistakenly telling you that we were available to come to your home Thursday evening for a good-bye dinner for the Smiths. I checked my calendar at work, not realizing that I had failed to update it for this month. This morning when I looked at the calendar at home I realized we have a conflict. Unfortunately, it involves an event that we are unable to reschedule.

Even though we are unable to come, we do appreciate the invitation.

After Jennie left, I began to wonder about the possibility of a "ninth-step person" in my own life. What about my older sister Virginia? We hadn't communicated for five years because of a family disagreement. The situation had bothered me, but as I'd explained to God many times, "It wasn't my fault." Now I swallowed my pride and wrote her a letter.

By the time I finished the letter, I realized how I'd been stumbling over that ninth step every time I approached God. No wonder he'd seemed so distant.

Has God seemed far away from you lately? Could it be that he's waiting for you to take that ninth step?

Father, thank you for showing me that I don't have to be a recovering addict to need the forgiveness and peace that comes from making amends.

P.S. Virginia and I have made a beginning in our now-cordial relationship by exchanging several letters since my first one to her.

And we would certainly be there if we hadn't already made another commitment. Please express our regrets to the Smiths. We will try to make other arrangements to get together with them before they leave.

Gratefully yours,

Delayed answer

Dear Margie,

Please accept my apology for not getting back to you sooner regarding your request for my help at the information desk. I would be delighted to help out a couple times a month. Just let me know the dates and times you need me and I'll be there to assist in any way I can.

Sincerely,

Postponed dinner

Dear Jerry and Judy,

I apologize for having to reschedule our dinner engagement. Jay and I will try to do better at coordinating our calendars so we don't make commitments for the same evening again. Thank you for your flexibility and willingness to change plans on such short notice. We appreciate having you as friends.

We love you,

Indiscretion

Dear Jennifer,

I let the cat out of the bag, and I'm sorry. I told Wilma your news before you had a chance to tell her yourself, and it was a thoughtless thing for me to do. Please forgive me. I've learned an important lesson through this, but it's one I should have learned in kindergarten.

Sincerely,

Even an Overdue Apology Is Welcome

Faye Field

For ye have need of patience. . . . — HEBREWS 10:36 KJV

IN my alumni newsletter at the state university where I taught for many years I read that Dr. Donald McDonald, now a retired professor, had been honored in an award ceremony for his services as an eminent school man.

I had not seen Donald since he was in my class the first year that I taught school. I wrote him a congratulatory letter and reminded him that I knew him when he was just a mischievous kid with apparently no goal in mind except to play pranks on a young, inexperienced teacher. Still, I added, I remembered him affectionately.

The prominent educator promptly replied in a most gracious, appreciative manner. Then he added a postscript: "I apologize for some of the trouble I am sure I caused you."

Fifty-five years I had waited for an impish boy to become a sensitive man aware of what had been offered long ago for his benefit.

How long have you waited to see someone you care about grow into a sensitive and mature person? Don't give up! Trust that your goodwill, seen or unseen, can effect change . . . in the other person as well as in yourself.

Dear God, with your help I can wait . . . and pray.

Incomplete project

Dear Patty,

I am sorry to have to report that the part of the project you assigned to me is way behind schedule. I will try to catch up between now and the end of the month, but I'm not sure I can. Is there someone you know who might be able to help out a bit? I know this is going to cause you a severe scheduling problem, and I apologize. This situation has taught me to be more realistic about the available time I'm going to have. Unfortunately I learned it too late to save you from the dilemma you're now facing due to my overcommitment.

If you have any suggestions that would help to get us back on schedule, give me a call.

With sincere apology,

Missed our date

Dear Lee,

I feel so badly about missing our breakfast date that I want to make it up to you somehow. Let's reschedule and instead of each buying our own meal, I'll buy both. When I realized what I had done I was extremely disappointed because I had been looking forward to our time together for weeks. What is the soonest we can reschedule? I'm free every day next week except Wednesday. How about you?

Sincerely,

Late report

Dear Carol,

I know you were hoping to have this information much sooner, and I am sorry I was unable to come through for you. Here is the material I have gotten together so far. I hope this will keep your people busy until I am able to complete the study.

Sincerely,

Wrong information

Dear Membership Secretary,

The information I included on my application for membership was incorrect. I was looking at the wrong document when I filled it out. Following is the correct information. I apologize for the confusion and delay this causes.

Sincerely,

Project failure

Dear Allison,

I'm not exactly sure what went wrong, but I'll find out so I can make sure it never happens again. I must have dropped some ball that I didn't even know was in the air. I know this failure will cast a bad light on you and I am willing to take responsibility for it because I know it was my fault, not yours. If there is anything I can do or anyone I can talk to to clear you of responsibility I will be happy to do so.

Sincerely,

11

Dealing with Neighbors

For it is your business when the wall next door catches fire.
                                                                    HORACE

You shall not give false testimony against your neighbor. You shall not covet . . . anything that belongs to your neighbor.
                                                        EXODUS 20:16–17 NIV

Jesus replied, "Love the Lord your God with all your heart and with all your soul and with all your mind. This is the first and greatest commandment. And the second is like it: Love your neighbor as yourself. . . ." MATTHEW 22:37–39 NIV

*E*ven though life in subdivisions, condominiums, and apartment buildings has brought people closer together physically than did life in the countryside, it has not done much to bring people closer together emotionally, psychologically, or spiritually. In fact, many people today know fewer of their neighbors than did people living in rural communities of earlier generations.

To gain the privacy that the wide open spaces gave our farming forefathers, we buy security systems, install deadbolts, and build privacy fences. Although we do indeed gain privacy, we lose intimacy. And our privacy degenerates into isolation. This increasing isolationism makes us more independent than interdependent. And our increasing independence makes us less God-dependent.

*For some people in some neighborhoods, isolation is part of survival, but it is not part of God's original plan. God intended us to live **in relationship** with other people as well as with him. In fact, the last six of the Ten Commandments cover our relationships with others, and two refer specifically to neighbors. He also intended that we would live **in harmony** with others as well as with him. Jesus stressed this concept when the Pharisees asked him, "Which is the greatest commandment in the Law?" Jesus answered, "Love the Lord your God with all your heart and with all your soul and with all your mind. This is the first and greatest commandment. And the second is like it: Love your neighbor as yourself . . ." (Matthew 22:37–39 NIV).*

When writing letters to neighbors, that is the best advice to keep in mind. "Love your neighbor as yourself." It sounds good. It sounds noble. It sounds . . . impossible! Yes, it probably is impossible. But that's no reason not to try. If we set low goals, those are the ones we will reach. And there is no virtue (and little satisfaction) in reaching goals that are so low they require no effort.

Before sitting down to write . . .

Make sure your own heart is right. *Before trying to change your neighbor's behavior, check your motives. Do you detect any selfishness, self-righteousness, lack of compassion? If so, deal with these first or they will come across in your letter.*

Make sure a letter is the best way to handle the matter. *Force yourself to answer these two questions honestly: "Am I trying to avoid personal confrontation? Am I taking the cowardly approach?" If either answer is yes, consider some other ways to handle the situation.*

As you write . . .

Consider the needs and viewpoint of your neighbor. The human tendency in a dispute is to attribute motives to the other person's behavior. For example, "She did that to make me mad" or "He's just trying to get even because I made him angry." Never assume that you know another person's motive or that you know all the details of a situation. Keep your mind open to new information and your heart sensitive to your neighbor's circumstances.

Consider harmony a higher priority than your own personal rights. Don't set out to get the good you believe you deserve unless you are willing to risk losing the good you already have. In other words, weigh the risks. Is the issue that has you upset worth putting at risk your relationship with your neighbor?

Don't make accusations. Approach the matter in a way that does not make your neighbor defensive.

Don't write while you are angry. Unless you are only using the letter as a way to deal with your anger in a healthy way and do not plan to send it, wait until you are calm before writing.

The above advice assumes that your purpose in writing to your neighbor is to complain, but perhaps that is not the case. Perhaps you just want to express appreciation. There are some samples here for that as well.

Thanks to conscientious pet owner

Dear Mrs. Jones,

I just wanted to thank you for being such a conscientious pet owner. I see you walking your little dog often, and the animal is always on a leash. And you never leave his droppings behind for someone else to step in or clean up. I can't think of a more neighborly gesture than a pooper-scooper in action.

Your neighbor,

Request to careless pet owner

There are responsible dog owners and then there are . . . well, the not-so-responsible ones. But maybe they're just unaware, not irresponsible. So be kind when you complain. Give them the benefit of the doubt. And when the pet owners are children, appeal to their desire to be treated as adults and write to them rather than to their parents. You might be surprised by the results.

Dear Robert,

    I have watched you playing outside with your new puppy and it is good to see how gentle and loving you are with him. He seems to be a smart dog, and I'm sure you'll have fun teaching him to sit up, shake hands, and roll over. And while you're training him, I wonder if you could teach him one more thing. It may sound difficult to do, but it's not; we've taught our dog to do it. Could you teach him to "do his business" in his own yard? I've had to clean up several of his messes, and if I don't see him do it and get them cleaned up quickly, they make brown patches in our lawn. My concern for our grass may seem unimportant to you, but being concerned for a neighbor's property is a part of growing up and learning to become a responsible citizen.

    Have fun with your dog. I know he'll be a good friend to you. And bring him over some day for a dog biscuit. I'd love to meet him.

Sincerely,

Commending parents for their honest child

Dear Susan and Steve,

    I never thought I'd write a thank-you note to the parents of a child who broke my birdbath, but I was so impressed by the integrity and

Measuring My Words

Lisa Isenhower

"For with the measure you use, it will be measured to you."
— LUKE 6:38 NIV

My grandmother taught me to cook when I was eleven. I stood at her kitchen counter and measured flour for cookies. "Does that look like a level cup to you, Lisa?" Gram asked. "It doesn't to me. Better measure it over again."

Exasperated, I'd dump the flour back in the bin and start over. Gram was strict about measuring. It frustrated me at the time, but I soon learned that careful measuring yielded delicious results.

Although I mastered measuring flour long ago, I still have trouble measuring my words. I sometimes blurt out a response too quickly, the verbal equivalent of slinging a haphazardly filled cup of flour into the bowl. But recently I decided to apply a little kitchen wisdom to help me stop and measure my responses more carefully. Here's how it works:

1. A scant reply. In a moment of anger, saying less than I feel like saying keeps me from saying more than I should.

2. Level words. Instead of beating around the bush, I strive to be direct when something difficult needs to be said.

3. Rounded with love. In complaints, apologies, and praise for others, it's best to be generous with love; always add a little extra.

This short communication recipe is a good reminder that carefully measured words yield satisfying results.

God, help me to be mindful of the measure I use when sharing my words with others.

sincerity of your daughter that I must commend you for raising such an honest child.

Most children I know would run away out of fear or disrespect after smashing a yard ornament, but your daughter Elizabeth came right up to our front door to apologize and ask my forgiveness.

You should be very proud. Elizabeth is truly a credit to you and to her generation.

Sincerely,

Complaining about rowdy child

Although there are plenty of responsible parents, there are some irresponsible ones as well. But maybe they are just overworked, overstressed, or near the breaking point. Or else just unaware of any problems. Look for an opportunity to help rather than harangue.

Dear Mrs. Brown,

We have only met in passing, but our children play together often at our house. We have always enjoyed having them around, but recently I have noticed that your son is becoming unnecessarily rough with the other children. I am concerned that something might be going on at home that has upset him. Is someone sick or in trouble?

I don't mean to pry, but I am concerned for your family's well-being as well as for my children's safety. I thought about asking your son if something was bothering him, but I didn't want to put him in the awkward position of feeling as if he were betraying a family confidence.

I'm no expert on child psychology, and I certainly don't know everything there is to know about parenting. But I do think that there is some truth to the cliché that "two heads are better than one," so I'm wondering if you would like to come over for coffee some afternoon or evening—whichever is convenient for you. We might not be able to solve all our problems, but at least we could share them and maybe then they wouldn't be quite so burdensome.

As Dependable as the Seasons

Marjorie Holmes

There is no one like Timothy. . . .
— PHILIPPIANS 2:20 TLB

EVERYBODY should have a neighbor like Margaret, the dear little pixie of a woman who lives next door to me.

She feeds our cat when we're away and brings in our mail. She keeps a bright eye on the house for us, and if anything seems amiss (like the time we left a window open during a storm), she scurries over to fix it, or calls us.

Her own house is immaculate, and so is her garden. In it she spends every possible waking hour. Like some elfin omen she marks for us the seasons' turning. We know it is spring when we see that woolly sweater and pixie hat as she crouches and digs with her trowel, preparing the soil. Summer, the hoeing and weeding and staking up. The harvesting: crisp lettuce and radishes and onions to be shared, squash and corn and scarlet tomatoes. Fall, the vigorous final gathering, along with the raking and mulching of leaves.

And now, in February, when the air is deceptively soft, and the last snowflake seems to have fallen but nobody's sure, we look hopefully out the window toward Margaret's garden. Let other people keep watch over a groundhog's hold, trying to lure him out and foretell spring's arrival by seeing his shadow. All we need is that tiny figure digging away in her pixie hat. A living symbol of joy and promise.

Spring is just around the corner!

We can count on Margaret.

Thank you, Lord, for a neighbor like Margaret. Help me to be someone on whom others can count, and let my work and life be an inspiration to them.

I will call in a couple of days to set up a time to get together. It's about time we get to know each other anyway.

Sincerely,

Noisy children in an apartment building

Dear 4C:

Let me introduce myself. My husband and I live in 3C. We know you by your footsteps and assume that you are the couple we sometimes see in the courtyard with the adorable children. I guess one of the oddities of city living is that people don't always introduce themselves.

I realize that in an apartment one doesn't know how noise travels. Since our apartments are identical, and since we raised our sons here in 3C, I know exactly how attractive that long hallway is to an active child. I enjoy hearing the "patter of little feet." But can you please keep them from practicing their roller-blading after 9 P.M.? We usually watch a little television and then like to read in bed—the sound of roller blades on the wooden floors is very loud.

We'll introduce ourselves the next time we see you, and we hope to have lots of opportunities to watch your children grow.

Thank you for your consideration.

Sincerely,

Snooping

Dear Neighbor,

Ever since we moved into this home last year, I have been uncomfortable with the level of interest you exhibit in the day-to-day routines of our family. While I appreciate the watch you keep over the neighborhood, particularly at vacation times, I sometimes feel as if I am under a microscope.

I value your friendship and want to keep our relationship intact, but I need more privacy. I hope you understand. It is not my intention to hurt your feelings, but to express mine in order to alleviate the tension that I feel growing between us.

Thank you for your understanding.

Your neighbor,

Warning on a zoning violation

Whenever you complain, it is good to include a possible solution.

Dear Nick,

I know that you've been trying to sell your old car for several weeks but without success. I'm wondering therefore if putting it in a different location might attract more potential buyers.

It's been parked in front of my house for five weeks now and apparently the people who visit me are not in the market for that type of vehicle. Perhaps it needs a more visible spot—maybe near the high school where teenagers would be more likely to see it.

One other thing that you might be unaware of is that the car is in violation of local zoning. I don't intend to report it, but I can't promise that other neighbors won't do so.

By the way, the name of the high school principal is Dan Lawson. He could probably tell you how to find out the school's policy regarding use of their parking lots.

Sincerely,

Requesting neighbors' cooperation

Dear Neighbors,

Recently there have been several reported acts of vandalism, break-ins, and car thefts in our neighborhood, and I believe it is time for all of us to take a little more responsibility for each other. We can do this by paying closer attention to people who are unfamiliar and to things that seem out of the ordinary. In addition, we can protect ourselves by following these safety tips:

- Lock your car, take your keys.
- Check window and door locks, especially when leaving your home, even if it's only for a short time. Do the same when you retire for the night.
- Install motion detector lighting around the house and garage.
- Keep your porch lights on.
- Be alert to unusual noises, people, and events.
- Notify neighbors about your vacation plans so they can keep watch.

If we show our local law enforcement agency that we are willing to accept part of the responsibility for maintaining a safe neighborhood, maybe they will be more inclined to patrol our streets regularly.

Let's be good neighbors and work together to make our streets safer for everyone.

Sincerely,

Asking a favor

Dear Sue,

I will be traveling to Europe with a group from my church later this summer and was wondering if you could feed my cat and keep an eye on the house while I am gone.

I will be leaving July 14 and returning July 28. Please let me know as soon as possible so I can find someone else if you are unable to help out.

Thanks for being such a great neighbor.

Sincerely,

Good fences and good neighbors

Dear John,

I was sorry to see that your fence sustained such extensive damage in the last thunderstorm. I noticed that some of the boards blew down, leaving gaping holes and exposed rusty nails. I am concerned that the fence in its present condition is a danger to children and a zoning violation as well, and I am wondering what plans you have for repairing it.

Since my family enjoys the benefits of the privacy fence, I would be willing to share the expense of replacing the missing sections. I am also willing to help out with the labor if you choose to do it yourself rather than hire someone to do it.

Please let me know your plans so we can resolve the matter before someone is injured.

Sincerely,

When leaves blow your way

Dear Neighbor,

Autumn is here again with all its beauty (and extra yard work). I noticed that you have piled up your leaves, but have not bagged them for disposal. This is unfortunate because your piles seem to blow in my direction with every passing breeze. Since I have finished the bulk of my yardwork, I was hoping to persuade you to finish the task and save me the additional job of raking again.

Thank you for your cooperation.

Sincerely,

Appreciating good neighbors

Dear Mr. and Mrs. Osmer,

I just wanted to tell you how much we appreciate you as neighbors and thank you for all the times you have pitched in to help us. Thank you for baby-sitting on the spur of the moment, for helping us rake the leaves the fall we had our new baby, and for lending us your new car when I got the emergency call from our son's school.

Please accept these golf balls as a small token of our gratitude.

Your neighbors,

Thanks for help while hospitalized

Dear Marie,

How can I begin to thank your family for taking over the responsibility of mowing our yard while my husband was in the hospital? It was a gift that will be remembered and passed along in the years to come. You are a blessing to us.

In the way of an update, my husband is healing nicely and hopes to return to work soon.

Gratefully,

Thanks for bringing dinner

Dear Jennifer,

Thank you for the delicious dinner you delivered to us last week. I hope that you will share the recipes as well.

I had no idea that having a baby would be so tiring, but apparently you did, and I thank you for anticipating my need with your kindness.

Sincerely,

Thanks for Christmas exhibit

Dear Tom and Connie,

I drive past your home on my way to and from work and feel compelled to write you a line of appreciation for the effort you invested in your Christmas display. I can't imagine the number of hours (or lights) that it took to create such an elaborate exhibit, but it was worth it!

Thank you for making my treks to and from work more beautiful.

An admirer,

12

Letters Expressing Anger

It is easy to fly into a passion—anybody can do that—but to be angry with the right person to the right extent and at the right time and with the right object and in the right way—that is not easy, and it is not everyone who can do it. ARISTOTLE

A man that does not know how to be angry does not know how to be good. HENRY WARD BEECHER

*A*nger gets blamed for a lot of the world's unpleasantness. People become angry over injustice, betrayal, dishonesty, mistreatment, intolerance, and a whole host of horrible things. But more often than not it is the misuse of anger that causes problems, not anger itself.

Anger is a legitimate emotional response to wrongdoing. When handled well, anger can have positive results. Unfortunately, few people learn to handle it well, and anger that is handled poorly turns into hatred and a desire for revenge, the true causes of many problems.

Because anger is the forerunner of hatred, people, especially Christians, *tend to put the two in the same category and conclude that both are wrong. The mistaken belief that anger is a sin causes people to deny that they are angry even when they have good reason to be. And by denying anger its true and rightful place, they exempt themselves from the responsibility of having to deal with it in a healthy way.*

Anger is a fuel that can empower us to make wrong things right.

Anger is emotional energy that can be used for good or bad. It can fuel a jackhammer that destroys things or a sander that smooths and polishes rough edges. Likewise, letter writing can be either a healthy way of dealing with anger or an unhealthy one.

To use letters in a healthy way, keep in mind the following:

A letter expressing anger is not . . .

- *an opportunity to get even.*
- *an opportunity to prove you are right.*
- *an opportunity to demonstrate that you are more virtuous.*
- *an opportunity to be unkind.*

A letter expressing anger is . . .

- *a way to right a wrong.*
- *a way to call attention to injustice.*
- *a way to encourage ethical behavior.*
- *a way to give someone the opportunity to improve their method of doing business.*

Letters that express anger in a healthy way have the following characteristics:

- *They state facts rather than make threats.*
- *They express concerns in an even tone rather than in emotionally charged words and phrases.*
- *They give only the necessary details and do not confuse the matter with broad generalizations. (For example, if you are writing about a snooty salesperson, don't sidetrack the issue with*

comments about the younger generation's lack of respect for the elderly.)

- *They look for a solution to a problem, not a release valve for hurt feelings.*

Psychologists tell us that the failure to deal properly with anger leads to all kinds of unhealthy physical and emotional side effects. On the other hand, expressing anger in a positive way, for a positive reason, to get a positive result, can heal relationships, free us from vindictiveness, and increase our self-respect as well as our respectability. As Emily Dickinson wrote,

> *Anger as soon as fed is dead—*
> *'Tis starving makes it fat—.*

To avoid the possibility of having your anger grow fat due to starvation, here are some letters that will help you feed it and, therefore, kill it.

A problem with the Post Office

Letters expressing anger should never leave recipients guessing as to what type of response you want. Be specific, not vague, about your expectations. Don't assume that someone will intuitively know what you consider a satisfactory response. On the other hand, don't set your expectations so high that they are impossible to meet. In the following situation, for example, it would be unrealistic to expect the Post Office to call all the people on your guest list who did not receive their invitations.

Dear Postmaster,

Before leaving for a two-week vacation, I drove to our local Post Office branch and mailed one hundred invitations to our daughter's open house, which was to take place the weekend following our return.

Two days after we got home I found out through a series of coincidences that several people had not yet received their invitations! Alarmed, I called several others to find out if they had received theirs. No one had. Consequently, my daughter and I had to call everyone on our list. Due to the short notice, many people were unable to come. Surely you can imagine our disappointment.

What I can't imagine, however, is how you could have lost such a

God's Love Never Ends

Daniel Schantz

David was angry at what the Lord had done. . . . David was now afraid of the Lord. . . .   — 2 SAMUEL 6:8–9 TLB

I WAS feeling bitter toward God about a project that had fallen through. As I finished breakfast I muttered my complaints under my breath. "It would have been so easy for you to make it work out, God," I complained. "It really makes me mad." As I headed for the car, I felt like a hurt little kid as I slammed the door behind me.

All day long I was nervous, as though I expected God to strike me down for being so angry with him. Instead, I had one of the happiest days of my life. Later, when I told my wife Sharon about it, she smiled and said, "Just because you are angry with God doesn't mean he is angry with you. After all, God is kind, even to his enemies."

"But I was furious . . ."

"Maybe so," she replied. "But all relationships are like that. You and I get upset with each other, but it doesn't mean that we really hate each other or want to hurt each other. It's just part of communication."

large bundle of mail. (We had even sorted the invitations by zip code and labeled all the bundles to make your work easier.)

As your employer, a taxpayer, I would like the following three things: an apology; an explanation of what happened to cause this system failure in your branch; and a report as to what you have done to keep it from happening again.

I look forward to hearing from you.

A dissatisfied taxpayer,

"But God is different," I insisted. "I didn't have any right to be angry at him."

"Oh, I don't know. I think if I were God I'd be flattered to think that you felt close enough to trust me with your strongest feelings," Sharon concluded.

Later that evening I read the Apostle Paul's instructions: "If you are angry, don't sin by nursing your grudge. Don't let the sun go down with you still angry—get over it quickly" (Ephesians 4:26 TLB). And that reminded me of the poet William Blake's words:

> *I was angry with my friend:*
> *I told my wrath, my wrath did end.*
> *I was angry with my foe:*
> *I told it not, my wrath did grow.*

Now I see that by telling God just how angry I was, I was being truthful. I also could let go of my anger, instead of nursing it. God doesn't quit loving me just because I'm mad at him or turn off the gifts of his wonderful grace. He calls me his dear child (Ephesians 5:1).

Lord, thank you that even when I'm angry and think of you as an enemy, your grace abounds, surrounding me with your love.

Poor package design

Whenever you are criticizing something, try to think of something good to say as well. Your complaint will be taken more seriously if you don't come across as someone who is impossible to please.

Dear marketing department,

"When all else fails, read the directions." But what do you do if you read the directions and still fail? That's what happened to me when I tried to open your cake mix according to the instructions on your newly designed package. "Lift tab," it said, "and pull back." But the tab was too short to grasp, so I had to pry it up with a knife. When I pulled the tab back, it simply tore off. Finally, I cut off the top of the package with my knife, but in the process I cut into the inner bag and spilled cake mix all over the counter.

Despite this inconvenience, I still prefer your cake mix over that of your competitors. But unless you improve your packaging, I'm going to start buying the other brand.

Cordially yours,

Delivery never made

To delivery-service manager:

The delivery you promised to make yesterday morning was not made until today—with no explanation or apology. I had to cancel two appointments for yesterday afternoon because, when I called your office, I was told the delivery would be made "sometime before 5:00."

In this day and age of cellular phones, it seems reasonable to expect that a delivery service would be able to keep in contact with its drivers at all times and thereby have an accurate, up-to-the-minute schedule.

If you find a way to make your schedules more precise, let me know. In the meantime I will request delivery by your competitor whenever I order something from out of town.

Cordially yours,

Hurtful remarks

A gentle reminder like the one that follows may be just what a person needs to cause him or her to take a closer look at how harmful negative comments can be.

Dear Vern,

All the people in our department were glad when you joined the company last year. We needed your enthusiasm and your good ideas then, and we still do.

But yesterday when you told several of us that our supervisor is incompetent and unaware of what's going on, I was disturbed. This man is one of the best I've ever worked for. Yes, he's low key, and he's not looking over our shoulders all the time. But in my seven years here I've come to know him as a man who knows what he's doing—and what we're doing.

Please be careful. Your remarks can hurt company morale.

Your friend,

Incompetent repairman

Dear Service Manager,

For many years the appliances we purchased from you have given us good service. They seldom need repair. And—until last week—we have been well satisfied with your repair people. But the repairman who came last Wednesday to fix the cycle-control mechanism on our washer was not up to your usual standards. He was clumsy and inept. He cracked the control knob and then spent an hour replacing the knob and getting everything back in running order.

We trust that you will do the right thing for him (perhaps giving him further training) and for us when you bill us for the time he was here working to correct his own mistake, not our faulty washer.

Sincerely yours,

Unsafe cab/bus driver

Dear Mr. Atkins,

When I hailed cab number 33 at the airport yesterday, I was not expecting a wild ride. Although I arrived home without mishap, the ride was one of the most unpleasant I've ever had. I told your driver that I was in no hurry, but he kept up his fast driving, often changing

Focus on Beauty, not Anger

Ellyn Baumann

Finally, brethren, whatever things are true, whatever things are noble, whatever things are just, whatever things are pure, whatever things are lovely, whatever things are of good report, if there is any virtue and if there is anything praiseworthy—meditate on these things.

— PHILIPPIANS 4:8 NKJV

A RELATIVE of mine was treating some people in my family pretty shabbily, and the more I thought about it, the angrier I became.

The worst part was that I had no defense against it. One minute I could be totally content, and before long I'd be steaming. But I began to notice that it always seemed to happen while I washed the evening dishes.

Finally, I asked the Lord to help me past it, so my joy would be secure and doing dishes could be a simple pleasure again. Not a full week passed before I received an unexpected gift in the mail. It was a beautiful photo of the sun setting over the ocean, with Philippians 4:8 printed on it. I immediately knew where it belonged: on the window frame right above my kitchen sink.

lanes and several times cutting off other drivers. One time he almost sideswiped a van. It was a white-knuckle ride for me all the way.

Is this recklessness something you encourage to increase the number of fares a driver can carry? If so, I suggest that you reconsider your priorities and put public safety above corporate profitability.

If you do not condone this recklessness, please remind your drivers of the importance of safety as well as good old-fashioned courtesy.

Sincerely,

The beautiful sunset gave me a place to focus my thoughts. From that day on, I had better control over my angry thoughts toward my relative. It wasn't that I didn't have any, but now I knew to think "Philippians 4:8 thoughts" in place of the angry ones. In addition, I found myself wanting to pray for my relative. I asked God to help him through the unhappiness that made him treat others unkindly. One day, I was totally awed to discover as I prayed that a tender, genuine acceptance of him had begun to grow in my heart.

Some time later, a friend was telling me about trouble she was having with angry thoughts. I smiled. "I know just what you need," I told her, and went to the window frame. "This picture and the Scripture have helped me change my thought patterns, and even to pray for the person I've been angry with. I want you to have it to hang over your kitchen sink."

I wonder if she, now healed, has passed the picture on to another who's having difficulty with angry thoughts.

Father, thank you for keeping us in victory and joy through high and noble thoughts, and for replacing our anger with love.

Discourteous bus driver

Dear Mr. Wallace,

I don't expect bus drivers to say please and thank you all the time. On the other hand, rudeness is never called for. Yet that is exactly what I observed yesterday in the driver of the Oak Street to Grand Avenue afternoon run. His attitude was downright obnoxious. Here is just one of the many examples of rudeness I observed in a few short blocks: When an elderly woman using a walker was trying to fold the walker and board the bus, the driver bellowed, "Hurry it up, lady. I don't have all day." He didn't even offer to help her get the walker up the steps. Another passenger had to do it. People already on the bus were rolling their eyes in disgust at his behavior.

Two weeks ago I started riding the bus to my new afternoon job, and this is the first time I have ridden with a discourteous driver. I hope it will be the last. I'm sure it will be if you will remind your drivers that passengers deserve to be treated with kindness and courtesy.

Sincerely yours,

Unpleasant restaurant experience

Dear Mr. Grant,

My family and I eat out often, and your restaurant has always been one of our favorites. The food is superb, the servers are efficient and pleasant, and your prices are reasonable. Lately, however, we have noticed a change that troubles us: You have put in a few extra tables—to reduce waiting time, one of your servers told us. We understand the reasoning behind this, but dining at your restaurant is less pleasant now. We long for the old congenial roominess.

Have you considered enlarging your restaurant or perhaps remodeling in some way that could increase capacity without compromising privacy? We strongly recommend that.

Cordially yours,

Incompetent tour guide

Dear Mr. Lance,

My friend and I heard so much good about your Holy Land tours that we decided to sign on with you this past summer. We were excited, eager to "walk where Jesus walked." We studied several guide books before we left and felt well prepared to make the most of the tour. We only wish that our guide had done the same. It became obvious that he had only a scant knowledge of the history and geography of Israel, and he knew very little about recent archaeological finds. Besides that, his knowledge of Bible stories and facts was minimal. We learned a lot, but we had expected to learn so much more.

You can be sure that before booking our next tour we will spend as much time studying tour packages as we do studying our destination.

Regretfully yours,

Tired of working for those who won't

Dear Senator Bradford, ,

Our family has a problem, and it seems that no one is doing anything about it. The poor, the minority groups, and the handicapped all have their advocates. Fortunately there are laws to help them. But where is someone to speak for another large group—the overemployed and underpaid? My wife has a part-time job and cares for our two children; I have one full-time job and two part-time jobs. This allows me to see my children only on Sundays. We are grateful for our jobs and our health, but high taxes are robbing us of time together. Does anyone care? What are you doing to help us?

A struggling constituent,

Corporate arm-twisting not appreciated

Dear Commissioner Lewis,

I do not understand why the city gave Marxon Manufacturing the zoning variance that allows them to build in our district. We had a public hearing, and I was sure the majority of the residents opposed the plans. Am I wrong?

If what I heard is true—that company representatives later met privately with community leaders and made a number of unspecified promises and indirect threats—I will be very disturbed. Please re-study this issue and bring everything out into the open. People may well agree with you, but when such matters are handled in seeming secrecy voters tend to lose trust in government. Please have someone write or phone me to explain the agreement the city made with Marxon Manufacturing. I anticipate your reply.

Sincerely,

Inconsiderate retail clerk

No matter how angry you are or how rudely you have been treated, avoid suggesting that an offensive employee be fired. If your complaint is the first one ever made against the person, your zeal may come across as an overreaction and your letter will be ignored. Suggest instead that the employee be monitored more closely or given additional training.

Dear Mr. Ellens,

Perhaps you know that I regularly shop for clothing at your store. Your selections and quality are outstanding, and your service has always been above average. Last Thursday a new salesperson waited on me, however, and he was impatient, inconsiderate, and sarcastic. I was appalled by his rudeness.

I won't let one bad experience keep me from shopping in your store. But if this is common behavior for him, he might be alienating other customers who might not give him (or the store) a second chance.

Given some coaching, perhaps he could develop the civility and consideration necessary for success in your business. I look forward to a better shopping experience next time.

Sincerely,

Intentional overcharge

Dear Mr. Warner,

Yesterday you helped me select a clock radio at your store, and you rang up the sale.

This morning as I was looking through your advertising mailer, I got a great surprise: prominently displayed was the very clock radio I purchased. It has been on sale this entire week for three dollars less than I paid for it. When I called to inquire about this, I was told that the overpayment will be refunded. Because you are a long-time employee I find it hard to imagine that this was simply a mistake. Can you please explain it? I have not spoken to your manager about it, but I will do so if you are unable to provide a satisfactory explanation.

With some concern,

A sticky rebate problem

Dear Mr. Hanson,

I am pleased with the new stereo system I bought from you earlier this month. The quality of sound is excellent. There is a problem with the manufacturer's promised rebate, however. Your associate assured me that I beat the deadline by two days, and it was this promise that persuaded me to buy that system. As it turned out, the deadline was the 12th, not the 15th.

I see two possible ways to resolve this matter: (1) I could return the equipment for a full refund; or (2) you could pay me the amount of the rebate. I will accept either arrangement. Please let me know which you prefer.

Respectfully yours,

Seeking help from consumer action column

Dear Consumer Advocate,

Can you help me? I bought a ceiling fan at a local department store about four months ago. It was one of their more expensive models. Now it has developed a squeak that is so annoying that we use the fan only when we are desperate for air circulation. The motor is sealed and cannot be oiled. The store manager refuses to do anything about the problem since this model had only a three-month warranty. I kept the sales slip giving the date of purchase.

Do I have any recourse?

Sincerely yours,

Letter to editor

Dear Editor,

Yesterday when I tried to park at the mall, there were two handicapped parking spaces available near the entrance I needed to use. But cars parked in adjacent spaces were so close that there was no room to maneuver a wheelchair. So even though I had room to park my van, I didn't have room to get out of it.

Perhaps it was lack of information, not lack of courtesy, that caused those drivers to park the way they did. So maybe my letter can alleviate the problem by reminding readers that areas marked with diagonal lines next to parking spaces designated for the handicapped are no-parking zones. Wheelchair users require these spaces. And vans with side lifts need the wider spaces for dropping their lifts and allowing the wheelchair-bound person to exit and enter the vehicle. When handicapped drivers return to their van and find that space taken by another vehicle, what are they to do?

We are not asking for anything more than we need, and we hope it is not more than others are willing to give.

Gratefully,

13

Letters to Clergy

And let us consider how we may spur one another on toward love and good deeds.   **HEBREWS 10:24** NIV

Clergy are men as well as other folks.   **HENRY FIELDING**

*S*ome church members have the attitude that it's the responsibility of ministers to be perfect (after all, they're being paid) and it's the responsibility of people in the congregation to tell them when they're anything less than that.

People in congregations take this responsibility very seriously, and their expectations for ministers are very high. In many cases, they expect ministers not only to preach well, but also to be good administrators, counselors, business managers, construction engineers, fundraisers, and social planners. They expect to hear sermons that are meaningful to believers as well as to unbelievers. And they expect ministers to carry the full responsibility of evangelizing their friends, neighbors, and relatives and of visiting the sick and elderly. In addition to all of this, ministers are expected to have perfect spouses and children.

If ministers are weak in any of these areas, one or several people in the congregation will feel "prompted of God" to point out the deficiency.

The purpose of this chapter is not to question whether God is prompting you to write to your minister; it is to help you do it with kindness, gentleness, love, and self-control (see Galatians 5:22–23 NIV). If you are unable to do so, assume that your urge to write is not coming from God. The last verse of Galatians 5 says, "Let us not become conceited, provoking and envying each other" (v. 26 NIV). It is never right to do something out of conceit (thinking you are better than someone else), and it is never right to do something that will intentionally provoke another person to feel angry or defensive.

This is not to say that you are never to criticize or call into question the behavior of a minister. You are. Every minister needs accountability. But accountability works best when there is mutual respect between the parties. In other words, criticism is taken more seriously when it comes from a person who has earned the right to criticize rather than from one who has "usurped" the responsibility.

Whatever the purpose of your letter, there is no reason to be cruel, sarcastic, or unkind (see section on criticism). And there is certainly nothing good to be gained from it.

And whatever the subject of your letter, whether positive or negative, your heart attitude will show through. So ask yourself, "How can I say this in such a way that it will spur my minister 'toward love and good deeds?'" (Hebrews 10:24 NIV).

The same rules of kindness and godliness that govern our behavior toward other people apply to our treatment of ministers. Just because we expect ministers to be spiritual is no excuse for being careless about our own spirituality in the way we behave toward them.

Notes on criticism

Before writing a letter of criticism, consider whether or not you have a relationship with your minister that gives context to your complaint. If criticism is the first impression you give of yourself, that may be the one thing your minister remembers. And if criticism is the only impression you ever give, it definitely will be the one that sticks in your minister's mind.

As you write, consider these questions:

Is what I am saying true? Are you positive you have accurate information or could some of it be based on mistaken identity or hearsay?

Can I state it in a kind, nonaccusing way? If not, don't write.

Is my criticism based on biblical truth or personal preference? Be sure to give proper weight to the issue. Recognize that matters of personal preference are not as critical as matters of biblical truth. Don't try to push your concern up the ladder of significance simply because it's important to you.

What is my motive? If you get what you want will it require someone else to lose what they have or need?

Which am I calling into question, my minister's behavior or his or her motives? Never assume that you know another person's motives. Only God knows the heart. It is dangerous to attribute motives to another person's behavior.

Is this the best timing? If your minister has had a week filled with tragedies and pressures unrelated to the subject of your letter, you might want to postpone sending it.

Would a face-to-face meeting convey the spirit of my criticism better than a letter? Make sure you're not putting your complaint in writing simply to avoid the discomfort of personal confrontation.

And remember, no matter how many complimentary letters ministers receive in a day, their minds will dwell longest on the criticism. So consider this: Is your complaint important enough to risk the possibility of distracting your minister from his or her spiritual mission and purpose?

Notes on encouragement

People complain when news organizations concentrate only on what is "negative," but most of us have this same tendency. We remain apathetic *and uninvolved until something bad happens (or something we don't like); then we become involved.*

But think how much healthier our churches would be if we acknowledged the good more often than we pointed out the bad. If you have failed to acknowledge good deeds recently, here are some things you might be able to thank your minister for:

- *treating everyone equally and not being a respecter of persons*
- *keeping the congregation focused on Jesus*
- *being available in an emergency*
- *being sensitive at a funeral*
- *setting a good example as a spouse*
- *setting a good example as a parent*
- *being vulnerable*
- *admitting failure*
- *being generous with gratitude and not hogging all the attention*
- *taking responsibility for a difficult decision and not passing the buck*

And while you're at it, don't forget the other people in ministry who seldom get the attention the pastor does. Church secretaries, custodians, elders, deacons, Sunday school teachers, sound technicians, ushers, parking lot attendants, and many other people contribute to the smooth functioning of the church. Maybe someone in one of these categories needs a word of encouragement today.

Regarding titles

When writing to a minister, it is sometimes difficult to know which form of address to use. Some ministers like the informality of being called by their first names. Some have been given honorary degrees and prefer to be addressed by that title. Others have earned doctorates but still prefer to be addressed by their first name.

If you know which form of address your minister prefers, use it. If not, choose one that fits the nature of your letter—formal if you're writing a formal, business-type letter; casual if you're writing a friendly, light-hearted letter. As long as you are respectful, your minister will not mind if the greeting is formal or informal.

Disruptive children

Dear Mr. Carlson,

Church music stirs my heart and the preaching of God's Word convicts my soul; but one thing bothers me. The spirit of worship is often broken by young children crying and older children coming and going. Many parents do not take advantage of children's ministries and apparently do not realize how disruptive their children's presence in church can be.

Certainly we cannot refuse to admit children into church, but isn't there a way to educate parents about common courtesies and common sense, such as taking screaming children out of the service and taking children to the restroom before the service begins?

I can't help but wonder how you manage to keep your own concentration? Perhaps if I knew how you stay focused, I could learn to do it too. Then I would not get so upset.

Thanks for taking time to read this and for responding, if possible.
                                    Sincerely,

If there is any area of church ministry that is likely to elicit criticism, it is music. And if there is any area of church ministry where personal preferences and spiritual convictions are likely to get twisted and confused, it is music. It is fitting, therefore, to include the following two letters, which express opinions on two sides of this controversial subject.

Why so much old music?

Dear Mr. Williams,

Joe and I have learned much from your recent series of sermons on Philippians. Thank you for investing so much time in preparing and studying. God has used your preaching to get our attention and cause us to make some drastic (and overdue) changes in our lives this year.

One thing we do still have some questions about, though, is the music we sing in church. Since we are new to the church scene, we're not familiar with many of the songs, and we are wondering why so many of them have such odd phrases. Two songs we sang recently had these words: "The fellowship of kindred minds is like to that above" and "Your festal banner wave on high." Are we the only two people in the church who don't have a clue as to what these words mean?

We love the shorter songs because they are easy to sing and easy to understand, but we're having a hard time warming up to some of the ones in the hymn book.

We don't want to complain; we just want to know why we still sing those old songs. Thank you for your time.

Sincerely,

Why so much new music?

If you have a constructive suggestion, include it in your letter.

Dear Don,

I've noticed recently that we are singing fewer and fewer of the old hymns of the faith in our worship services. Is this intentional or is it just coincidental? I don't mind the choruses—a few of them are fine— but I miss singing the great old hymns. Did you ever read what Augustine said about them?

When I remember the tears that I shed on hearing the songs of the Church in the early days, soon after I had recovered my faith, and when I realize that nowadays it is not the singing that moves me but the meaning of the words when they are sung in a clear voice to the most appropriate tune, I again acknowledge the great value of this practice.

That's pretty much how I feel. I know everything has its time and place, and I'm not against change; but sometimes I wish it didn't have to happen so fast.

If there isn't time in our worship services to sing more hymns, do you think we might be able to have an old-fashioned hymn sing sometime and sing all of our old favorites?

Sincerely,

Music appreciation

And every once in a while, the music pleases someone.

Dear Jim,

Our hearts are thrilled by the music in our Sunday worship services! On the way home our family marvels at how well the theme of the music coordinates with the subject of the message. I don't know how much time you and John have to spend together to make this happen, but it is worth every minute because we are always prepared to listen when you step up to preach.

My husband and I come from different church traditions and musical backgrounds, and we both appreciate the wide variety of musical styles that are used. And the fact that so many people are allowed to use their talents is heartwarming.

May God continue to bless your service for him.

Respectfully yours,

Let's not forget the older folks

Dear Keith,

How thankful I am that you are starting a program for the senior adults of our congregation! I am nearing retirement and am caring for my aging parents as well, so I know how much people will benefit from opportunities to fellowship with one another and to care for each other. In fact, I have a few ideas for service to shut-ins that you may be able to include in your planning. For example, how about a "morning out" for care-giving mates?

Am I Doing This Right?

Marion Bond West

And a little child will lead them.   — ISAIAH 11:6 KJV

NO one except God knew how inadequate I felt being newly married to a minister. I didn't really know how to be a minister's wife. I tried to keep my insecurities from showing by smiling a lot, but inside I wasn't smiling. I always wondered, *Am I doing this right? Why did I ever think I could be a minister's wife? Does it show how new I am at this?*

My husband, Gene, pastored a church where I met a very needy four-year-old boy who, along with others, attended service as part of our community outreach program for children. Paul came from a non-churchgoing, very poor family, and his parents were divorced. He needed tangible things such as shoes and food, but he also needed encouragement and acceptance. Probably because I needed acceptance, too, I often sat with him and his sickly grandmother in church. He colored pictures, sang from the hymnbook, and sometimes slept on my lap. His needs were so great, I hardly knew where to start.

If you have any brainstorming sessions, I would be glad to participate. May God bless your efforts.

Sincerely,

Paying a compliment

Dear Mr. Johnson,

How I look forward to church each Sunday! Your series on the Ten
Commandments has been especially helpful, even though I thought
when you started that I already knew everything about them.

I decided to begin with a home visit one cold and windy Sunday
afternoon. The small yard, close to a busy street, was cluttered with
broken toys and empty drink cans. I walked across the tiny wooden
porch and knocked on the door. No answer. I had just turned to leave
when the door with peeling paint opened slightly. Then more. Finally,
it was thrown open wide.

There stood the beautiful little boy. He was barefooted. He came
out on the porch and looked me over for a moment, and then a
tremendous smile touched his face. He announced for those inside,
"Hey, everybody! It's the preacher's wife! The preacher's wife has
come to see us!" He grabbed me by the hand and led me inside, where
I was warmly received on that chilly day. The little boy squeezed my
hand and announced once again like a circus barker, "I said, 'It's the
preacher's wife!'" Paul's grandmother, sister, father, and aunt scur-
ried toward the front to greet me.

My smile suddenly went all the way down to my toes. Instantly,
unexpectedly, I felt like a preacher's wife—at last. It was wonderful!

*Oh, Father, it's true. You do often speak and minister to us
through little, unsuspecting children.*

Recently I invited a new neighbor to attend with me. She does not go to church regularly, but she felt comfortable at our church. You really helped her by giving the page number of the Scripture text so she could find the place in the pew Bible.

Thank you for being sensitive to the needs of people who might otherwise be uncomfortable in church.

Keep on keeping on,

Great job with youth

Dear Randy,

After seeing our church's youth group working so hard in my back-yard during their help day for senior adults, I have had a change of heart about "young people these days." You are doing a great job with them—not only teaching them the Bible, but also instilling in them the desire to serve others. The cookies and milk I served them were a small "thank you" for all the time they spent washing windows, trimming bushes, and raking leaves.

Thank you for giving our teens a chance to help others. I am reminded through their good deeds of my need to pray more for them and for you as you continue to seek God's direction in your work with them.

Gratefully,

Need to hire additional staff member

Dear Dennis,

Having been in the church for thirty years, I have observed several pastors, each with his own special gift and heartbeat for a certain area of ministry. I know that your heart's desire is to see the young people of our church give their lives to the Lord's service, but there is too much for you to do to concentrate on that one area.

We are a small church with a small budget, but with the the increasing number of teenagers coming to our church perhaps we should consider hiring someone to minister solely to them.

If you are looking for someone to support you in this, you can depend on me. I believe we need to move forward on this matter quickly, while the kids are still interested.

Sincerely,

Recommending candidate for youth pastor

Dear Dr. Allen,

Since you asked the congregation to pray with you about hiring a youth pastor, I have taken this very seriously. My grandchildren will soon be teenagers, and I want them to have the right kind of spiritual leadership during those important years.

I would like to suggest a person for you to contact. His name is James Smith, and he is the son of good friends of ours. Jim graduated from a highly respected Christian college and has worked in a youth camp for several years, but he now wants a more stable, long-term setting for his discipleship ministry. I believe it would be worth your while to find out if he is interested in the position our church has open. His phone number and address are . . .

If you need more information, please feel free to call me.

Sincerely,

Requesting participation at event

Dear Mr. Anderson,

I am writing on behalf of the Rockland Rotary Club to invite you to offer the invocation at our luncheon on Wednesday, January 27. Some of the club members are also members of our church, and we would be honored if you would join us for lunch. We appreciate your ability to present biblical truth in a way that is not abrasive or offensive to people of other religious backgrounds, and we are confident that you will honor the Lord in everything you say. We place no restrictions on what you say.

Thank you for considering this request. Please respond by January 3.

Sincerely,

Assurance of prayer

Dear Dr. Davis,

Our church family has been aware of the heavy burden you have been under in the last week, and I want you to know that I am committed to praying for you more diligently than ever. Even though I have tried to pray regularly for you and your family each morning after breakfast, I now feel the urge to pray specifically for you as you come to mind throughout the day.

Sometimes I forget that ministers are subject to the same temptations I am. So in the past my prayers have concentrated more on asking God to bless your ministry than on asking him to meet your own spiritual and personal needs. That is changing now with my own spiritual growth.

May God strengthen you for every need.

Sincerely,

Requesting help in handling church problem

Dear Ms. VanDyke,

For the past year I have watched with concern as our fifth and sixth grade Sunday school department has gone steadily downhill. Mr. Hill, who has been the superintendent for more than twenty years, does not realize that he can no longer handle things as well as he once did. His temper is short, he forgets important details, and he is having trouble working with the teachers. Even though most of us are trying to compensate for his difficulties, the department is beginning to suffer.

Is there a way to facilitate a "changing of the guard" without doing harm to Mr. Hill's dignity? He's been so faithful. Any help you or the board could offer would be appreciated.

Sincerely,

Creative Listening

Marjorie Holmes

In the beginning was the Word. . . .   — JOHN 1:1 NIV

HOW often we hear, or have said ourselves, "I'm not going to church this morning. The minister is so boring." Or its happy opposite, "Our priest is marvelous. I hate to miss a single Sunday."

Our own parish had been blessed with an unusually vibrant, gifted rector. Ray had a radiant personality, and his sermons were so enthralling I dreaded the times when he was away. Few substitutes were in his class. One year, one of these, a kind but quiet man, preached sermons that seemed so dull I found myself daydreaming and glancing at my watch.

I confided this to Ray when he returned. "I almost stayed home. You are so much better!" He smiled, but he wasn't flattered. Instead, he gave me a valuable insight. "Marj, I understand. But let me tell you what we tell our children. You don't go to church to be entertained. You go to hear God's Word. Go with the expectation of hearing it and you will, no matter how it's presented. After all, you wouldn't go to the house of your dearest friend and say, 'Entertain me, be original, or I won't come again!'"

Now every time I enter a church, I remember those words. The building doesn't matter, whether humble or a great cathedral—this is the home of my dearest Friend. The "messenger" doesn't matter either—whether dynamic and colorful or plain and ordinary, I can be a creative listener, ready to hear what God has to say to me.

Father, help me to listen carefully, creatively. Make me a responsive instrument to the encouragement and comfort you know I need.

Appreciation

Dear Jerry,

Recently I heard on the radio that this is "Pastor Appreciation Week." Frankly, I had never thought of telling you how much I appreciate your ministry, but I really do, and I want to share some good news.

I have been sending tapes of your messages to a relative in prison. He is growing in the Lord and passing the tapes on to other inmates. You never know how far reaching your ministry may be.

Even though your true rewards will be in heaven, I am enclosing a gift certificate to the Christian bookstore as my way of saying, "Thank you for all you do."

Sincerely,

Thanks for spiritual sensitivity

Dear Ed,

Thanks for your sermon a week ago Sunday and for your promise to explore until Easter the magnitude of God.

We spend so much time these days trying to convince people that God is interested in the minute details of our lives that we have reduced him to the deciding vote in debates about what to drink, what to wear, and what political party should be in office. We have made him so relevant to our tiny piece of the world that we have made him irrelevant to the rest of the universe. We have struggled so hard to convince people that he is timely that we have completely obscured his timelessness.

Your preaching reminds me of how wonderful and glorious God is, and when I focus on that I don't need anyone to remind me how insignificant and sinful I am.

Thanks for keeping your heart right with God.

Sincerely,

Appreciation to pastor's wife

Dear Lorna,

Although your work is often done behind the scenes, I want you to know that I appreciate all the many things you do to support our church and to support your husband as he ministers to us weekly. I also want you to know that I pray for you as well as for him.

I know that much of what he does for other people in times of crisis keeps him away from you and your family, and without your support he would be unable to minister to us so effectively. Your attitude of selflessness has been a blessing to me personally.

Since I don't usually know what specific needs you have or what challenges you are facing, I generally pray that you and your husband will deepen your relationship with each other and resist the temptations that might tear your family apart. I trust that this is happening and that our lives bless you as richly as yours does us.

With love and appreciation,

Thanks for special assistance

Dear Mr. Johnson,

Our family is deeply grateful for the assistance you gave us during our recent crisis. Faced with difficult decisions that seemed too hard to make as our father lay dying, we were glad that you could spend some time with us. You pointed us to Scriptures of comfort and gave wisdom that helped us make several difficult decisions.

Graciously, God prepared each of us in a different way for Dad's death. Your willingness to help at a critical time will always be remembered. Your presence was a source of strength when we felt very weak.

May your strength be renewed as you continue to give so generously to others.

With appreciation,

Requesting advice

Dear Dr. Smith,

How thankful I am for the spiritual growth I have experienced in the last few months as a result of your preaching. But now I am faced with a dilemma. Although I have been a Christian for several years, I never realized until recently that I should be giving more than a few dollars a week to the ministry of the church. This conviction has come from my own personal Bible study, which your sermons have encouraged me to do. But I haven't been able to figure out what God expects from me, and I've never heard you preach on the subject. I want to be obedient in this area, but I need some help.

Could I come in and talk to you about this sometime? I'm going to be out of town for a few days, but I'll call your office when I get back to set up an appointment. I hope you can straighten out my thinking on this matter.

Sincerely,

MATTERS OF BUSINESS

From search committee

Dear Dr. Connelly,

Central Community Church has been without a pastor since Reverend Jones moved to Japan as a missionary last November. After several church members submitted your name, we discovered that two search committee members have followed your ministry for many years and that both believe you would be an excellent candidate for the position of senior pastor.

After prayerful consideration, we are requesting that you talk to our committee about the possibility of being a pastoral candidate.

Information about the church's history, our church constitution, and our doctrinal statement are enclosed along with a questionnaire

The Old and the New

Marjorie Holmes

Pastors who do their work well should be paid well and should be highly appreciated, especially those who work hard at both preaching and teaching.
— 1 TIMOTHY 5:17 TLB

FAR from home one Easter morning, our family followed the bells to a little country church.

People hastened to make us welcome, seat us, hand us songbooks already open to the proper page. The building had the smell of most old wooden churches—worn hymnals, pews, carpeting, coffee from countless suppers. Familiar, so familiar . . . the fellowship, the organ, the choir coming down the aisle and the fervor of their "Allelujahs!" I didn't feel a stranger. Rather, as if I'd come home to something lost.

Then the minister rose, bringing the slight shock of something new: the sideburns, the longish hair sprouting the nonsequitur of a boyish cowlick. For he was so young (still in seminary, somebody whispered). After this service he would dash off to another church. Meanwhile, his enthusiastic presentation of the Easter story: "He is not here; he as risen!"

I was really stirred. It was almost like hearing this incredible news for the first time. At the door I tried to tell him so. "Your sermon was marvelous, very inspiring." Such inadequate words for what I was feeling.

As I pondered this juxtaposition of old and new a great tenderness filled me—and a hopeful concern: that fiery youth would continue to preach such powerful sermons about the old, old story.

Lord, bless all ministers as they carry your message of resurrection. Help the rest of us to encourage them, and help all of us to keep the message fresh, always new, always energetic.

for you to complete if you would like to be considered for this position. I will call within the next few days to determine your level of interest.

With anticipation,

Letter of call

Dear Bill,

This letter is simply a matter of formality to confirm our recent conversations. After many months of searching and praying, we are delighted to issue a call to you to become our pastor. As I stated yesterday, we were very pleased that 96 percent of our congregation voted to invite you to become our next pastor. The fact that you were able to give us an affirmative answer the same night also confirms that our journeys have led us to the same place.

You will receive a call this week from Don Smith, who will give you the final details of your financial package.

May God bless you in the days ahead as you anticipate ministering with us on his behalf.

Joyfully,

Welcome to our congregation

Dear Bill,

We are pleased that you have accepted the invitation of our congregation to become our pastor, and we welcome you to our community of believers.

Be assured of our prayerful support as you and your family face a time of adjustment. Many church members are eager to help in practical ways, such as meals and child care during the week you move. We hope that you will have a smooth transition and experience a warm welcome from our church members as well as from our community at large.

We look forward to many years of service together.

Sincerely,

14

Requesting Donations

By this kind of hard work we must help the weak, remembering the words the Lord Jesus himself said: "It is more blessed to give than to receive." ACTS 20:35 NIV

Money is like muck, not good except it be spread.
FRANCIS BACON

No one would have remembered the Good Samaritan if he'd only had good intentions. MARGARET THATCHER

*L*ife would have been easier for all of us if God had taken the initiative to distribute wealth equally, but he didn't. He gave us a few principles to follow and then left it up to us to figure out the best way to do it.

Well, our best ways are far from perfect, but at least we have his original principles to give us direction. Here are a few of them that tell us how (and how not) to use our income. Knowing the proper use of our own resources will keep us from asking others to use theirs improperly.

- *Give a minimum of a tenth of your income (Malachi 3:10)*
- *Take care of widows and the fatherless, the poor and oppressed (Psalm 82:3)*
- *Be generous (Proverbs 11:25)*
- *Don't hoard your wealth (Matthew 6:19)*
- *Be kind to the needy because it is the same as being kind to Jesus (Matthew 25:40)*

There are many types of motivations: some are good and some are bad; some are selfish and some are unselfish. But when we get down to the motives for charitable giving, we can summarize them in four basic categories: fear; guilt; pride; and goodness (which includes love and obedience). Consequently, there are four basic types of fundraising strategies: those that appeal to people's fearfulness; their guilt; their pride; or their goodness.

People motivated by fear believe that something bad is going to happen but that they can prevent it by giving money to an organization that promises to fight whatever evil they are afraid of. People motivated by guilt believe that they did something bad (or failed to do something good) and that they can make up for it by giving to a worthy cause. People motivated by pride believe that they are better than those in need, so they give because giving makes them feel good about themselves. People motivated by goodness believe that God gives all good things and that they are to use what he gives them to make life better for others, so they give out of obedience and love.

Of the four, it is easy to see that the fourth, goodness, is the highest form of motivation; it is also the highest form of fundraising appeal.

But when money is tight it is tempting to resort to one of the others because "the pool" is bigger; more people are plagued by guilt and fear and consumed by pride than are devoted to goodness.

But if your fundraising appeal plays on people's fears, you are, in a sense, selling them a false sense of security. Or if it implies that giving to your organization or cause can in some way right a wrong, you are offering to relieve guilt, which only God has the right to do. And if it suggests that giving to your cause will prove that they are kind, caring Christians, you are offering them a false sense of personal value. If, however, your cause is one for which you can legitimately appeal to their love for God, their desire for justice, and their concern for the poor and needy, you should be able to write a convincing (and ethical) fundraising letter.

When you prepare to write your letter, think about the type of people you are writing to and answer the following questions:

- *On a scale of 1–10, what is their level of awareness of this cause? What can I say that will raise their awareness?*
- *On a scale of 1–10, what is their level of interest in this cause? What can I say that will arouse their interest?*
- *What healthy emotions are attached to this cause (e.g., love, compassion, loyalty)? Is there an honest, ethical way to use this emotional attachment to get people to sense the urgency of the need? (***Honest*** and ***ethical*** are key words here. Many fundraisers use emotional appeals in unethical ways.)*
- *What unhealthy emotions are attached to this cause (e.g., anger, fear, hatred, jealousy)? Have I used any of these for my own selfish ends?*

Some fundraising manuals will tell you to "create a crisis" whenever you ask for money. This advice may be based on the idea that people are more likely to give money to keep someone alive than they are to keep the lights on in your building. Even though this may be true, it does not justify deceit. And "creating a crisis" to raise funds for any organization is indeed deceitful.

When writing your fundraising letter, keep in mind these principles:

Be honest. *Don't exaggerate the need. If the truth won't motivate people to give, you shouldn't be asking for their money.*

Be straightforward. *Don't ask for prayer when you're really asking for money.*

Be clear. *Give all pertinent facts in a logical order.*

Be concise. *You are asking people for their money, so be polite and don't take any more of their time than is absolutely necessary. This too* *goes against the advice of "professional" fundraisers who say that longer letters give the impression of being more important and thus get a higher percentage of response.*

As mentioned earlier, the best motive for giving money as well as for asking for it is goodness. And a guide for this is found in the apostle Paul's letter to Timothy:

> *Command those who are rich in this present world not to be arrogant nor to put their hope in wealth, which is so uncertain, but to put their hope in God, who richly provides us with everything for our enjoyment. Command them to do good, to be rich in good deeds, and to be generous and willing to share. In this way they will lay up treasure for themselves as a firm foundation for the coming age, so that they may take hold of the life that is truly life.*   *—1 Timothy 6:17–19 NIV*

LETTERS TO ACCOMPANY DONATION

Thanks for good work

Dear Friends,

    I am glad to be able to send you this check for $100.00. I have been following your growth and accomplishments for some time, and I believe the Alpha Women's Center is a great service to the women of Grand Rapids and to the community as well.

    Keep up the good work.

Sincerely,

Offering to give time as well as money

Dear Zoo Director,

I have been a contributor to the John Ball Park Zoo for several years. Recently I retired from my job and am now interested in volunteering some time to the Zoo as a clerical support person or a tour guide. My schedule is flexible, and I love animals. I hope you can put me to work.

I look forward to hearing from you soon.

Sincerely,

Suggesting other ways to raise money

Dear School Board Member,

My children have attended your school for several years, and each year I notice further cutbacks and diminished resources for education. Is it possible that some of the services could be restored if we were to use some innovative fundraising efforts? For example, in addition to our annual bake sales, we could sponsor a craft fair in May and an auction in October.

I would be willing to chair a committee to get these programs organized. Please contact me at your earliest convenience to discuss these possibilities. My phone number is ___-___.

Sincerely,

REASONS FOR NOT GIVING

Budget limitation

Dear Station Manager,

I received your letter requesting contributions to pay for a new transmitting tower for your radio station.

While I enjoy your radio station immensely, my own budget limitations prohibit me from contributing to this project.

Sincerely,

Disagree with project

Dear Campaign Chairperson,

I am confused by your concern for the Snow Owl when thousands of American children do not have enough to eat. The poverty level in this country is growing faster than the Snow Owl is disappearing. I cannot, therefore, in good conscience, contribute anything to your campaign to save the Snow Owls.

Sincerely,

Annoyed by too-frequent requests

Dear Events Coordinator,

I am delighted that the Chicago Symphony has been invited to perform in China. But I have already made my regular contribution for the year and, in addition, have been asked to support your building renovation and your scholarship fund to bring underprivileged children to the symphony. Now you are in my mailbox again, wanting more help.

I am writing to tell you, without apology, that you will have to get to China without my assistance.

Sincerely,

FUNDRAISING—LIBRARY

Need for new books

Dear Friend of the Library,

Our building expansion is nearly complete and the requests for additional resource materials have been met.

But we have fallen short of our goal to raise the necessary funds to purchase new books to complete our fiction and nonfiction sections. Without supplemental funding from our loyal members, the new wing will remain closed indefinitely.

Please help us to complete the project by sending a tax-deductible

A Giving Heart

Arthur Gordon

Do not turn away from the one who wants to borrow from you.
— MATTHEW 5:42 NIV

GLENN Kittler was a wonderful, warmhearted man whose wit and wisdom cheered all of us who worked with him. Glenn has been gone for several years now, but many readers of Daily Guideposts will remember him and his cat Louie.

Glenn said something once that I've never forgotten. We were walking together along an avenue in New York City when we were approached by a wistful woman who said she needed money because her children were hungry. Glenn took out a handful of coins and gave them to her.

As we moved on I said disapprovingly, "That woman's here every day with the same story. She'll probably just buy a drink with the money you gave her."

"Perhaps she will," Glenn said. "But you know, I think God sometimes sends people like that just to test our sense of charity." We walked a little farther, and then he said, almost to himself, "The act of giving is more important than the merit of the receiver."

Jesus knew that, too.

Lord, use me to show your love to others.

contribution. A postage-paid envelope is enclosed for your convenience.

Thank you for your support.

Sincerely,

Need volunteers

Dear Sir or Madam,

The Kent County Library system provides many services that are unavailable in libraries around the country. For example, our on-line computers that are linked to the downtown library and our full-time staff members to help research hard-to-find information are not found in many libraries.

Unfortunately, funding cuts have put these services in jeopardy.

We are calling on you, a loyal patron, to help us preserve these services by volunteering your time at the library. Your help with some of the routine, nontechnical assignments will allow experienced staff members to spend more time in the technical areas that require expertise.

Free training sessions will begin in two weeks, so call soon if you can help out on a regular basis. My phone number is ___-____, ext. ___.

Sincerely,

Need additional staff

Dear Library Member,

The Stedman Library has always prided itself on having the finest resources and the most up-to-date equipment. Due to government cutbacks to programs such as ours, however, we are now understaffed. Without the appropriate staff to handle the flow of materials and research for our patrons, our library will fall far short of your expectations.

In a small community like Stedman, there are few resources available to students and educators, so it is imperative that we maintain our level of excellence.

In order to cover the cost of hiring additional personnel, we are asking members to consider giving a one-time, tax-deductible gift.

We believe the educational future of our community is as important to you as it is to us, so we ask that you will give generously.

Thank you for your consideration.

Sincerely,

Need additional equipment

Dear Library Member,

At the Grover Library, we have been as prudent as possible with regard to our budget. We have solicited and received funding from private corporations, contacted publishers to purchase overruns, and managed to get by with a venerable cataloguing system that simply will not do any longer.

The Library Purchasing Committee has received several bids from computer companies who can install a new cataloguing system and train us to use it for a reasonable price: $12,000.00.

We need to raise this money by July 1 if we are to have the system up and running by fall.

Your contribution, large or small, will make a difference. Please consider a tax-deductible gift to the Library Fund. A postage-paid envelope is enclosed for your convenience.

Thank you for your support.

Sincerely,

FUNDRAISING—CHURCHES

Campaign for specific project

Dear Members,

For the past several years, we have had to say no to people who have had the vision and energy to start new programs for our youth simply because there has been no place for them to meet. Our building is being used to full capacity every night of the week. Although we are pleased about that, we are not pleased that so many good things are being left undone.

After careful consideration of our spatial limitations and the growth of our congregation over the past three years, it has become clear to the Board that we need to expand our facility. If we want to keep our doors open to the community as an outreach for Christ, it is essential that we take immediate action.

A meeting to discuss the planned expansion will be held Sunday, August 4, in the sanctuary at four o'clock. The chairman of the building committee will summarize the thinking that has led us to this place, and there will be a time for questions. After this we will pass out pledge cards for you to use to let us know your commitment.

Between now and then, please pray about how you and your family can contribute to this project.

Sincerely,

Budget can be met

Dear Member:

Thank you to all of you who have pledged your support to St. John's and have been faithful in your giving. It is your generosity that enables us to provide youth programs for our children, to support missionaries around the world, and to meet the physical and spiritual needs of people in our church and community.

Due to some unexpected maintenance expenses, we are behind in this year's budget by about $3,000.00. If in your family's budget there is some discretionary money that you could put toward making up this deficit, we would certainly be grateful. If you are able to contribute, please make a note on your check that it is to be used for special maintenance expenses.

Thank you for your support in the past year. We hope you will

Faithful in Small Things

Mary Lou Carney

You have been trustworthy in a very small matter.

— LUKE 19:17 NIV

SEVERAL months ago I saw a sign on the cash register of my local supermarket that read: "ROUND OFF FOR THE NEEDY."

"What's that?" I asked the checkout girl, pointing at the sign. She said, "If people want to donate the odd change from their grocery bill, we funnel it to organizations to help feed needy people."

Odd change? "Here," I said, smiling as I dumped my thirty-six cents back into her hand.

While doing my grocery shopping this week, I was amazed to see a huge banner: "OVER $10,000 RAISED FOR THE NEEDY. THANKS!" Ten thousand dollars? From small change? Incredible!

Later, as I put away groceries, I thought of my life. Was I discrediting the "small change" opportunities that came my way? I didn't have time to direct the children's pageant at church, but I could spend a few evenings painting sets. I couldn't chaperone the week-long ski trip, but I could make a giant batch of chocolate chip cookies for them to take along. My offering when the missionary visited was small, yet daily I remembered her in prayer. Little things. Christ knew how important they were—and I'm learning.

Father, still the part of me that yearns for grand displays. Keep me faithful in little things.

continue to be partners with us in our mission to spread the Good News of Jesus Christ at home and around the world.

Sincerely,

Delinquent pledge

Letters about delinquent pledges have a high likelihood of leaving a bad impression and, as a result, of having the opposite effect of the one you desire. There are few good ways to write this type of letter without sounding insensitive and greedy. One way, however, is to assume that the person has a reason other than negligence for being late. Rather than write a letter reminding the person of his or her obligation, write one offering to provide what he or she needs, which, after all, is also the work of the church.

Dear Mr. Jones,

Thank you for pledging to support First Church with a monthly donation. We appreciate people like you and your family who are willing to make a commitment to support the ongoing work of our church.

Our treasurer has noticed, however, that you have missed your last few pledge payments. This causes us some alarm because we wonder if you are going through a time of financial trouble or personal crisis. If so, we want to offer our services to help in any way we can. We have people available to give financial, emotional, and of course spiritual help. Please don't think you are alone. We want to help. You are part of our family, and we are part of yours.

If you need to talk to someone, please call the church office at ___-____. We hope to hear from you soon.

Sincerely,

Appeal to faith

Dear Member,

Calvary Church has been praying for over a year regarding the possibility of adding to our facility. So far we have found no other way to ease the cramped conditions and relieve the burden on maintenance personnel who spend hours setting up and tearing down the same rooms for different events. This problem alone accounts for overtime dollars that could be used elsewhere in ministry.

The new addition will provide educational space and a chapel for weddings and other special events. There will be new kitchen facilities and an elevator to make the wing accessible to the handicapped. We believe these additions will make Calvary Church better able to serve the congregation and the community.

We are enclosing a pledge card for you to fill out. You will notice that it does not have a space for your name. We are asking you to decide what you can afford to give toward the cost of the addition, fill in the amount, and return the card to the church. We will tally the pledges and then destroy the pledge cards. We trust you to honor your pledge without any oversight from us.

Thank you for your support.

Sincerely,

Sponsor a kid who can't afford camp

Dear Member,

Missionary work takes many forms. Some people go overseas to spread the gospel of Jesus Christ, and some work at home to support those who go.

Both aspects are important. But consider this third possibility: supporting a child who needs to hear about Jesus.

We are writing on behalf of twenty-five children who want to spend three weeks at a Christian Summer Camp on Lake Geneva. There they will hear a gospel message every day and see it lived out in the lives of counselors and staff members. This may be the only chance they ever have to get away from the noise and chaos of their life in the inner city to a place where they can hear what God has to say to them.

Wouldn't you like to make this happen for one child? Please give generously to Kids Camp and give these children a chance to see and hear what a difference God can make in their lives.

Enclosed is a contribution card. Please fill it out and return it by May 6. Thank you for your support.

Sincerely,

Short-term mission trip

When asking for money to cover the cost of going on a mission trip yourself, be sure to include specific details as to what you will be doing, what your qualifications are for doing it, and how much you personally are contributing to the cost. People will be more likely to give if you demonstrate the importance of the trip by putting up some of your own money (and if they have some assurance that they are not funding your summer vacation to some exotic location).

Dear Mr. and Mrs. Smith,

I am a student at the University of Wisconsin-Madison, studying English Literature. During the past two years, I have learned effective ways to witness and serve God through opportunities and training sessions presented by my church. Being on a secular campus has opened my eyes for the first time to see what a difference it makes in life to have a personal relationship with Christ. And I have developed a deep compassion for people who don't have a clue as to where to look to find meaning in life.

Sensing this void in my classmates and professors, I have developed a passion for evangelism. When I came here to school I was timid and afraid, but now I am bold because I know I have something they desperately need.

Now I have an opportunity to go with a group from my church and use my gift of evangelism in Lithuania. I believe I am at a time in my life when I need to leave my comfort zone and see how God can use me as part of his plan. The team will be gone for four weeks and will visit twelve cities.

Giving Good Gifts

Penney Schwab

Defend the cause of the weak and fatherless; maintain the rights of the poor and oppressed. — PSALM 82:3 NIV

THE clothing rooms operated by our ministry are stocked through donations from generous Christians who give wonderful, love-filled gifts! We just received fifty handmade baby quilts to supply warmth for infants whose cribs may be cardboard boxes. We have bright knitted caps and mittens for schoolchildren, "in" shirts and slacks for teenagers, and sturdy work clothes for job seekers.

But we get other "gifts," too. Yesterday a woman brought in a bag of ripped, threadbare jeans covered with oily stains. When I wrinkled my nose (they smelled terrible!), she snapped, "Poor people shouldn't be picky! If they are really in need they'll wear these and be grateful."

Her comment reminded me of the story of a little girl who came home from Sunday school and asked her mother for some food to fill a Thanksgiving basket for a poor family. The mother rummaged through the pantry and fished out a couple of cans of anchovies. "Take these," she said. "They've been on the shelf for years, and none of us likes them anyway."

The child's face fell. "But, Mother," she said quietly, "if we only share what we don't want, we're not helping the poor. They're helping us."

When you give gifts do you take time to ask, "Will my gift glorify Christ? Will it help the receiver? Or does it only help me?"

Lord Jesus, giver of all good things, help me to give wisely, compassionately, and with love.

I have earned $1,000.00 to put toward the cost of the trip and need to raise another $2,000.00 to be able to go.

If you would like to participate in this ministry by supporting me financially, please fill out the enclosed card and return it to me. I need to have 100 percent of my support in place by May 1. Thank you for your interest and support.

Sincerely,

Missions project

Dear Member,

Our church has the rare opportunity of sending a missionary team into Uzbekistan, an area not previously open to Christians. We have accepted the challenge of getting a team together, complete with resource materials, by August 15.

We are excited about the opportunity of telling people about Jesus for the first time, and we want to invite you to have a part in this once-in-a-lifetime venture. We are trying to raise $7,500 by May 1. If you can help, please complete the enclosed card and return it to us. Thank you in advance for what you are about to do.

Sincerely,

FUNDRAISING—SCHOOLS

Give more than last year

Dear Parent,

The Cleveland Academy has always maintained that the cost of our education cannot be covered by the price of the tuition, but that no value can be placed on education.

Cleveland Academy is at a crossroads. For us to survive and to continue to provide the caliber of education we offer, we have two options: drastically increase the cost of tuition; or find individuals to offset the rising costs.

I am pleading with you to search your hearts and evaluate your child's education. Compare our program and its results to what you see elsewhere. If you believe as I do, that the education at Cleveland Academy is worth more than ever, please give generously this year. We are asking everyone to reach deep and, if possible, to give even more than last year.

Thanks for being a part of the Cleveland Academy family. I know that you already give much more than money. You give your time and talents and emotional support. And believe me, they do not go unnoticed.

Sincerely,

Funding for extracurricular activities

Dear Parent:

As you know, the Cleveland Academy is committed to quality education. And we believe that quality includes balance. Therefore, we offer more than the traditional subjects of reading, writing, and arithmetic. We also offer classes in drama, music, and art so children can explore their hidden gifts in these areas. To withhold these programs from elementary age children could, we believe, put them at a disadvantage in the years to come.

Please help us give our children every advantage for a promising future. We are asking you to consider supporting our Arts Program with a donation. We have enclosed a pledge card for you to fill out and a postage-paid envelope to use in returning it to us.

Thank you for your support in this area.

Sincerely,

Library needs

Dear Parent,

By choosing the Cleveland Academy you have made a statement about the value you place on your child's education. We believe that every one of our students will get the best education available. Last year the Academy installed a new computer lab, and kindergartners through sixth graders have regularly scheduled class times in the lab.

This year we would like to computerize our library to make more educational materials available to our teachers and students and to make it more accessible.

I am writing to ask you to support this improvement with a donation. Please complete the enclosed pledge card enclosed and return it to the administration office.

Thank you for your support.

Sincerely,

Alumni association

Dear Alumni,

Many alumni like yourself want to give today's students the same opportunity for a quality education that you had. As you know, the spirit and quality of Brunwood College have remained a constant since it began in 1924. For many years the generosity of friends and benefactors has made it possible for Brunwood to offer one of the most comprehensive Liberal Arts programs in the Northeast.

Can we count on your support to ensure a spirit of learning for the generations to come? We have enclosed a pledge card and a postage-paid envelope. Please fill in the card and and return it to us so we can budget and plan wisely for next year and the years to come.

Thank you for your support.

Sincerely,

Haven't given yet

Dear Parents,

We are nearing our goal of $50,000.00 for the Library Computer Fund and are eager to begin installation. For those of you who have not had a chance to donate to this worthy cause, there is still time. We need everyone to pitch in a little or a lot to make this project come together.

As you know the library is crucial to the education of our children. Without up-to-date reference materials and on-line services our children are at a disadvantage. Please consider making a generous contribution to the future of your children. Thank you for your support.

Sincerely,

Minorities program

Dear Community Member,

If you have ever skipped a meal for any reason, you know how difficult it is to concentrate on anything when your stomach is telling you it's time to eat.

Imagine, then, being a child who is sent to school without having had breakfast and is expected to sit quietly through three class periods before lunch time. Can we legitimately expect hungry children to concentrate on studies when we can hardly do it ourselves? Also, children without adequate protection from the weather are not likely to put school work at the top of their priority list.

It is a sad fact that many children come to school unprepared to learn and suffer severe disadvantages as a consequence.

The Chapter for Learning is calling on you to help these underprivileged children. Your gift will allow us to begin an early morning breakfast program in the schools and a community clothes closet stocked with warm clothing and boots for children who do not have them.

Please respond generously this year. Your gift is very important to the future of our children. Thank you for your support.

Sincerely,

Building fund

Dear Parent,

We have exciting news! Enrollments are up over thirty percent! This means that more children than ever are experiencing the difference a Walden education makes. Walden has always prided itself on providing a Christ-centered, quality education for children in grades K–12. As you know, it is considered to be one of the finest college preparatory schools in the nation.

But with growth come growing pains. We do not have room for the number of students who want to attend next year. This leaves us with three options: (1) limit enrollment; (2) use the music and art rooms as regular classrooms; (3) add to our facility.

Since you are already familiar with our school and its philosophy, you know that either of the first two options would be a last resort for us.

Within the next few weeks, you will be contacted by a representative of the school who will answer your questions and ask you to help us finance additional classroom space.

Between now and then, please consider how you can help. Your support will make the difference.

Thank you.

Sincerely,

Student union building

Dear Mr. and Mrs. Norman,

Do you remember the friendships you made and nurtured around the fireplace or over a cup of coffee at the snack bar in the Student Union? It is one of the few places on campus devoted to the social life of students, and it's a place where lifetime friendships are kindled, where networking and bonding take place, where stimulating conversation flows, and where a diversity of opinions are expressed. You know as I know that the Student Union is the heart of the university.

For nearly sixty-five years, our Student Union has sustained the comings and goings of students while undergoing only minor renovations. But now it needs attention. Its age is beginning to show.

The Board of Regents has agreed to install a new floor and to upgrade the kitchen if half the funds can be raised from the private sector. It is our hope that you will contribute to this project to preserve the Student Union.

Please consider the amount you can donate. Then fill in the enclosed card and return it with your gift in the postage-paid envelope.

Thank you for your support.

Sincerely,

Religious appeal

Dear Parent,

You hear a lot about school choices these days, but are there really choices? The public school systems are in a state of moral decay at a time when it is more important than ever for children to have a moral and ethical foundation for their behavior and choices.

The Foundation for Moral Education was established to put morality back in our public school systems. Parents should not have to pay exorbitant private school tuition to have their children in a safe environment. Every parent and child in America deserves a safe school, and our program, which teaches teachers how to incorporate commonly held social and moral values into every subject, has been tested and proven effective in more than fifty public schools.

Won't you help us in this endeavor by making a donation? Your gift will make a difference in the morality of the next generation, and they are the ones who will be making decisions about our future in just a few years.

Please, think ahead and give now. Thank you for your support.

Sincerely,

Financially disadvantaged student

Dear Mr. and Mrs. Jones,

I am writing on behalf of Jimmy Johnson and children like him all over our city. Jimmy lives in a rundown apartment with his mother and six siblings. He is a bright boy, but he needs someone like you to care about him if he's ever going to learn to make wise choices.

In this land of abundance, it is shocking that so many of America's children live in poverty. But if you would donate just $20.00, we can make sure that Jimmy has a nutritious breakfast and decent clothes to wear to school. This will enable Jimmy to spend his classroom time concentrating on the subject matter rather than counting the hours until lunch.

Won't you show that you care by sending your donation? Complete the enclosed card and mail it back soon. We want to make sure that Jimmy is on his way to a brighter future. Thank you for your support.

Sincerely,

Pledge not received

Dear Mr. Johnson,

Thank you for taking our phone call and pledging to support The Right to Life Foundation. Your pledge could not have come at a better time.

Right to Life is producing and financing a series of commercials that promote adoption as an option to abortion. We want to air these commercials as often as possible and during programs young women watch. Every pledge is important, therefore, because it means one more airing of the commercial and one more opportunity to keep a frightened young woman from aborting her unborn child.

Please honor your pledge of $250.00 and help us save lives. We look forward to hearing from you soon. Thank you for your support.

Sincerely,

Personal letter requesting one-time donation

Dear Jim and Janet,

You know I hate writing letters to ask for money, but I am making an exception in this case because I urgently need your help. I have recently learned of two teens who need professional counseling for totally different problems. Both sets of parents have tried everything they know to do to help their children but have reached the end of their own resources. Their health insurance is limited and does not cover anything psychological. I have looked into various treatment programs, and the ones that I believe will help could cost as much as $10,000.00 for outpatient therapy—more if inpatient treatment is necessary.

When the need came up I thought of you because I remember the concern you had for your daughter when she was struggling and how pleased you were with the results of the counseling you and she received.

I'm making this need known to only a few people who I know will have empathy for the situation and the financial means to make a difference. If you have any questions, call me at the office. I'll be happy to give you more details.

Sincerely,

Thank you for bequest

Dear Mrs. Wilson,

Thank you for your hospitality last Wednesday and for the tour of your lovely garden. It is always a pleasure to spend time with you.

As we discussed, I am sending you the enclosed confirmation form that you need to complete and have notorized. This will confirm your intention to bequeath $1,000.00 to the Meijer Arboretum at the time your estate is settled.

Thank you for your support. Your generosity is very much appreciated.

Sincerely,

Worthy project

Dear Mr. Smith,

I am writing to you on behalf of the Grand Rapids Museum. As a long-time supporter of the museum, you are aware of the financial burden of our daily operations and you have been generous with your contributions in years past. You also know how important it is to keep changing exhibits and adding new ones.

This year the museum would like to undertake the renovation of a carousel, complete with the original forty-four animals. We have the opportunity to purchase such a carousel from the Louisiana Park Commission. I am contacting you in the hope that you will pledge the funds necessary to renovate one of the animals, which we have estimated will cost $1,000.00. The enclosed picture shows the carousel in its prime. It brings back memories, doesn't it?

I will be contacting you by phone next week to find out your decision. Thank for your generous support over the years and for your consideration of this project.

Sincerely,

15

Letters about Children

Who takes the child by the hand, takes the mother by the heart.
                                                    DANISH PROVERB

Every beetle is a gazelle in the eyes of its mother.
                                                    MOORISH PROVERB

At every step the child should be allowed to meet the real experiences of life; the thorns should never be plucked from his roses.
                                                    ELLEN KEY

*P*arents, especially mothers, are not known for their objectivity
  when it comes to their children. And that is good. Children, by
virtue of their defenselessness, need fathers to protect them and mothers
to defend them. But doing this effectively can be a difficult balancing act.
Perhaps the greatest temptation parents face is that of wanting to "pluck
the thorns from the roses of childhood." Every parent knows that experience can be the best teacher, but it's far less painful and much less
stressful for parents to rescue children from difficult circumstances than

to guide children safely through them. But that is what good parenting is all about. And that is what parents need to keep in mind when writing letters concerning their offspring. While striving to protect and defend their children, they must maintain the objectivity necessary to keep from being labeled overprotective, for that is a kiss of death. If a label like that sticks, parents lose their ability to truly protect their children because their concerns will never be taken seriously.

Therefore, whenever you need to write a letter concerning a problem with your child, keep in mind these guidelines.

Be objective. Try to see both sides of the issue. Make sure you have all the correct information before you take sides. It does not help children to side with them when they are wrong. In such cases, it is best to help your child work through the problem toward a solution that has the fewest negative consequences for all parties involved (not just for your child). Remember, you are not being disloyal to your child by insisting that you get all the facts before taking up his or her cause. Children, like everyone else, have a point of view that tends to focus on their own self-interests.

Be fair. Even when you or your child is right, you gain no long-term advantages by making unreasonable demands or by making people lose face. Work toward win-win solutions.

Don't cause defensiveness. Comments that put people on the defensive are roadblocks to solutions. Avoid phrases such as "I was appalled to find out . . . ," "There is no excuse for . . . ," or "I will not tolerate . . . ."

Offer solutions as well as opinions. When you see a situation that you believe is less than satisfactory, don't dump the problem in someone else's lap and expect it to get fixed. People who see the problem are generally the best ones to fix it because they already see the need and believe in the importance of it.

No matter what the subject of your letter is, always think of something good to say. Doing so probably will not be easy, but it is a good habit to get into and it is a good example to set for children. It also is a good way to force yourself to look at things from a perspective other than your own or that of your child.

And remember, if you have a history of writing letters of gratitude and appreciation, your letters of dissatisfaction will be more readily received. So don't wait until you have something to complain about to refer to these sample letters. Read some of the positive ones and then try your hand at writing one of your own.

IN SCHOOL

Requesting information about preschool

Dear Mrs. Colburn,

We are new residents in this city and have a three-year-old daughter who is very eager to go to school and make new friends. Your preschool has been highly recommended to me by my neighbor, so I am writing to request information about enrollment, including details about class sessions, parent involvement, and child-readiness requirements. I know that a school as popular as yours will fill up quickly, so please send me the materials as soon as possible. Amy and I want to be part of your group. Thank you.

Sincerely,

Checking on enrollment

Dear Mrs. Colburn,

Thank you for sending the preschool enrollment information to me so promptly. My husband and I have looked over the material and are very pleased with your curriculum and with the safeguards you have in place to assure the well-being of your students.

Please reserve a place for our daughter Amy in your morning sessions starting next September. I have completed the enrollment forms and enclosed them with this letter.

If you need additional information, please call. Our phone number is ___-____, and our E-mail address is _____ .

Sincerely,

Day care

Dear Mrs. Cohen,

Whenever I ask friends or neighbors about day care in our community, your name comes up. Everyone I have talked to confirms that you offer loving, Christian care in your licensed home. This is exactly what we need for our two preschool sons, ages two and four. We also have a six-year-old daughter who needs a "launching pad" each morning before boarding the bus for first grade. My workday ends at three o'clock. Please consider adding our children to your extended Christian family.

Could we schedule a meeting with you in your home so that we can get acquainted and discuss possible arrangements? I will call you this week to set a time.

Sincerely,

Parent/teacher follow-up

Dear Mr. Henry,

My husband and I were happy to meet you at the recent parent/teacher conference. Your preparation for our meeting was thorough and very helpful. We are thankful that you see our son as more than just a name on an attendance roster and that you want to help him develop his strengths and also encourage him to improve in areas where he is less confident.

Be assured that you have our confidence and full support. Please call us anytime to offer advice or to request our help.

Sincerely,

The Proper Response to Spilled Milk

Aletha Jane Lindstrom

And be ye kind one to another. — EPHESIANS 4:32 KJV

ONE summer day when I was eight, my mother sent me to buy milk. She wanted it in a hurry, so I rode my bike to the grocery store down the road. While carrying the glass quart bottle in my hand, I hit a bump, and went sprawling. The bottle shattered, and milk spilled everywhere.

My knee was scraped up and I hurt all over, but I was even more afraid of being yelled at when I got home. My family didn't have money to waste. But when I wheeled my bike into our yard, my father rushed toward me. "Are you all right?" he asked, seeing my forlorn face. "Did you get cut?" Only after carefully checking me over did we go to clean up the glass.

When my son Tim was eight years old, he wanted to help me by feeding the horses. After carrying a big armful of hay through the gate, he forgot to close it behind him, and all the horses escaped.

When he told me, I started to yell, "Tim, how c—" But a picture came to my mind of my father's face. He too had had to make a split-second choice: to yell at me for my mistake or to react with love and concern.

I took a deep breath and reached my hand out to touch Tim's tear-stained cheek. "Are you all right, son?" I asked.

Lord, when the people I care about make mistakes, let me react with love and forgiveness—just as you do with me.

Appreciation to teacher

Dear Mrs. Stanley,

Thank you for making us aware of Pam's problems in socializing with other girls in her class. The suggestions you made at our recent parent/teacher conference led us to explore possible causes for this difficulty.

Pam is happy to know that you observe these incidents of exclusion and are concerned about her happiness. She is cautiously willing to reach out to others, but will be strengthened in these attempts by any encouragement or feedback you can give her. We appreciate your kindness to our daughter.

Sincerely,

Working out conflict between child and teacher

Dear Mr. Conley,

After last night's parent/teacher conference, we talked with our son about his late assignments. Philip vigorously defended himself, claiming that the assignments are excessively long. We know that other students are managing to get them done, so we're not convinced that length is the real issue.

We will continue to try to determine the true cause of the problem and, in the meantime, will work more closely with him on assignments for your class.

Please alert us to any new developments, either favorable or unfavorable, regarding this issue, and we will do the same with you.

We believe that we can help Philip work through this problem if we keep the lines of communication open and if we all strive to maintain honest and direct communication with one another.

Thank you for calling this problem to our attention, and please let us know if you think of anything else we could be doing to solve it.

Sincerely,

Proposal to principal for after-school club

Dear Ms. Smith,

Our son Jason has watched quite a few educational television programs about threats to the environment, and Mr. Conley's recent unit on the importance of wetlands has added to Jason's interest. He wants to do something to help and would like to involve his friends in some activities to preserve the local wetlands. Would it be possible to begin an after-school club for children who want to pursue these interests? We don't know how to make a formal proposal and would appreciate your input.

Our goal would be to have the club members learn ways to preserve the environment and, of course, to have some fun while they're doing it.

We are willing to help launch this group if you believe it is feasible. Please call us with your response to this idea and with information on how we could implement it. Thank you.

Sincerely,

Need to control rowdyism

Dear Mr. Bast,

I am writing to express my concern about rowdy behavior in the hallways and on the playground. Older children are intimidating the younger ones by stealing their books, homework assignments, and items of clothing. Then they threaten the children with physical harm if they tell anyone.

If this behavior is allowed to continue it is just a matter of time before someone gets hurt. I know several parents who would be willing to serve as hall monitors if you think that would help.

Please let us know what you decide. Many parents are concerned, and we all will appreciate your firm, positive action in dealing with this problem.

Sincerely,

To teacher about unwise handling of situation

Dear Mr. Andrews,

I'm sure you were greatly frustrated last Friday when your expensive fountain pen disappeared from your desk. You had every reason to be upset and to take action. I wish, however, that you had found another way to deal with the problem.

Keeping all the students after school did not resolve your problem but it did cause problems for others.

Because Susan missed the bus and didn't get home to babysit her sister, I missed an important doctor's appointment. Surely there is a better way to deal with such problems in the future.

I realize how important it is to communicate and to support each other in the educational process, so I do want to resolve this matter and try to figure out a way to keep it from happening in the future. Please call me so we can discuss other options.

Sincerely,

To principal about teacher's unwise decision

Dear Mr. De Boer,

Last week our daughter's homeroom teacher, Mr. Andrews, made the whole class stay after school because someone had taken his expensive fountain pen from his desk. We realize that something had to be done, but his decision to penalize the whole class at the end of the school day created multiple problems for many people. Parents had to find alternate ways to get their children home because they all missed their buses, and I missed an important doctor's appointment because I was depending on Susan to care for her younger sister.

I have already talked to Mr. Andrews about this matter and his response was unsatisfactory. He believes he acted appropriately. I disagree. Please arbitrate this matter so we can avoid future problems and misunderstandings. Thank you.

Sincerely,

To teacher about need to encourage students

Dear Mrs. Jones,

Thank you for your commitment to good writing and clear communication. We need teachers like you who uphold standards of excellence in the classroom.

As you well know, our son Matthew is never very excited about writing assignments, but he was unusually discouraged after you returned his last essay. The red marks and sarcastic comments gave him little reason to believe he will ever be able to write well enough to please you.

We know Matthew needs help in appreciating the importance of good writing and clear communication, and we have been trusting you to help him overcome his dislike for English. But your comments had the opposite effect. He dislikes the subject more than ever now.

We believe Matthew would make more progress in your class if you would encourage him with some positive comments. They may be difficult to find, but surely you can think of something good to say about his work that is not dishonest.

Please call us if you have other suggestions or concerns. Thank you for all you do to prepare students for a successful future.

Sincerely,

To principal about problems on buses

Dear Mr. Henderson,

I am writing to alert you to the fact that older students are harrassing younger children on the school buses by ridiculing them and physically forcing them out of their seats. I understand that it is impossible for the driver to deal with these problems because she must keep her attention on the traffic. But someone must do something to stop this bad behavior. Perhaps some responsible high school students would be willing to monitor the buses or maybe a parents' volunteer group could get involved. I am willing to help in any way I can. Please let me know how you decide to handle this problem and if you need my further involvement.

Sincerely,

Field trip suggestion

Dear Ms. Schultz,

Many parents of students in our school are employed in the furniture industry. Therefore, I would like to propose a series of field trips adapted to various age groups to teach students about this local business. They would learn about the many facets of the work—from design to manufacture, from product development to distribution. At the same time they would learn about career opportunities and would develop familiarity and a sense of identity with local products. They also would gain appreciation for the work their parents or neighbors do.

As an employee of Herman Miller, I am very familiar with the office furniture business and would be willing to serve on a committee to organize these field trips. Please contact me with your response to this idea. Thank you.

Sincerely,

Need for more supervision

Dear Mr. Seger,

Food wars may be funny in movies, but they're not funny in real school lunchrooms. When I visited our school last week, I was appalled to see how much food was being wasted. Not only was good food being thrown away, a lot of it was being thrown around. Some of it landed on clothing; more of it landed on the floor, creating slippery conditions and a high possibilty of injury.

I realize your staff has a challenging workload, but please arrange for more supervision in the lunchrooms. If you need someone to recruit volunteers to help, please call me.

Thanks for your attention to this matter.

Sincerely,

Abusive patrol person

Dear Ms. Dawson,

My second grader has been telling me disturbing things about the patrol person on duty after school. According to my daughter, this person screams at the children to hurry, jerks their arms to hold them back from the street, and sometimes whacks their bottoms to get them moving across the street.

I consider this inappropriate behavior. Please observe this person at work to find out if these complaints are valid.

I know that you believe as I do—that children should be treated with kindness and respect—so I'm sure you do not condone this behavior.

Thank you for your concern for the well-being of our children in and out of school.

Sincerely,

Concern about textbooks

When you are addressing a controversial issue, don't write in an accusing tone that puts people on the defensive. Doing so will defeat your purpose. Ask yourself this question: Am I putting more energy into proving that I am right (or that someone else is wrong) or into solving the problem? As surprising as it may seem, proving you are right is not always a necessary prerequisite for (and is sometimes counter-productive to) problem solving. Often you can make a difference without having to make a scene. Many educators welcome good suggestions. And common sense tells us that everyone is more likely to take a suggestion offered out of a spirit of good will than one that is shoved on us out of spite.

Dear Mr. Grafton,

I have been involved in several discussions with friends and neighbors regarding proposed curriculum changes at the high school and I always feel as if we are all just sharing ignorance. Do you have any information you could send to me that would help me get a balanced view of the issues involved?

I know that any change tends to alarm people, so you are probably wary of releasing too much information prematurely. But I believe that parents will be your advocates, not your adversaries, if you keep them informed and involved. No one wants to usurp your authority; we just want to make sure we are fulfilling our own responsibility to our children, to you, and to our community.

Unfinished Forgiveness

Ellyn Baumann

The Lord reproves him whom he loves. . . . — PROVERBS 3:12 RSV

ONE night, while I did laundry, my nine-year-old son Zeb and I played rummy. I left to change loads during one of his turns, and when I returned Zeb's manner told me something was up.

The possibility that he'd looked at my hand took me by surprise. *Zeb wouldn't do that,* I thought. But his big, blue eyes opened wide when I asked him, and with an embarrassed grin, he said, "I only peeked at your first card, Mom!"

After I gathered up the cards and called off the game, I talked to Zeb about honor and trust. He listened and agreed, then was ready—too ready—to start the next game. "No, son," I said, with a standoffish air.

I do not believe it is at all reasonable for parents to expect schools to be in perfect accord with all of their values. I do, however, believe it is imperative for parents to know what values their children are being taught so they can knowledgeably help them process and evaluate the information.

Anything you can do for us to make us better parents will make our schools better as well.

Thank you in advance for providing the information I need to be a responsible parent as well as a valuable member of the community.

Sincerely,

"I'm sorry, Mom," Zeb replied and started upstairs to his room.

Usually corrections at our house end with hugs, not separation. *What's wrong here?* I wondered as I went over a mental checklist of how the Lord corrects me:

1. He loves me, so he corrects me (Proverbs 3:12).
2. When I confess, he forgives and cleanses me (1 John 1:9).
3. Then he forgets it (Isaiah 43:24).

Of course! There was more I needed to say. I called Zeb back downstairs. "Zeb," I said, hugging him, "I forgive you, and the Lord forgives you. Now, let's put this behind us and play another game!"

"All right!" Zeb said. His joyful relief was evident as we shuffled and cut the cards. I was relieved, too. More than just learning right behavior, I wanted him to learn about love. Me, too.

Father, let my correction always be with love. Thank you for loving me—both firmly and tenderly.

Request for building improvements

Dear School Board Members,

I know that the scope and variety of problems you deal with to ensure quality education within fiscal restraints in our school district are complex. Each school has needs to consider. But the need for remodeling and repair at the Henry Street buildings must be made a priority. Roofs leak, floor tiles are loose, and the walls are dirty and dingy.

Since it is unlikely that tax money can be allocated for the construction of new schools, we appeal to you to allocate funds for improvements to existing buildings. Please guard the investment citizens have put into these properties, and please work actively to create a safe and cheerful environment for the students, especially those in Henry Street school who are disadvantaged in many ways. Thank you.

Sincerely,

Request for policy change

Dear Mr. Everly,

We are writing to ask you to reconsider the policy regarding unexcused absences for students whose parents want to extend vacation periods beyond the days allocated in the school calendar.

Many parents are forced to schedule family vacations during the school year due to the seasonal restraints of their employment. Is it possible, therefore, for you to adapt the policy to allow excused absences for students who keep up with their school work and cause a minimum of inconvenience for their teachers? It is important for families to spend time together, and travel is very educational. We believe that a change in policy would, in the long run, be to everyone's advantage.

Thank you for your dedication to quality education and your equal concern for family enrichment. Thank you also for considering our request. We will look forward to your response.

Sincerely,

Need to update equipment

Dear Mrs. Rose,

Some of the papers Kimberly brings home are barely readable, and it's not because of her sloppy work; it's because they are produced on an old mimeograph machine. The blue ink on these copies blurs and fades, making the letters and words difficult to distinguish and causing unnecessary stress on the eyes of students and teachers.

Most offices now have plain paper copiers that are reasonably priced and highly efficient. Our teachers need access to a quality copy machine supported by a good service contract. The speed and readability of a new machine is worth whatever added expense might be involved.

Please consider putting money for the purchase or lease of new copy machines into next year's budget.

Sincerely,

Request to use classroom

Dear Mrs. Koster,

Neil will be celebrating his tenth birthday on February 21, and we want to invite everyone in his class to a party. But the size of our home and the distance from school make it inconvenient for us to have the party here. I'm wondering if we could have an after-school party in your classroom. We will provide games and refreshments for a one-hour party. Please let me know if you think this is a workable idea. Thank you.

Sincerely,

Notifying school bus driver of change

Dear Mr. Randolph,

We have given our daughter, Stacy Anderson, permission to spend the night with her friend, Keri Smith, on Friday, January 18, so they will both be getting off the bus at the Plymouth Street stop after school.

Thank you for your constant, watchful concern for the children in your care.

Sincerely,

Notifying preschool of change

Dear Ms. Stiles,

My husband and I will be out of town for a few days, so our daughter, Abby, will be picked up from preschool by her grandmother, Linda Bloem, on Tuesday, March 5. She will have the required security call card for Abby.

Thank you for your watchfulness for the safety of our children.

Sincerely,

Requesting early dismissal

Dear Mrs. Nelson,

Please excuse our daughter, Sara, at 2:15 P.M. on Wednesday, April 4, for an orthodontist appointment.

Thank you.

Sincerely,

Absence due to illness

Dear Mr. Dykema,

Our son, Bill, stayed home with the flu on March 4 and 5. Please mark on his attendance records that this was an excused absence.

Thank you.

Sincerely,

Absence due to injury

Dear Mr. Timmer,

Please excuse our daughter, Mary, from participating in phys. ed.

classes this week. She injured her back in a sledding accident and the doctor has advised her to limit her physical activity.

Thank you.

Sincerely,

Advance notification of absence

Dear Mr. Klein,

My parents will be celebrating their fiftieth wedding anniversary with a family reunion in Florida on March 26–30. Our family will be taking vacation time during that week in addition to the week of spring break, so we will be taking Beth out of school for those days. In accordance with your policy for excused absences, we have made arrangements with all her teachers regarding daily assignments, and after we return we will arrange for her to take any tests she has missed.

Thank you for understanding the importance of this special vacation.

Sincerely,

Thanks for pointing out problem

Dear Ms. Kimble,

Thank you very much for alerting us to our son's vision problems. We were unaware of the many ways he was hindered and had to adapt to his nearsightedness. His new glasses have opened a new world to him and made him more confident and outgoing.

We sincerely appreciate your concern for him.

Sincerely,

Thanks for patience

Dear Mr. Post,

We want you to know how much we appreciate Miss Ten Broek as a teacher. Her patience and good nature have made typing class less trying for our son Robert. His resulting improvement in this skill has greatly encouraged him. He'll look back to these class sessions thankfully as he uses these skills in many typing and computer applications. Please express our thanks to her and place a copy of this letter in her personnel file.

Thank you.

Sincerely,

Request for college information

Dear Dr. Vanden Berg,

Our daughter will be graduating from high school in 1997, and we are exploring college options with her. Since your college has such a fine reputation for quality education and personal attention, we would like information about curricula, financial aid, housing, and extra-curricular activities that will help us choose a college that meets her needs. Please send the information to the address below. Also, please let us know the dates of senior visiting days that you have scheduled.

Thank you.

Sincerely,

Choosing another college

Dear Provost Marshall,

I am honored to be accepted as a student at Beaverton State, but I must decline this opportunity as I have also been accepted at the University of Michigan, which offers a program more in line with the major I have chosen. I appreciate all the time you took with me to help me make my decision. While I regret passing up the benefits of a smaller, more personal college, I know some other student will be very happy to take my place.

Again, I thank you.

Sincerely,

Lessons Taught by Children

Dolphus Weary

But Jesus called the children to him and said, "Let the little children come to me, and do not hinder them, for the kingdom of God belongs to such as these." — LUKE 18:16 NIV

IN the first few days of kindergarten, my youngest son, Ryan, came home almost every day with notes from his teacher regarding some disturbance he had caused in class. He brought home more notes the first week than his older sister and brother had brought home in a year.

When I discussed with Ryan the problem of his talking in class, he looked into my eyes and said, with absolute innocence, "But, Dad, she told us not to talk to other children in class. I wasn't talking to other children. I was talking to myself!"

I had to stifle a grin as I explained what the teacher said versus what she meant, and that whenever he's in class he needs to talk less—both to himself and to others.

Later, as I thought about his five-year-old innocence, I wondered, *When was the last time I took people at their word? Wasn't I always reading a meaning into a mere glance and whole attitudes into a turn of the head?*

Maybe my youngest son had something to teach me about taking people at their word. His problem understanding what the teacher meant has prompted me to speak more clearly, to try always to say what I mean, and to make sure my words match my intention.

Thank you, Lord, for the blessing of children and for what they can teach us when we stop long enough to listen and to learn.

IN OTHER ACTIVITIES

Appreciation for coach

Dear Mr. Mac,

You are a great coach! Our David may never play in the big leagues, but he will always look back with pleasure at his first experience of team play. Your patience, understanding, and encouragement will help shape his attitude and approach to many other challenges in life. David loves you, and we admire and appreciate you for the time and attention you have given to our son.

Sincerely,

Appreciation for sports coordinator

Dear Mr. Martin,

As manager of our girls' Little League team, I want to thank you for your work as league commissioner. The challenges you faced this year due to the many games that had to be rescheduled caused you a lot of stress, I'm sure. Yet you managed to work around time and place complications and pull the whole season together. Your many volunteer hours and your patience are appreciated by our team and our league. Thank you!

Sincerely,

Incompetent coach

Dear Mr. Bill,

I am writing to express my dissatisfaction with Len Green as coach of the Little League Redhawks. In my opinion, his behavior is such that he should not be given the privilege of working with children. He is late in coming to games, erratic about enforcing rules, and harsh when players fail to perfom well. This has not been a recreational experience for players or parents. Please recruit a better coach for this team next year. Thank you.

Sincerely,

Incompetent umpires

Dear Little League Commissioner,

We, the undersigned parents, wish to protest the poor quality of umpiring our teams experienced this season. These young players give their best and try to follow the teaching and advice of their coaches. They try to be good sports, but it is difficult for them (and for parents) to see results determined by umpires who don't know the rules of the game. We are depending on you to hire better people next year so that the hours invested in Little League will be time well spent. Thank you for attending to this matter.

Sincerely,

Appreciation for Little League volunteer

Dear Chuck,

I value the Little League experience for our kids and would like to participate in this work but am unable to do so since my travel schedule makes me so unreliable. My absence makes me appreciate even more your faithful presence at all these practices and games. Thank you for doing patiently and well what I cannot do and what I know is so important for our kids.

Sincerely,

Need to break down prejudice

Dear Director,

Our daughter loves her Girl Scout troop, and she's learning many valuable things about the environment and about helping other people. But she and her friends are not learning to accept others regardless of race or ethnic origin. Is there a learning unit available that would encourage more acceptance of differences? I know that the scouting program has great potential to break down walls of prejudice, and I hope our local group can be used for that purpose. Please do all in your power to promote more understanding among the girls. Thank you.

Sincerely,

Appreciation for scout leader

Dear Scoutmaster,

You give so much of your time and energy to the scouting program that I know we can never adequately express our appreciation. You receive very little public recognition for your work, but what you are doing for these young people will make them fine, responsible citizens. They are the leaders of our future.

Thank you for doing such a wonderful job.

Sincerely,

Too much pressure

Dear Scoutmaster,

Your scouting program has taught my daughter many useful skills and many important values. I am concerned, however, about the pressure she is feeling to sell cookies this season.

I realize it is important to raise funds for the scouting program through cookie sales, but the object of the program is not to turn out super salespeople. Please lessen the pressure of competition in this project and concentrate on the other fine aspects of the scouting program. Thank you for hearing my concern about this.

Sincerely,

16

Making Requests

Men become attached to us not by reason of the services we render them, but by reason of the services they render us.
EUGÉNE LABICHE

A favour well bestowed is almost as great an honour to him who confers it as to him who receives it.
RICHARD STEELE

[W]elcome him as you would welcome me. If he has done you any wrong or owes you anything, charge it to me. . . . I will pay it back. . . .
PHILEMON :17–18 NIV

*T*he independent spirit that built our nation could also lead to its *downfall. Our cultural identity is that of helper, giver, fixer; we are not good at asking, receiving, taking. Unfortunately that includes the category of advice. We are a nation of know-it-alls and do-it-yourselfers. We would rather get lost than ask directions; we would rather do* *something wrong than ask for advice; and sometimes we even would rather die to prove we are right than to admit we might be wrong.*

But Proverbs says, "Wisdom is found in those who take advice" (13:10 NIV). And it goes even further by saying, "Make plans by seeking advice" (20:18 NIV).

In other words, asking advice should be part of the planning process, not just part of the repairing process; we should make requests to keep from getting into trouble, not just to get ourselves out of it; we should ask for help before we need it, not when we're in such deep trouble that we have to holler for help to get out.

For some reason, the whole concept of requesting anything is fraught with negative connotations, such as weakness, dependency, fearfulness, and helplessness.

But failing to make requests is more often a symptom of weakness than is asking for help. It's the weakness known as "pride." We want to say, "I did it myself," "I did it my way," "I don't need anyone else," "I deserve the credit."

Parents chide their children, "If you needed help, why didn't you ask?" But plenty of adults model the same behavior, and they wind up spending more time, energy, and money undoing what they did wrong than it would have taken to find out how to do it right in the first place.

So before you start anything new or decide to do anything different, make sure you have enough information, knowledge, and know-how to pull it off. If you don't, get in touch with people who do and ask for help.

Requests for help fall into several categories:

Information. *You have an idea you want to pursue but you're not sure it is feasible, so you need to ask for information.*

Advice. *You have all the information you need but you're not sure you know enough to process it accurately, so you need to ask for advice.*

Assistance. *You're convinced your plan is a good one but you can't pull it off alone, so you need to ask for help.*

The first two are the easiest to ask for because they are the easiest to give; they require little or no investment from the giver. Most people are happy to supply information, and nearly everyone feels honored when asked to give advice. But a little bit of soul-searching needs to precede requests for assistance.

- *Who is the the best person to ask?*
- *Do I have the kind of relationship with this person that entitles me to ask for help?*
- *Can I expect to get this kind of help free of charge or should I offer to pay?*
- *How can I ask in such a way that shows I respect and value the person's time and expertise?*
- *Is there something I can offer other than money that will make my request more like an equal trade?*

As Jean de La Fontaine wrote, "People must help one another; it is nature's law." To help another person is to fulfill not only nature's law but God's as well, as we read in 1 Corinthians 12:28 NIV:

> *And in the church God has appointed first of all apostles, second prophets, third teachers, then workers of miracles, also those having gifts of healing, [and] those able to help others. . . .*

To ask for help is to give others the opportunity to fulfill God's law and to exercise their spiritual gifts. In fact, it was a plea for help that determined the direction of the spread of the gospel. We refer to it as the Macedonian call, and it is recorded in Acts 16:9–10 NIV:

> *During the night Paul had a vision of a man of Macedonia standing and begging him, "Come over to Macedonia and help us." After Paul had seen the vision, we got ready at once to leave for Macedonia, concluding that God had called us to preach the gospel to them.*

Not all requests are as strategic as that one, of course, but it does show how important it can be to ask for help when we need it.

So swallow your pride and ask for help—before you get into such a fix that it will take a whole army of helpers to get you out.

Requesting information, asking questions

The following type of letter can be sent to more than one company at a time if you want to "comparison shop" by mail. By getting people to give you specific answers to specific questions, you can compare costs and services more accurately.

Manager, Sales Department:

I am interested in hiring a landscaping firm to design a plan for our three-quarter-acre lot and would like to find out more about the services you offer. Do you have a brochure you could send me that describes the areas in which you specialize?

Also, I have the following questions that I am using to screen prospective landscaping firms:

- Can you develop a master plan that I can implement over a period of a few years?
- Do you have on staff or would you recommend someone to do the "hard labor," such as building fences, gazebos, or water ponds?
- Could you design a plan to fit my budget?
- Do you bid on the whole project or charge an hourly fee?
- In which of the following areas do you have expertise?
    perennials
    herb gardens
    shade gardens
    fragrance gardens
    cutting gardens
    vegetable gardens

ground covers
shrubs
water ponds

I have a rather elaborate plan in my mind, but I need help to keep from making costly mistakes. Would your people enjoy helping me perfect my ideas?

As soon as I have enough information I will call to set up an appointment to discuss doing business. You have earned a fine reputation among my friends, and I hope we can work together.

Thank you very much for your helpfulness.

Sincerely,

Requesting additional information

Dear Mrs. Wallace,

I certainly appreciate the time you spent with me the other day. You answered my questions clearly and thoughtfully. I was impressed by your understanding of the subject and by your patience with my lack of knowledge.

But as I thought about our discussion I came up with several additional questions I need to have answered before I can make a decision.

I know it is inconvenient for you to make another trip to our town, so it would be fine with me if you would like to try to answer my questions by phone. I am home most evenings after 6:00 and my phone number is ___-____, and our E-mail address is _____ .

Thank you very much for your help. I look forward to hearing from you.

Regards,

Responding to a request for additional information

Dear Mrs. Morris,

After our last meeting, you raised several interesting questions con-

Paul's Letter to Philemon

I, Paul, am a prisoner for the sake of Christ, here with my brother Timothy. I write this letter to you, Philemon, my good friend and companion in this work—also to our sister Apphia, to Archippus, a real trooper, and to the church that meets in your house. God's best to you! Christ's blessing on you!

Every time your name comes up in my prayers, I say, "Oh, thank you, God!" I keep hearing of the love and faith you have for the Master Jesus, which brims over to other Christians. And I keep praying that this faith we hold in common keeps showing up in the good things we do, and that people recognize Christ in all of it. Friend, you have no idea how good your love makes me feel, doubly so when I see your hospitality to fellow believers.

TO CALL THE SLAVE YOUR FRIEND

In line with all this I have a favor to ask of you. As Christ's ambassador and now a prisoner for him, I wouldn't hesitate to command this if I thought it necessary, but I'd rather make it a personal request.

While here in jail, I've fathered a child, so to speak. And here he is, hand-carrying this letter—Onesimus! He was useless to you before; now he's useful to both of us. I'm sending him back to you, but it feels like I'm cutting off my right arm in doing so. I wanted in the worst way to keep him here as your stand-in to help out while I'm in jail for the Message. But I didn't want to do anything behind your back, make you do a good deed that you hadn't willingly agreed to.

Maybe it's all for the best that you lost him for a while. You're getting him back now for good—and no mere slave this time, but a true Christian brother! That's what he was to me—he'll be even more than that to you.

So if you still consider me a comrade-in-arms, welcome him back as you would me. If he damaged anything or owes you anything, chalk it up to my account. This is my personal signature—Paul—and I stand behind it. (I don't need to remind you, do I, that you owe your very life to me?) Do me this big favor, friend. You'll be doing it for Christ, but it will also do my heart good.

I know you well enough to know you will. You'll probably go far beyond what I've written. And by the way, get a room ready for me. Because of your prayers, I fully expect to be your guest again.

Epaphras, my cellmate in the cause of Christ, says hello. Also my coworkers Mark, Aristarchus, Demas, and Luke. All the best to you from the Master, Jesus Christ!

Reprinted from *The Message, The New Testament with Psalms*. © 1994 by Eugene H. Peterson. Published by NavPress Publishing Group, Colorado Springs, CO 80935.

cerning the effectiveness of energy-saving technologies for the home. These questions deserve a well-researched response.

I've examined all the written information I have on the subject and have thought about my own personal experience with such devices. The written information is enclosed. As you can see, it addresses many of your concerns. My experience in the field may also be helpful, and that is too broad to put in writing, so I would like to meet with you again to discuss your questions.

I'll call soon to see when you might be available. Thank you for your interest and for posing some challenging questions.

Best regards,

Response to inquiry

Dear Mr. Irving,

Thank you for your note requesting more information about our programs. We value each individual who shows an interest in our work, and we appreciate the ongoing support of people in our community.

I am enclosing several of our brochures that address the questions you raised. If other questions occur to you as you read this information, please feel free to contact me. If I don't hear from you, I will call you in a few days to make sure you found the information satisfactory.

Once again, I appreciate your interest in our work and I will try to reach you soon.

Regards,

Procedural change

Dear Maggie,

I've been on the board of the women's center for several months and have regularly attended its meetings. I appreciate the dedication of the board members and am aware that the meetings have been conducted in their present fashion ever since the center began many years ago; however, I'd like to suggest a change.

I believe that our growing numbers and increasing presence in the community demand a more formal structure both for our meetings and for the way we handle our external affairs. I've enjoyed the informality of our meetings, and I believe we are trustworthy in financial matters. But the amount of work we have to accomplish within a limited time demands that we bring some formality to the proceedings. Also, our financial records reflect a lack of regular attention, which could become a problem if we are ever called on to explain our expenditures.

I suggest that for our board meetings we follow Robert's Rules of Order. We can set aside time *after* the meeting for visiting, or else we can schedule a separate time for socializing. I also suggest that we hire an accountant to set up a professional bookkeeping system, which our treasurer could then maintain.

I realize these changes will be difficult for some members, but the future success of our group depends on our wise oversight and good stewardship.

My best,

Time extension

Dear Tom,

Well, it seems I've bitten off more than I can chew! I was certainly excited to take on this project, and I was pleased that you asked me to do it. But my preliminary research has revealed the project to be much more extensive than I had anticipated.

In order to do a thorough job and to provide you with good results, I'm asking for a little more time. Judging by the information I've uncovered, I estimate it will take me two more weeks to pull everything together.

Please let me know if this will inconvenience you. I could speed things up somewhat, but I want to make sure that every area is adequately examined. I'll check with you in the next couple of days to make sure this is acceptable.

Thank you for your patience.

Sincerely,

Shorten deadline

Dear Rick,

We are really excited about the brochure you're putting together for us. Your ideas are excellent, and you have a good understanding of how to present our services to potential members.

Recently, however, we've been deluged with requests for information about our programs. Due to this unexpected interest, I'm writing to ask if you could intensify your efforts. If possible, we'd like to have the finished brochure in three weeks.

This unanticipated demand coupled with our mandate to serve people well puts pressure on all of us, and I realize the revised schedule could be difficult for you. All I ask is that you do what you can and contact me if this new deadline is impossible.

If I don't hear from you by Friday, we'll expect to receive your work within three weeks.

Thank you very much for your cooperation.

Sincerely,

Meeting deadline

Dear Jennifer,

Our committee has several important events coming up, and we need to establish some deadlines and priorities and check on each other's progress.

I'd like to meet with everyone on Monday, July 10, at 9 A.M. in room 233. Please be prepared to update us on your part of the project and to discuss ideas for future events.

The Courage to Ask for Help

Vicki Schad

Pride goes before . . . a fall.   — PROVERBS 16:18 NIV

WHEN my father was a little boy, he became the proud owner of a battered red bicycle. Proud is the right word to use, for more than one reason. He was the only boy in the family at that time, and he was too proud to ask his big sisters to teach him how to ride. He mounted the bike from the doorstep, and managed to keep it fairly steady as he steered down the driveway. But he had a problem: He didn't know how to stop!

He could have asked for help, but his pride kept him from doing so. Instead, whenever he wanted to stop, he would steer the bike behind the farmhouse and "bump" into the woodpile. His plan worked fine for a while. Then one day he was gone for so long that people started looking for him. They found him down by the woodpile, in a heap with his bike, just beginning to regain consciousness! His was the kind of pride that literally "goes before a fall."

Some of Dad's self-reliance has been handed down to me. A few months ago I became the proud owner of a computer. How I hated to ask for help in learning how to use it! I too ran into a few "woodpiles" before I admitted my need. In fact, I lost several documents before I finally called on my younger brother for advice.

What woodpiles have you been crashing into lately? Isn't it time to admit you need help? God is waiting for you to ask.

I admit it, Lord. I need you to help me with _____.
Please show me what to do next.

It's important that we all attend the meeting, so let me know right away if you have a conflict.

Regards,

Rescheduling order

Dear Mr. Jefferson,

Last Monday I ordered several rolls of wallpaper which I asked to be delivered next week. But we have been unexpectedly called out of town and won't be home to receive the order. Could you hold the wallpaper and deliver it on the 15th of the month instead? If this is not feasible, please contact me to make other arrangements.

As always, I appreciate your good service. Thank you for your attention to this matter.

Sincerely,

Share experience

Dear Mrs. Wetherby,

I'm a member of a small Bible study for women that meets every Monday morning in a member's home. Occasionally, we gather with other women's groups for fellowship and to exchange notes about our groups (e.g., how we began; what we were formed to do; tips for keeping our groups vital).

We have found these meetings to be both helpful and entertaining. We all leave feeling refreshed and energized, and we make new friends in the process.

I am writing to invite your group to attend a get-together next month during our regular meeting time on Monday morning. We'll all discuss the purpose and experiences of our respective groups and have refreshments afterward.

Would you present our invitation to your group and then let me know if you would be interested in meeting with us? We can solidify the details when you call.

Thank you for considering our idea.

Sincerely,

Business guidance

Dear Ms. Carlson,

In a recent issue of our local newspaper I read an article about the mentoring program for entrepreneurial businesswomen that you have spearheaded. As I read about your program, I was delighted to discover that I may qualify for the type of mentoring you offer.

Last month I began my own bookkeeping service targeted toward small to mid-sized businesses. I'm realizing I need both advice and moral support to progress successfully, and perhaps even to survive!

Until I read about your program, I was unsure where to get that advice. A mentor who could guide me over some of the rough spots in my new venture would be a tremendous help.

Could you send more information about your program? I'm enclosing additional information about myself and my business to help you assess my eligibility.

Thank you for providing this service and for considering my request.

My best,

Permission to reprint article

Dear Permissions Manager,

As president of a local civic organization, I produce a quarterly newsletter detailing our club's activities. I often include bits of information that I think our members might enjoy or find useful.

I found just such information in your article titled "Ten Tax Tips to Remember" by Dan Wilcox in the July issue of *Home Office Computing*. I enjoyed the article, and I'm sure our members would as well.

I am writing to request permission to reprint the article in our fall newsletter, which is distributed free of charge to our mailing list of one hundred members.

I will, of course, acknowledge the author and include whatever credit line you prefer. We are also willing to pay a permission fee for the one-time use of the material. Please let me know your requirements soon so I can complete the layout for our fall newsletter.

Thank you in advance for your help.

Regards,

Obtaining an interview

Dear Dr. Wilkinson,

When I passed your office the other day, I noticed that you are advertising for a new receptionist. I have held similar positions in the past and am ready to return to work now that my youngest child has entered first grade.

I am writing to request an appointment to discuss with you your expectations for the job and to find out if my qualifications satisfy them. I'm enclosing my résumé and letters of reference. I will give you a few days to review this material, and then I'll call to set up an appointment.

I'm excited about the prospect of returning to work and hopeful that my skills will match your needs.

Thank you for your attention to my request.

Sincerely,

To speak

Dear Ms. Inglis,

Could any scene rescue a group from the winter doldrums faster than the white sands and clear, blue waters of a tropical island?

That's what I propose to bring to your Homemaker's Club—the Bermuda Islands. I have just returned from an extended tour of the islands during which I poked about in little-known and breathtakingly beautiful nooks and crannies.

Now, with a series of professional-quality slides and an entertaining and informative monologue, I've visited dozens of local groups to share the beauty I discovered in Bermuda and to temporarily remove us all from slushy streets and the morning alarm clock. Armchair travel does indeed have its delights!

My fees are reasonable, and I have a long list of happy customers. Please call if you're interested in being whisked away to warm breezes and white sands. My résumé and references are enclosed.

Looking forward to hearing from you.

Best regards,

Getting speakers

Dear Mr. Hart,

I recently acquired a list of the speakers your company represents and was interested to note that you have several individuals who specialize in topics related to child development.

A women's study club that I belong to frequently invites speakers to lecture on a wide variety of subjects. Next month we will be studying early childhood development and are looking for a speaker on that subject.

Our meetings are informal as well as educational, so we like people who are down-to-earth and entertaining rather than strictly academic.

Although our funds are limited, we can pay a modest honorarium. I'll call later this week to discuss our needs and perhaps you could suggest a speaker who would be appropriate for our group.

Sincerely,

Entertaining a friend

Dear Margery,

Did I tell you that my college roommate is spending the week with me? I'm absolutely thrilled, and I can't wait to introduce her to you, another of the good friends in my life.

I will be showing Bea around our city, and I have outings planned to the museum and the botanical gardens. I also purchased theater tickets for Friday night.

Recently, however, our school board has scheduled a special session for that same evening to discuss some pressing issues. Since I will have to attend the school board meeting, I thought I would ask you to accompany Bea to the theater. Would you mind?

You'll love the show, and I know you two will really hit it off. Check your calendar and let me know if you can be my friend's "date" for the evening.

It's great to have such wonderful friends.

My best,

Alleviating fear, a request

Dear Ellen,

You'll probably think this is a really silly request, but I need a confidence booster. Dave has a business trip to New York City next month, and I am going along. We are both excited about this because the two of us haven't done much traveling alone since the kids were born.

But I am really apprehensive about being alone in the city all day while Dave does business. I don't want to sit alone in a hotel room for a week, but I'm not sure I have the courage to venture out. I know you survived a whole summer there, so I'm wondering if you have any tips or recommendations that would make me less fearful? I don't want to ruin what could be a great experience by behaving like a frightened little girl. Can you help?

I will be grateful for any advice you can give me that will make me more confident. Thanks for listening. Admitting my fear has made me feel better already.

Your cowardly friend,

Alleviating fear, a response

Dear Carla,

Your upcoming trip to New York sounds marvelous. I'd love to be able to tag along and be your tour guide. I absolutely loved the summer I spent in Manhattan.

Being a country girl myself, however, I can relate to your apprehension. I remember how lost I felt on my first taxi ride through the city. The sight of all those crowds and cars and skyscrapers overwhelmed me. I figured I'd have to spend the rest of my life on the streets because I'd never be able to find my way out of the concrete jungle at the end of the summer. But I did—even though by that time I didn't want to.

Since you have a week to spend there, I'd advise you to do the regular tourist stuff for the first few days. Take one of the bus tours offered by Big Apple Tours so you can learn your way around without having to navigate on your own right away. By that time you'll feel confident enough to venture out by yourself.

And believe me, you'll have a great time. There is no city like New York, New York.

If you'd like any more tips or moral support, give me a call. I'd enjoy chatting with you. And do call me when you get back. I'm eager to hear how it goes.

Best wishes,

Board a relative

Dear Mike,

I've told you so much about my family, you probably feel as though you know them. But now it can become a reality. My younger brother will be here next month, and I have a problem. I'm afraid he will feel out of place in an apartment full of "girls," as he calls me and my roommates. So I'm wondering how you would like a ready-made little brother for a weekend (July 21–24)? I know he would be thrilled to stay with you, a "big guy" and a basketball player to boot. And I think you would really enjoy him, too.

I have lots of activities to keep him busy, so I'd be picking him up early and dropping him off late. He'd have so much more fun with you than dodging hair dryers and mascara wands over here.

Give it some thought and get back to me as soon as you can. I'm really looking forward to having you meet him.

My best,

Job for a relative

Dear Dr. VanBuren,

Several years ago I worked for you as a filing clerk and thoroughly enjoyed the job and the friendly atmosphere of your office. You often mentioned that you were very satisfied with my work as well.

It is those fond memories that prompts this letter. My daughter has just completed her first year at Michigan State University and will be coming home for the summer. Since she must pay part of her tuition for next year, she would like to begin work quickly.

Elizabeth is a responsible girl who has always done well in school and at her previous jobs. I know that you would be very pleased with her attitude and abilities, and I know that she would enjoy working for you.

I'm enclosing her résumé and letters of reference. I've suggested to her that she call you soon to set up an interview. I hope this works out since I know you two would be a great match.

Thanks for a good relationship in the past and for considering my present request.

Sincerely,

Child care

Dear Sue,

I have been considering the possibility of doing volunteer work one day a week at our local hospital, but I haven't been able to figure out how to take care of Alex and Joel. The other day an idea finally came to me and it involves you.

I've heard you say several times how much you miss gardening now that you live in a house with hardly any yard. Then I read in the newspaper that the new arboretum is looking for volunteers to work in their greenhouses and visitors' center.

So that brings me to my proposed plan. If you are interested in working at the arboretum one day a week, I would take care of your two children on that day if you would take care of mine on the day I work at the hospital. That way we both would get to do work we love, have a day to spend with adults, and give our children an opportunity to play with others their age.

How does this sound to you? I'll give you a few days to think about it and then give you a call to discuss it. Thanks for at least considering it.

Your friend,

Feed the cats

Dear Tom,

Our family has been blessed with a new grandchild, and we are going to Dallas to see her! We'll be leaving this Sunday and returning Friday night.

Would your little Sarah be willing to come over every day after school to feed and water our cats? I know she is very conscientious, so I wouldn't worry at all if I knew she was looking in on them. And it would be an opportunity for her to earn some spending money as well.

If you are both willing, would you call me tomorrow? Then I will stop by and leave the key to our house and give Sarah some instructions.

My best,

Watch the house

Dear Sally,

Well, you always said our ship would come in, and it finally has! Ted and I are going on a two-week cruise at the end of the month. I simply can't wait to bask in the sun on the deck of a luxury liner.

Would you be willing to help us out while we're away? I'm stopping the mail and the paper, and the lights will be timed to go on in the evening. But could you watch the house and make sure that the lights do go on, the mail and paper do stop, and that everything else remains as it ought?

I doubt that anything will happen while we're away, but it would be a comfort to know someone was keeping an eye on the house.

I'll call you in a couple days to see if this will work out. Maybe we can also make plans to get together for an evening before we leave.

I'll talk to you soon.

Your friend and neighbor,

Closing a request with confidence

The following sentences can be used to say politely and respectfully that you expect a response.

- I appreciate your prompt attention to this matter.
- You have been so kind and helpful. Thank you for going out of your way to assist me. I look forward to your response.
- Since your establishment promotes the integrity of its service, I am confident that you will give my request thorough consideration.
- I thank you in advance for your help and await your reply.

17

Letters about Vacations

Rest is the sauce of labor.   PLUTARCH

There can be no high civilization where there is not ample leisure.   HENRY WARD BEECHER

My soul finds rest in God alone; my salvation comes from him.   PSALM 62:1 NIV

*H*aving fun can be a lot of work. If you've expressed that sentiment recently, you may be a candidate for a stay-at-home vacation. But even that is no guarantee of restfulness because at home you will be surrounded by all the work that needs to be done there, and that will make relaxation nearly impossible.

Instead of trying to simplify your life by staying home, why not simplify your plans for getting away. Resist the temptation to pack every minute of your vacation with activities.

The best way to simplify your vacation and to make it less stressful is by planning ahead. Decide what you want to do, where and when you *want to do it, and how much of it you want to do. Then start collecting information far enough in advance so that you can make decisions based on what you want rather than on what is available.*

Some places—like Big Bend National Park in Texas over the Christmas holidays—are booked many months in advance, sometimes a year or two. Plan well in advance to avoid disappointment if there is something specific that you and your family members have your hearts set on doing.

When requesting information always include enough details to make sure you will indeed get the right information. The Who? What? When? and Where? questions are useful here. Also, having other people in the family answer these questions will help you find out if they have expectations different from yours. If they do, you can work the details out ahead of time and avoid nasty confrontations in faraway places.

Who? *Who will be traveling? How many will be traveling? How old are the travelers?*

What? *What is the main purpose of your trip? Is it sightseeing, education, action/adventure, shopping, sunbathing, sailing, hiking, skiing? What type of accommodations are you looking for? Hotels, motels, bed & breakfast inns, or campgrounds? What means of transportation is best? Plane, train, automobile, or motorhome?*

When? *Are you locked in to a particular time or can you adjust your schedule to take advantage of "off season" rates?*

Where? *Have you already decided where to go or are you flexible? Is the "where" more important than the "what" to you? How about to the rest of your family? Do they agree?*

TIP: *Don't assume that you can plan a vacation everyone will enjoy without asking for their input. People who have participated in the planning and have worked through the necessary compromises before leaving home will be less likely to complain when they get away from home.*

TIP: *Travel information is easily found on the Internet, and many travel reservations can now be made by E-mail.*

Invitation to bed and breakfast

Dear Sue,

I learned from your sister that you and Sam are planning a brief vacation in our area. This is a delightful place to get away from business pressures, and I can make your getaway even more delightful by offering accommodations in the Bed and Breakfast owned and hosted by our family.

We offer privacy and friendly help in a charming Victorian home. Our breakfasts are tasty and generous, and we are within walking distance of quaint shops, a lovely lake, and restaurants of all kinds. If you are interested in making reservations, please send for our attractive brochure. We wish you a fine vacation.

Sincerely,

Requesting general information

Dear Sir/Madam,

We are seeking accommodations in a bed and breakfast establishment near the shore [or business or historical district] in your community. Ideally we would like a quiet, historical home in an attractive, quaint setting. We would like to be near public transportation if possible. Since we will be spending several days there, we are hoping also to enjoy a friendly, smoke-free environment. Please send us any brochures or information that will help us select a place. Also, please include information about area churches. Thank you.

Sincerely,

Offering to exchange houses

Dear Mr. and Mrs. Brown,

We have learned that you are interested in exchanging houses with someone in our city for the month of August this year. Since we are planning to vacation in your area during that time, we would like to explore the possibility of exchanging homes with you.

Our home is in a quiet neighborhood near public transportation, a small shopping area, and several neighborhood churches. We would welcome two to four people to stay at our house in our absence. Further details on the house, possible costs, and available dates can be provided if you are interested. Please furnish us with information about your house. It would also be helpful if we would exchange area maps, tourist brochures, and a picture of our homes.

We look forward to working out arrangements that will be mutually satisfying.

Sincerely,

Requesting resort brochures and rate information

Dear Sir/Madam,

Please send us information and brochures listing the types of accommodations and activities your resort offers and the various rate schedules. Are your facilities barrier-free? Do you offer smoke-free rooms? Special rooms that accommodate wheelchairs?

We have heard many favorable comments about your resort and look forward to spending our vacation in your area. Thank you for your help. Our address is below.

Sincerely,

Requesting information from chamber of commerce

Dear Chamber of Commerce Personnel,

As we make plans for our next vacation, we are thinking of including a few days in your city. Please send information concerning your area's history, industry, religious or educational facilities, accommodations, and transportation.

We will have two small children and two early teens in our group, and we are especially eager to receive information that will help us

Putting People Ahead of Things

Fred Bauer

Come and dine. . . .   — JOHN 21:12 KJV

SUMMER," someone said, "is when we take time off from making a living in order to do some living." From a family standpoint some of our most memorable times together have come during summer.

One of the kids recently reminded me of such a moment that occurred on a family hiking trip several years ago. It was a hot day, our canteens were empty, and our mouths dry when we came down a mountain into a lush valley. Several cars had parked nearby, the occupants of which were gathered up the way at the face of a rocky wall, where cold, clear water was bubbling from the stone. We licked our lips and waited our turn. The mountain's gift did not disappoint us. We buried our heads under the flow and took long, satisfying drafts. "Water never tasted any better," my son reflected.

Memories of times spent with friends and loved ones at play are like scrapbooks by a fireplace on cold winter nights—they thaw frozen hearts. Maybe it's the slower pace of Junes, Julys, and Augusts that make the atmosphere more conducive to conversation and caring. These languid days offer a great opportunity for reaching out to people. "Come join us for a cookout," "How 'bout a picnic?" or "Meet us at the beach" are all icebreakers for overdue reunions. When on a trip, take time to visit old friends along the way. Fifty miles or a couple of hours may seem a lot, but such get-togethers will make nicer memories than a few missed museums and monuments. Summers in particular are a good time for putting people ahead of things.

Teach me the value of things present, Lord, so in the future I won't regret the past.

make their vacation an enriching, memorable experience. Thank you in advance for your help. Our address is below.

Sincerely,

Inquiring about overseas accommodations

Dear Travel Information Personnel,

My husband and I plan to spend two weeks in your country in September of 1997. We need information about accommodations (preferably bed & breakfast inns), public transportation, car rental, and points of interest. Please send us any booklets, maps, and brochures that will help us understand your land and culture. I am enclosing a check for $3.00 American to cover the cost of sending this information. Our address is listed below.

Thank you for your help.

Sincerely,

Confirming reservation

Dear Ms. Briggs,

The information you sent about your resort was very helpful in shaping our vacation plans. As a follow-up to our phone conversation of April 10, we wish to confirm our reservation for two adults and two children in first-floor, smoke-free rooms for June 11–18 at your quoted rate of _____. I have enclosed a check for the required deposit and will get back in touch with you two weeks before our expected arrival date to confirm these plans. We are looking forward to this vacation.

Sincerely,

Thanking host for thoughtfulness

Dear Helen and Paul,

We will never forget the many kindnesses you included in our house-

A View from Eternity

Linda Ching Sledge

You care for the land and water it; you enrich it abundantly. . . . for so you have ordained it. — PSALM 65:9 NIV

OUR two-week drive along the Atlantic coast had left my husband, Gary, twelve-year-old son, Geoffrey, and me exhausted. We had gone through our itinerary at top speed, yet the perfect vacation spot continued to elude us. Faster and faster we sped on our quest until somewhere in the backwoods of northern Maine we were hopelessly lost. We wandered along narrow gravel roads, growing more and more frustrated as precious hours ticked by. We had a schedule to keep, an itinerary to follow. When would we ever find the place we were supposed to be?

Then we rounded a curve, and there before us stretched a breathtaking expanse of water with a small green island floating on its silvery surface. We pulled our car onto a strip of sand to find our location on the map. Two hours later, we had forgotten that we ever needed maps or itineraries or schedules. There was a beach to explore, water to wade in, rocks to climb, and small round stones to skip along the shore.

I have two pictures of that blessed and unnamed place. Yet I do not have to look at them to recall the lake, the trees, and the faces of three contented travelers who finally found the best place to be.

Searching madly for your heart's desire? Rushing around won't get you there any faster. Instead, take the long, slow, scenic route toward your true destination—the one the Lord planned for you all along.

Slow me down, Lord, so that I may see, really see, eternity all about me, and your hand leading me down each lane.

exchange arrangement. The little notes we found telling us how to work the washer, find extra towels, and how to tenderly care for your plants made us feel you were there as our cordial hosts. Even more unforgettable was the welcome we received in your church. Your thoughtfulness in alerting several of your friends and your pastor to our visit made us feel the fellowship of Christians in a warm, loving way. We thank you and we thank God for this evidence of Christian family care.

Sincerely,

Thanking resort owner for service

Dear Ms. Briggs,

Your brochures did not do justice to the beauty of your resort. Please compliment your groundskeepers for us. We also ask you to encourage your staff by telling them how much we appreciated their smiling responses to our questions and requests. You gave us royal treatment and we will enthusiastically recommend your place to our friends.

Sincerely,

Requesting information about national park

Dear Sir/Madam,

We are planning a trip to the Great Smoky Mountains National Park in your state and would appreciate receiving information on points of interest and available accommodations. We are considering camping in the area and would like to know how many sites are available, what amenities are offered, and what the cost is. Our family of five is interested in moderately challenging hiking and also in learning about the environment through ranger talks or guided services. If possible, please also include information about national historical sites in the area.

Thank you for your help. Our address is below.

Sincerely,

Rest Is Not a Naughty Word

Kathie Kania

My people have been lost sheep; their shepherds have led them astray. . . . They wandered over mountain and hill and forgot their own resting place. — JEREMIAH 50:6 NIV

VACATIONS. A time of rest. Yet how many of us actually do rest? As I look out at the trees with their open arms, standing serenely, I am saddened again by a mind-set that I've had since childhood: the admiration for overwork.

"She has high blood pressure," the ladies would whisper. "Works all the time. House neat as a pin." Amazingly, this was supposed to be a compliment. I was a child then; I thought high blood pressure was a desirable trait.

"He's a workaholic," a colleague intimated recently, adding, "I wish I was more that way myself!"

If you listen, you even hear status associated with diseases caused by stress and overwork. Diseases that prove what hard workers we are.

Many people (myself included) feel guilty or lazy if we sit and "do nothing." Is it any wonder that some have the feeling that God is too busy for them? But nowhere in Scripture do I find God to be a rushing, hurrying, hard-pressed God; his handiwork—from plant to planet—travels serenely within its cycle. Ought we be different?

This week I plan to stare long at the trees. Taste my toast and coffee. Read my Bible, not with a prescribed amount in mind, but letting the verses sink slowly into my heart.

Why don't I do this more often?

Dear Lord, rest is not laziness. Help me to remember this as I find ways to gather serenity for myself and my family.

Requesting road maps from state tourism office

Dear Madam/Sir,

I am in the process of planning our family vacation and would like to visit your area. Would you please send a map of your state along with brochures about special tourist attractions and historical sites? I would also appreciate receiving any available city maps. Please send this information to the address below. Thank you for your help.

Sincerely,

Checking on item lost in hotel—a follow-up letter

When inquiring about a lost item, be sure to describe it clearly, giving size, color, and any other pertinent information.

Dear Mr. Stone,

This letter is a follow-up to our phone conversation of earlier today when I called to inquire about an item we left at your hotel while we were guests there last week. As mentioned, on June 16 our family concluded a stay in room 223 of your hotel. Upon our arrival home we discovered that we do not have _____. We could have left it at the pool or in the bathroom of our room. Would you ask your staff members to check carefully for this item? Please call us at the number below to let us know the results of your search and we will make arrangements to have the item returned at our expense. I appreciate your prompt and careful attention to this matter. Your successful search would make memories of our stay even better than they already are.

With sincere thanks,

Requesting compensation for lost luggage

Dear Sir/Madam,

Your airline got me to my destination safely and on time, but my luggage did not get the same service. Airport personnel informed me that my luggage would be located soon and delivered to my hotel. This did not happen.

Ordinarily I could have borrowed or bought suitable clothing to get by for a few days. But this time was different. Lost in my luggage was a specially ordered dress that I was to wear in my friend's wedding. Also lost was the wedding gift I had purchased.

Your company represents itself as consumer-friendly, so I am trusting you to resolve this matter. My flight information and address and telephone numbers where I can be reached are listed below. I have already filled out claim forms for lost luggage, and I am enclosing copies of receipts for the items mentioned above.

I look forward to hearing from you within this week with a report on your search for my baggage and the compensation you will offer for my inconvenience and possible loss.

Sincerely,

Lost luggage settlement unacceptable

Dear Madam/Sir,

You recently informed me that my baggage, which was lost on flight 611 on January 9, cannot be found. Your representative offered _____ as compensation for my loss and inconvenience. This sum does not begin to cover my loss. I have stated the value of the lost goods and, as much as possible, have validated the expense to replace them. I did this in good faith expecting your company to make things right. Since you have not yet made an offer that accomplishes this, I cannot accept this settlement. Please contact me this week to discuss the matter.

Sincerely,

Requesting compensation after being bumped from flight

Dear Sir/Madam,

My attendance at several important meetings was jeopardized when you bumped me from flight 617 from O'Hare to Los Angeles on May 7 due to overbooking. Although I was not happy, your policy of offering fair compensation for this inconvenience made me willing to work with the problem and accept the delay.

As of this date, however, I have not received fair compensation from your company and I believe that this must be due to an oversight. Please contact me within a week to resolve this matter.

Sincerely,

Seeking refund from hotel

Dear Madam/Sir,

My original vacation plans called for me to be in your city from May 3–8, and I made reservations in your hotel for those dates. On April 26 my plans changed, and I phoned your hotel to notify you that I would need accommodations for May 3 and 4 only. But my credit card statement, which I received today, shows that I was billed for six days. Please check your records and refund my credit card account for the charges made on the nights I did not use your facilities.

You have an excellent reputation for customer relations, so I know that you will make this adjustment immediately and inform me in writing and with documentation that you have refunded this amount. I thank you for resolving this matter.

Sincerely,

When illness forces a cancellation

Dear Sir/Madam,

When illness forced me to cancel my participation in your group tour to the Grand Canyon, I was extremely disappointed. I am following your cancellation policies by sending verification of my illness so that a portion of my payment can be refunded. The enclosed notarized letter from my doctor should satisfy your requirements.

Sincerely,

Canceling flight and requesting refund

Dear Madam/Sir,

This letter is to confirm my earlier phone call in which I informed your agent that injuries from a recent car accident leave me unable to travel. Therefore, I have canceled my reservation on flight 321 from Detroit to Denver on September 2, 1996. If there are forms I must fill out to have the price of my ticket refunded, please send them to me at the address below. I appreciate your prompt attention to this matter.

Sincerely,

Telling friend of illness and canceling vacation plans

Dear Sue,

We have been having a great time making plans for our weekend getaway and the thought of it has pulled me through some tedious hours. But now I have sad news: I must cancel my part in these plans as I have had to schedule surgery during the week preceding our planned vacation. It's minor surgery, and I'll let you know the outcome, but I'm sure it will make me a less-than-ideal companion for your long-awaited vacation.

I hope there is still time for you to find someone to take my place or, if you prefer, for us to reschedule our mini-vacation following my recovery. Please understand how sorry I am to upset the plans and how much I want you to have a good time even though I cannot share it with you. Perhaps we can enjoy a weekend together later this year.

Sincerely,

Complaint about tour package

Dear Madam/Sir,

Most of my memories of the Central European excursion tour I took with your company are very enjoyable, but a very important memory is missing. One of the trips I looked forward to the most was a visit to the medieval walled city of Rothenburg in Germany. As we approached the city we ran into a thunderstorm, and the tour manager decided to go on to the next city because only a few people had umbrellas or raincoats. To me, that was a small reason for making the big decision to leave out an important part of the trip we had looked forward to and paid for. Is it your company policy to allow guides to make decisions in this way?

Since the fees were paid in advance as part of the tour expense, I feel cheated. Please explain your policy in regard to this type of situation. I want to be assured that this will not happen again if I decide to take another tour with your company.

Sincerely,

Inquiry about tour operator

One of the best uses of letter writing is to clarify your thinking and to give the recipient time to respond. If you have a list of questions, you can take the time to be sure the list is complete. The recipient will have the leisure time to think through the questions before answering and to add any additional information as needed.

Dear Helen and Jim,

World Tours is offering a vacation package that really appeals to me, and I am writing to ask your opinion of the company. You have often told me how much you enjoy group tours, and I'm wondering if you know whether this company delivers what it promises. Here are some of my questions:

- Have you been satisfied with the guides World provides?
- Does the company include everything promised on the itinerary?
- Is it true that I won't have to "lug my own luggage"?
- Are the meals adequate (as promised)?
- Is there good security in the hotels they reserve?

- Do you consider this tour operator to be honest and solvent?
- Are the personnel concerned about the welfare of each tour participant?

Your answers to these questions, and any other information you can provide, will help us decide if this tour is the best one for us. I sincerely appreciate your help and look forward to sharing trip experiences and pictures.

Sincerely,

Requesting information about insurance

Dear Mr. Martin,

I am planning a trip to Europe and have received information about insurance policies that would cover me in the event of illness or accident abroad. Since I already have insurance policies with your company, I would like to know if your policies will adequately protect me in Europe. Please inform me as to any limitations in my policies so that I can decide whether or not to buy another policy. I want to be well-protected but I have no desire to duplicate my coverage.

Thank you for your help.

Sincerely,

Requesting help from consumer action group

Dear Consumer Advocates,

My husband and I returned yesterday from a tour of France, and our experience was far from satisfactory. Our first clue that something was wrong came when we learned that our guide did not speak French any better than we did. And the situation deteriorated quickly from that point. If we hadn't paid so much money for the trip we would be laughing about it, because it really turned into a comedy of errors. But few people can afford such an expensive joke. It certainly wasn't what we thought we were paying for when we wrote our check.

We are debating whether or not to pursue legal action to try to recoup some of our money, but in the meantime we hate the thought that others are being taken advantage of in the same way we were. Is there something you can do to warn people about _____, the tour company? If you would like more details, please call.

Sincerely,

Complaint about unsanitary restroom

Dear Sir/Madam,

If I had ventured into your restaurant's restroom before eating my dinner, I would have walked out the door. The restroom was uncared for, unsupplied, and filthy.

A genuine concern for health and sanitation applies not only to the kitchen but also to the restrooms. My experience causes me to question the sanitary state of your kitchen. I will not eat at your restaurant again until I am assured that sanitation is as important to you as it is to me.

Sincerely,

18

Credit Matters

Interest works night and day, in fair weather and in foul. It gnaws at a man's substance with invisible teeth.

HENRY WARD BEECHER

One of the mysteries of human conduct is why adult men and women . . . sign documents which they do not read, at the behest of canvassers whom they do not know, binding them to pay for articles which they do not want, with money which they have not got. **GERALD HURST**

Let no debt remain outstanding, except the continuing debt to love one another, for he who loves his fellowman has fulfilled the law. **ROMANS 13:8 NIV**

*P*erhaps it is a spirit of optimism that leads us into debt. Our belief in a better tomorrow convinces us that next month we will have the money to pay for what we cannot afford this month. But when next month comes it is seldom accompanied by cash.

So each month we slide further and further into indebtedness.

If the spirit of optimism got us into debt, only a sense of realism will get us out. But the problem is, reality is what most people are running from when they fall into debt in the first place.

The adjectives we use to describe reality reveal why we tend to avoid it. We speak of painful reality, harsh reality, and cruel reality—not exactly goals to strive for. But reality has its positive side, and "people who shut their eyes to reality simply invite their own destruction", (*James Baldwin,* Notes of a Native Son*).*

When it comes to debt there is one reality: Unless you start climbing out you will fall deeper in. And to face this reality is to take the first step out of debt.

"Melancholy and remorse form the deep leaden keel which enables us to sail into the wind of reality," wrote Cyril Connolly in The Unquiet Grave. *Debt does inevitably lead to melancholy, remorse, and depression because debt is a constant reminder that we have lost control of our lives. But by choosing to "sail into the wind of" this reality we regain control and, at the same time, we regain a sense of personal value and worth.*

"The wicked borrow and do not repay, but the righteous give generously" (Psalm 37:21 NIV). Even before reading this verse, we know it is true, and we cannot have any respect for ourselves until we learn to control our spending.

When going into battle against debt, the good news is that we can fight it on two fronts simultaneously. We can hit it from the spending side and the earning side. It's kind of like fighting a weight problem with both diet and exercise.

One of the keys to working with creditors (and getting them to work with you) is communication. To them, no news is NOT good news. No news means someone has skipped town with their money. So even when you can't make a payment (especially when you can't make a payment), call or write to assure your creditors that you do still plan to pay in full.

Matters of credit and debt can be difficult and unpleasant to deal with, but avoiding them will only make them worse. When it comes to debt, honesty, straightforwardness, and sincerity combine to make the best policy.

Slow pay

Dear Dr. Lassater,

I apologize for the delay in paying our bill. We do plan to pay it in full, but we have fallen a bit behind due to these unexpected medical expenses.

Enclosed you will find a check for twenty dollars. We will contact your office soon to work out a payment schedule.

Thank you for your patience.

Sincerely,

Credit report

Dear Mr. Kent,

We were very surprised to be informed that our application for a home-improvement loan has been turned down. Please send us a copy of our credit report so we can determine what erroneous information led to your decision.

Sincerely,

Cancel

Dear Card Services,

We wish to cancel our credit card immediately. Please do not send us a new card, and do not charge the annual fee.

Thank you for your prompt attention to this matter.

Sincerely,

How to Manage Mammon

Faye Roberts

Store up for yourselves treasures in heaven. . . . For where your treasure is, there your heart will be also. — MATTHEW 6:20–21 NIV

FOR two years after my husband died, I tried to fill the void in my life with material things. I went shopping, applied for credit, received charge cards, and kept buying things. Soon I owned a new washer, dryer, microwave, garden tiller, and a small pickup truck. And before long I found myself deep in debt. There were more bills in the mailbox than money in the bank, and I worked in that bank! I knew better.

In desperation, I went to my loan officer for help, and between the two of us we worked out a plan to get me out and keep me out of debt. It was a struggle, but I finally succeeded. In the process, I discovered that principles of good money management go back as far as King Solomon. If you have a problem similar to mine, here are some suggestions you might find useful. (And look what inspired them!)

1. "The soul of the diligent is richly supplied" (Proverbs 13:4 RSV). Divide your desires into two categories: wants and needs. For me, the house and utilities were definite needs. Everything else I put to the test. My wants I put aside, and my needs I tried to meet in a less expensive way. I shopped for a lower-priced insurance policy and gave up my membership at the athletic club. My old winter coat got me through one more year.

2. "The prudent looks where he is going" (Proverbs 14:15 RSV). Give yourself achievable goals—ones you can reach in a few months. My first goal was to pay off the smallest bill. Instead of going to the movies, my kids and I stayed home and played Monopoly, and I put twenty dollars toward my goal. The exhilaration I felt writing "paid in full" on one bill gave me the incentive to tackle larger ones.

3. "Go to the ant . . . consider her ways, and be wise" (Proverbs 6:6 RSV). Be diligent, rely on your resources. I rented a carpet cleaner and did the work myself. I stayed away from high-priced convenience foods and clipped coupons. The money I saved went to the specific goals I had set. Instead of giving twenty dollars to a local charity, I donated two hours of my time.

4. "If your hand causes you to sin, cut it off" (Mark 9:43 RSV). Taking the cards out of my wallet wasn't enough. I had to completely get rid of the temptation by cutting them up.

5. "Better is a dry morsel with quiet than a house full of feasting with strife" (Proverbs 17:1 RSV). A family needs to work together to become debt-free. Without alarming the kids, I let them know that we needed to be more frugal.

Of course they were disappointed when we didn't go to the movies, but playing games at home and popping popcorn became just as much fun as a night out. We made economizing a family project. Mandy, who was seven, became an expert coupon-clipper. They all learned to save aluminum cans. They no longer badgered me about having the latest thing advertised on television. When we worked together, a measure of peace entered the house.

6. "No one can serve two masters. . . . You cannot serve God and mammon" (Matthew 6:24 RSV). The worst thing about being in debt is feeling mastered by money. I found, though, that the more I sought God, the less I had the urge to spend. I knew I had achieved a minor victory when a friend asked me to go with her to a sale at my favorite store. I stayed home and baked a cake for a neighbor instead. As King Solomon said:

7. "Commit your work to the Lord, and your plans will be established" (Proverbs 16:3 RSV). Mine were.

Thank you, Lord, for revealing to me your priorities. Work in my heart until all of mine are exactly the same as all of yours.

Need more information

Whenever you are asked for additional information, send it along with a brief note itemizing the material you are sending and what pieces, if any, are still missing. By doing this you can avoid time-consuming misunderstandings.

Dear Sirs,

    I am enclosing the information you requested regarding our application for a mortgage.

- A set of the house plans
- Specifications
- Legal description of land

We will send the purchase agreement as soon as it is completed.

Sincerely,

New in area

Dear Mrs. Wheeler,

    My husband and I are in the process of moving to Kalamazoo, where we are building a home. We are interested in establishing a line of credit at your store because we intend to buy most of our new furnishings there. Please send me the necessary forms to fill out.

    Thank you for your help.

Sincerely,

Lack of work record

Dear Mr. Anstett,

    My lack of employment history may cause you to think that I am a poor credit risk. But there are other factors I would like you to consider. Being a mother and a housewife for thirty years has been a career that I have taken very seriously. My work has included menu planning, schedule balancing, and maintenance management. I have

Putting God First

Patricia Lorenz

The purpose of tithing is to teach you always to put God first in your lives.
— DEUTERONOMY 14:23 TLB

WHEN my mother died a few years ago, Dad gave me a box of papers from her desk. Included were her down-to-the-penny household statements for each month of my childhood years.

Every month Mother paid eleven bills by check and placed the rest of the family income in ten separate envelopes labeled: church, school expenses, clothes, gifts, repair and improvement, dues and licenses, doctor/dentist, Dad's allowance, Mom's allowance, and savings.

The June 3, 1960, ledger reveals that our family of five was living on $404 a month. In spite of the tight budget, Mother and Dad were giving more to the church than they were keeping for themselves. Mom kept $10, Dad kept $10, and $24 went to church.

Have I followed in my parents' footsteps? Hardly. The excuses come too easily. Four children to put through college. A big mortgage. An emergency that might come up. The vacation fund.

As a child I never had the slightest notion that my parents inched their way through on such a tight budget. And every month they never gave any thought to doing less for the church than the absolute maximum their tiny budget could stand. Maybe that's why I felt so rich as a kid.

Lord, give me the courage to tithe and then to trust my budget concerns to you.

been a comfort giver, hostess, nutritionist, counselor, referee, and teacher. I have managed all our household finances and successfully maintained my own checkbook and charge accounts for many years.

Enclosed you will find letters of reference to validate that I am a responsible, trustworthy person. I am confident that you will approve my loan application after you review them.

Cordially yours,

19

Letters of Complaint

Criticism should not be querulous and wasting, . . . but guiding, instructive, inspiring . . . **RALPH WALDO EMERSON**

A small bird will drop frozen dead / From a bough / Without ever having felt sorry for itself. **D. H. LAWRENCE**

Therefore I will not keep silent; I will speak out in the anguish of my spirit, I will complain in the bitterness of my soul. **JOB 7:11 NIV**

*T*o be called a complainer is certainly no compliment. The word in fact is most often used as a term of derision, so it is little wonder that so few people have learned how to complain well.

Complain well? The very idea calls for a question mark. The two words seem oxymoronic, mutually exclusive. Most of us were taught that the only virtue associated with complaining is in stifling it. After all, to complain is to express an attitude of ungratefulness.

Such a conclusion is only valid, however, if there is no hope of improving the situation. To complain about such things as the weather is of course a waste of time because, despite all our modern-day meteorological accomplishments in forecasting it, scientists are still powerless to change it.

But what about things that can change? And what about things that should change? Are not these legitimate targets of complaint?

Certainly.

Jonathan Swift, an English churchman and writer, expressed a thought-provoking sentiment in his work entitled Thoughts on Various Subjects *(1711). "Complaint," he wrote, "is the largest tribute Heaven receives, and the sincerest part of our devotion."*

To help us understand what he might have meant by this mysterious comment, we can look at statements made by two familiar Old Testament characters: Job and David. Though known for their godliness, they were also known to complain. "Therefore I will not keep silent," said Job during his time of suffering. "I will speak out in the anguish of my spirit, I will complain in the bitterness of my soul" (7:11 NIV).

And David wrote this: "Hear me, O God, as I voice my complaint; protect my life from the threat of the enemy. Hide me from the conspiracy of the wicked, from the noisy crowd of evildoers" (Psalm 64:1–2 NIV). Later David voiced this complaint: "I cry aloud to the LORD; I lift up my voice to the LORD for mercy. I pour out my complaint before him; before him I tell my trouble" (142:1–2 NIV).

The complaints of Job and David have one thing in common: They were directed to the one who could change things. Perhaps this is the solution to the mystery of Swift's comment. Complaint is a tribute to God in that it acknowledges his power to change (that is, improve) our circumstances.

Both Job and David complained for a good reason. They wanted God to make things better.

Our reasons for complaining are seldom that noble. Most of us complain simply to vent bad feelings rather than to accomplish anything good, and perhaps that is why complaining has such negative connotations.

To improve its image we need to do two things. First, we need to agree never to complain about circumstances that cannot be changed and never to complain to someone who has no power to change them. Second, we need to improve our skill as complainers.

To do this, we can follow Emerson's rules for criticism. They are just as applicable today as when he wrote them in 1847, and they apply equally well to complaints. Good complaints are . . .

Instructive. *Your letter of complaint should explain what is wrong.*

Guiding. *Your letter of complaint should show how the situation can be improved.*

Inspiring. *Your letter of complaint should create a desire to improve.*

When you write letters of complaint that accomplish these three things, you can change the world. Well, maybe not the world, but at least your small part of it.

MAKING COMPLAINTS

Transit damage

Dear Service Department Manager,

Today I received an engraved Waterford crystal bowl I ordered from your company. You can imagine my disappointment when I found it broken into several pieces.

I'd like to know how to proceed in this situation. Would you like me to return the pieces? Will you be able to replace the bowl quickly? I had intended to give it as a wedding gift in less than a month, so a rather difficult time element is involved. I would very much like a replacement of this beautiful bowl if that is possible.

Thank you for your prompt attention.

Sincerely,

Cost of purchases

Dear Pharmacy Owner,

I was thrilled when your establishment moved into our neighborhood. I appreciate the convenience and personal service that your family-run business provides. Your store is always clean and well-stocked and your workers are always attentive and knowledgeable. It's also nice when a business contributes so much to a community, as yours has.

But I would like to bring one consideration to your attention, and that is the cost of your merchandise. I realize that a family-run business will be more expensive than a chain store, and I've been willing to pay that difference. Frequently, however, your prices are nearly double what I would have paid at other stores.

I want to continue shopping at Medi-Rite, but I'm not sure I can consistently afford to pay such high prices. If you could reexamine your prices and bring them more in line with your competitors, I would gladly continue to patronize your store. Please let me know your thinking on this.

Thank you very much.

Sincerely,

Inadequate explanation

Dear Angela,

I'm sure it was difficult for you to give me an accounting of your actions yesterday afternoon. Be assured it was also difficult for me to demand an explanation. Yet, as your employer, I am entitled to an honest accounting of your time.

As I listened, I could not ignore my suspicion that you were not completely forthcoming in your explanation. So, I am giving you another opportunity to set things right. I am not so concerned that your actions may have been unrelated to work as I am disturbed that you may have been dishonest with me.

I make every attempt to treat my employees with fairness and integrity, and I expect that same integrity in return.

Please meet me in the conference room at three o'clock this afternoon. I trust that you will then be able to tell me honestly why you were away from your desk for three hours yesterday.

I am sure that we can work this problem out. And I'm looking forward to doing so.

Sincerely,

Messy area

Dear Day Shift Clerks,

Every day, those of us on the evening shift come to work hoping for one simple change—a clean break area!

We understand that after an eight-hour work day, you are eager to get home. But it is disheartening for us to have to begin our day by cleaning up your mess, knowing that we will have to clean up again before leaving.

We don't mind leaving the break area clean for you, but we do wish that you would reciprocate. We have a simple system that works for us. We each wash our own cups and we take turns washing the coffee pot and utensils. This way everyone shares the task fairly.

We are simply asking for some courtesy and thoughtfulness regarding this matter.

Best regards,

Manufacturing error

Dear Sir,

Recently we received our special order of personalized nameplates for our association Christmas party. They are every bit as beautiful as we had hoped. The brass nameplates and walnut stands look elegant together, and the engraving is first-class.

There is a problem, however: When we tried to stand the nameplates up, we discovered that they were attached upside-down! They will stand up only on their heads.

We are returning the nameplates promptly and requesting your assessment as to whether they can be reattached within the time we agreed upon.

We are hoping you can rectify the problem, since we'd love to distribute such an attractive gift to our members. We look forward to your immediate reply.

Sincerely,

Manufacturing problem

Dear Mr. Swift,

When we worked with you to develop the hinges for our custom-made Oriental screens, we emphasized that quality and durability were our first concerns.

We took a chance on using the lighter-gauge brass hinges that you suggested because they were more attractive, and you said they would hold up well. We've been testing the screens, however, and we're finding that the hinges are disintegrating under normal usage.

We suspect that they may need to be redesigned and made of a heavier material as well. Let's meet again to review the results of our performance tests and to begin developing a solution.

We've appreciated your attention to our project in the past and look forward to continuing our successful partnership.

Best regards,

Billing error

Accounts Receivable:

Several months ago I received a bill from your laboratory for some blood tests my physician had ordered. I paid that bill promptly, as the enclosed copy of the canceled check indicates.

If Only . . .

Linda Neukrug

Give ear to my words, O Lord. . . . — PSALM 5:1 KJV

WHEN I was unemployed, I thought I would be happy if only I had a job. So I prayed, "Dear God, just let me get a job and I will never complain about anything again." But only weeks after starting a new job I was unhappy with some of my co-workers, swamped by my workload, and even annoyed that my chair wasn't comfortable enough!

When I was single, I thought if only I had a husband life would be better. Then, only a few months after Paul and I were married, an argument about the right way to slice carrots had me wondering if this was the happily-ever-after I'd prayed for.

Who knows what I might have wished for next as the "answer" to all my problems if a well-meaning friend hadn't given me a needle-point pillow that read, "Happiness is not getting what you want—it is wanting what you get."

Surprisingly, that simple message even enabled me to give up my "If-I-lost-ten-pounds-my-life-would-be-perfect" fantasy. It also caused me to stop making my prayers into a "gimme" list for God, and instead to be appreciative of the many good things already in my life—including my cozy apartment (small enough not to require too much work to keep clean), my good health (including a zest for food), and a caring husband (even though he cuts carrots wrong!).

God, help me to remember to thank you for what I do have rather than remind you of what I don't have.

Recently, however, I was notified by a collection agency that you had turned my account over to them for nonpayment of this bill!

On the basis of my canceled check, please correct your records and notify the collection agency of your error.

Collection notices are always disturbing, but even more so when the financial obligation was met months ago.

Thank you for your immediate attention to this matter.

Regards,

Catalog order

Customer Service Department:

I received my first catalog order from your company, and there is good news and bad news. I am very pleased with how quickly I received my order and with the quality of most of the items. But there is one problem: The sandals do not fit. Even though the label identifies them as the size I ordered (which is the size I always wear), they are much too small. Also, the strap on one of them is defective.

I am returning the sandals for a refund. I do not want them replaced. The remainder of the order is delightful, and I'll look forward to receiving your next catalog.

Thank you for your prompt attention to this matter.

Sincerely,

Computer error

You seldom have anything to lose by admitting that you might be partly responsible for an error. Don't go overboard on this, but don't always assume that someone else's incompetence is the sole cause of all mistakes.

Dear Ms. Greer,

Thank you so much for sending us a computer printout of our

church members. Our development committee is eager to begin work on the fund drive for our church's new facility.

In looking over the list, however, I noticed that the names appear to be arranged by birth date rather than alphabetically. This would mean we would have to alphabetize the entire list before we could address our mailings or update our other lists against that printout.

I suspect that, with your fancy computer equipment, you can arrange these lists in many ways. Would you be able to provide us with a list of church members alphabetized by surname?

I'm sorry I wasn't more clear about our needs in the beginning, and I hope that providing us with this new printout isn't too great an inconvenience. Please let me know if this will be a problem for you.

Thanks very much for your patience.

My best,

Misrepresentation

Dear Mr. Oliver,

Last Saturday, I read your store's advertisement for a fifty percent discount on a pair of Drexel nightstands. Your ad ran without qualifiers or limitations of any kind. I clipped the ad and arrived at your store within an hour of its opening, but there were no nightstands. According to your manager, they had sold out and would not be reordered. He advised us to select nightstands from the other merchandise—at full price.

I was, of course, disappointed to have wasted my time and energy driving to your store, but I was outraged by the dishonesty implicit in your advertisement. I do not believe that the advertised item sold out that quickly, but I do believe that you understand the meaning of the phrase *bait and switch*.

Surely you also know that merchants who do not stand behind their promotional specials can't be trusted in other matters, either. I am a small-business owner, and I know that a company's survival depends upon the integrity of its owner and the trust of its customers. This does not bode well for your store.

I will give you one week to respond to my letter before I decide what further action to take.

Regards,

Parking in driveway

Dear Paul and Mary,

Over the five years we have been neighbors we have all worked very hard to remain on good terms with one another. Living as close as we do, each of us has had to make an extra effort to be thoughtful and to nurture our good relationship.

That's why I don't want a minor problem to jeopardize our mutual good feelings.

Lately, we've had a hard time getting into our driveway because your motorhome has been parked in such a way that it blocks our access to the street. Several times I've had to drive across my front lawn just to get in or out of the driveway.

I know our driveways are small, and the cul de sac makes parking angles especially difficult, but if you could be a little bit more careful about where you park your vehicle it would certainly keep stress from building in our relationship (and it would save our lawn).

Thanks for being so great in so many ways. I'm sure we can work this out.

My best,

Meetings out of control

Dear Matt,

I realize that this is your first year as president of our rambunctious little group and that there's a steep learning curve at the beginning of any new job. But while this is occurring, we must still conduct our board meetings in a manner that results in wise and well-thought-

Give Someone a Pat on the Back

Phyllis Hobe

Now I praise you, brethren. . . .   — 1 CORINTHIANS 11:2 KJV

I WAS in the express line at the supermarket and it wasn't moving. The checker was new and needed assistance with almost every item she rang up. When she saw my two tubes of toothpaste, she hesitated. "It's a buy-one-get-one-free," I snapped.

"Yes, ma'am," she said, "but they aren't properly marked and I can't ring them up until I get the right code number." When she called to the other checkers for help, they ignored her. So did the manager, who was all the way across the store. I was about to complain when suddenly I wondered, *What would Jesus do?*

I knew the answer immediately. He would see that the checker was close to tears, and he would identify with her struggle. It's hard enough to start a new job, and when no one is there to help you it can be miserable.

"Take your time," I said, changing my tone of voice. "You're doing a good job."

"But I don't like to keep people waiting," she said.

"That's all right," I told her. "Next week you'll be a whiz."

That brought a little smile to her face. To mine too.

And a week later, she really was a whiz!

Amazing, isn't it, how good a little encouragement feels—not only when you get it, but when you give it?

Teach me today, Lord, to be slow to complain and eager to praise.

through business plans and decisions. When we engage in lengthy debate and fruitless discussion we shortchange the group and waste our time.

As president, you are the one responsible for keeping us on track. Doing so with this board can be a challenge, as I well know. But by the time I got to year three of my three-year stint as president I had learned a few tricks that were helpful. Maybe they will help you as well.

First, I distributed an agenda with time limits for discussion on each subject. Second, I was very firm (some said rigid) about sticking to the agenda. I even set a timer to go off at the end of the allotted time. At first this was annoying because we had to postpone decisions until future meetings. But when people got used to the idea that "the clock was running," they surprised themselves with their ability to tune in on what were the really important issues of each item.

Perhaps these suggestions will help you improve the efficiency of our meetings. Please call me if I can be of further help to you.

My best,

Newspaper not delivered

Manager, Circulation Department:

A new carrier has recently taken over our rural route, and I am not certain that he is fully aware of our account. For the past two weeks we have received our paper only sporadically. Last Sunday's paper was not delivered at all. We paid a month in advance so you owe us a refund for the missing papers, but I'm not sure what is the best way to reconcile accounts. This week I began keeping track of the missing papers, so we can settle our account definitively at some point.

Please have someone from your department contact me and let me know how you will remedy this situation.

I have always had very good delivery service in the past, and I am sure this is just a temporary difficulty.

I look forward to hearing from you.

Best regards,

A Lesson in Gentleness

Dolphus Weary

A gentle answer turns away wrath. — PROVERBS 15:1 NIV

AT age fifteen, my son Reginald got his driver's permit and began practicing to drive the two blocks to church. One Sunday after the service, my wife Rosie and I began to wonder where he was when he didn't immediately come home. Finally, we saw him walking down the road with a friend. As he approached, I could see despair in his eyes and with a trembling voice he said, "Mom, Dad . . . I wrecked the car." He then proceeded to tell us about a drag race around the local junior high school.

My wrath was immense and harsh words were ready to tumble from my mouth. How could he be so irresponsible? How could he—

"Are you all right, Reggie?" Rosie asked quietly.

A gentle answer turns away wrath.

Reggie nodded and began to cry. "I'm so sorry. It was a dumb thing to do!"

A gentle answer turns away wrath.

My angry words sputtered. Rosie's response made me think about the countless times God had provided gentle words and gentle hands to guide me back to himself. I remember how many years ago as a teenager I drove the ministry's Volkswagen to various places to conduct vacation Bible school. One day, as we were returning home, the motor blew up because I'd failed to check the oil. The words I heard from John Perkins, my boss, were gentle, understanding, and caring. I learned then, and try to practice it now, that gentle words calm a person's heart.

Lord, today and every day, help me to use gentle words regardless of the circumstances.

Delivery person

Delivery Manager:

We recently began using your company to deliver our milk because you assured us of the highest quality product. Your recycling program for milk bottles also appealed to us.

We've run into a snag, however, and that is with our delivery man. Our milk may come at any time of day—or night, for that matter. Sometimes he takes the empty bottles; sometimes he lets them accumulate for days. He has occasionally missed our order completely, and once he left the wrong order.

When we have mentioned these problems to him, he becomes surly and uncommunicative. Thus, we have little hope that the situation will improve.

We hesitate to jeopardize an older man's job by complaining, but speaking to him has brought no change. The only other alternative we see is to cancel our milk delivery. Instead we are making this last attempt to redress the situation. We would like to continue having our milk delivered, but we would like some assurance from you that your service will be more reliable. Please see what you can do to help Mr. Cutler improve his work habits and his disposition.

Thank you for handling this problem.

Sincerely,

No stop light

Director, County Road Commission:

As I'm sure you know, there has been another fatal accident at the intersection of Washington and Arbor streets. That intersection has had at least one such tragedy every year since I moved to this area five years ago, not to mention the many less serious accidents.

Our neighborhood has begun calling the corner "Death Row," and we are all tired of witnessing so many preventable tragedies and of exposing ourselves to danger every time we go through that intersection.

We have asked for a stop light before. This time we are organizing a neighborhood association to address the issue. Since our informal requests have been ignored, perhaps our united and organized voice will be heard.

We ask that you approve at your next meeting our request for a stop light at that dangerous intersection. If this is not feasible, please attend the next meeting of our association to explain the county's position on the matter. We will schedule the meeting for a time that is convenient for you. This letter will be followed within one week by a phone call to set the date.

Thank you for your service to our community.

Regards,

ANSWERING COMPLAINTS

Accountability

It is a cliché, but it is true: The best defense is a good offense. If you know someone has made a complaint against you, don't go into withdrawal, go into action. Take the initiative to resolve the matter. Admit what fault is yours and express your desire and enthusiasm for doing better.

Dear Mr. Wasser,

It has come to my attention that someone has complained about my work. Although I do not know the nature of the complaints or who has made them, I am sure you want to get to the bottom of the problem. So do I.

While I may be unclear as to all the details of my new responsibilities, I am very eager to do my job well. I take my work seriously and want to be regarded as dependable and honest. If accountability is lacking in my work it is because I am acclimating to a new job, not because I am sloppy or uncaring.

Would you talk with me about this problem? I want to see things from your perspective, and I really do want to know the areas in which I am not performing well so that I can improve.

I will look forward to our meeting.

Best regards,

Disturbed retail customer

*When taking responsibility for a misunderstanding, do so without quali-fication. The tendency in letters like the one that follows is to apologize "for **any** inconvenience we **may have** caused you." It is better to avoid this avoidance technique and simply say, "I apologize for the inconven-ience we have caused you." After all, people who complain believe they have been inconvenienced, so there is nothing to be gained by introduc-ing the "may have" clause.*

Dear Mrs. VanHaaren,

I received your letter expressing dissatisfaction with our service. I assure you that we take all communication from our customers very seriously and do everything we can to rectify the problems that occur.

I have discussed the situation you described with the clerk in-volved, and I am convinced that part of the problem was due to mis-communication. This employee has been with us for many years and has been a conscientious worker and courteous to our customers.

She expresses her regret for the misunderstanding, and we both apologize for the inconvenience or unhappiness the incident caused you. Please accept the enclosed coupon for a free lunch. And please accept our sincerest apologies once again.

Sincerely,

Our mistake

Dear Mrs. Williams,

Despite our best efforts to satisfy our customers, we still make mis-takes.

Whatever You Look for Is What You Find

Walter Harter

I complained, and my spirit was overwhelmed.   — PSALM 77:3 KJV

FIRST there was a plumbing problem. Then a garage door had to be replaced. Finally, the car stalled on the highway and the repair bill was outrageous. "Life is just one misfortune after another," I bellowed.

My wife, Edna, let me know that she had heard enough. "Okay, I've heard all your complaints," she said. "Now how about the good things that have happened?" She showed me a small notebook she'd been keeping of "happy stuff," as she called it. In it she'd written, "Our friend gave us a bunch of camellias to brighten up the house; I received an unexpected phone call from a long-lost high-school friend; we are both mobile. . . ."

Edna was right. Despite the inconveniences, more good things than bad had happened to me. I started making my own list: "a surprise visit from a faraway relative; Edna's wonderful birthday dinner; the clear night when she and I stayed outdoors and counted the stars. . . ."

The misfortunes, especially the insignificant ones, came into perspective against the backdrop of pleasant experiences I had been ignoring.

Are you feeling hemmed in by circumstances? Stop and take inventory of the "happy stuff" that surrounds you. Get a pencil, start your list, and watch your scowl change into a smile.

Lord, even when unpleasantries abound, let me focus on the goodness.

We apologize that the paint we gave you is the wrong color. We are revising our labeling and warehousing system to prevent these kinds of mistakes, but in the meantime things are in a state of upheaval.

We sincerely regret the frustration and inconvenience this mix-up has caused you, and we hope it won't undermine your trust in our establishment.

We will, of course, replace the paint. Please accept as well a discount coupon good on your next purchase.

Thank you for your patience.

Sincerely,

Misunderstanding

Dear Mrs. Christenson,

The look of surprise on my face when you came in on Tuesday was due to the fact that I wasn't expecting to see you until Thursday. In my appointment book, your name was penciled in for Thursday with a note that you would call Tuesday to confirm it. So I was expecting your phone call, not your smiling face, on Tuesday.

I don't know where our communication went awry, but the result was that you were inconvenienced, and I am sorry for your long wait. I will make sure we are in complete agreement the next time you call for an appointment.

It was delightful to see you anyway, even unexpectedly. Let's make sure we have time to visit the next time you come in.

My best,

20

Special Situations

All virtue is summed up in dealing justly.   ARISTOTLE

Turn from evil and do good; then you will dwell in the land forever. For the LORD loves the just and will not forsake his faithful ones.   PSALM 37:27–28 NIV

The King is mighty, he loves justice. . . .   PSALM 99:4 NIV

*I*f we lived in a perfect world, there would be no selfishness, no greed, no injustice. We would never have disputes or conflicts to resolve because everyone would do what is fair and right without the threat of fines, lawsuits, or imprisonment for failing to do so.

But, alas, we don't live in such an ideal world, so we do have conflicts. People do lie and cheat and steal, and society pays a high price for it. Part of this price is economic. The cost of law enforcement, the justice system, and prison management keeps our taxes on the increase. But the economic cost is only part of the price we pay for "sin in the camp." The other cost, and perhaps the higher one, is measured *not in dollars and cents but in social and psychological consequences. When selfishness, greed, and injustice begin to characterize a society, people begin to expect that type of behavior. And when people expect it from others they begin to rationalize it in themselves.*

Thus begins a deadly downward spiral. On the way down we hear such phrases as "Every man for himself," "Gotta look out for number one," "I'm just fighting fire with fire," and "If I don't look out for myself, no one else will."

These slogans are not straight out of Scripture.

In fact, the role of the Christian in society is to reverse this direction. But how? What can we do to counteract greed, selfishness, and injustice? What can we do to make the world a better place? How can so few people overcome so much evil?

*Some popular voices proclaim that through **politics** we can legislate good behavior; others say that through **persuasion** we can convince people to be good; and still others declare that through **power** we can force people to be good.*

But none of these is what God says. His solution is much more basic. He says that our task is to "overcome evil with good" (Romans 12:21 NIV).

That's right. The solution to evil and injustice in the world is not found in politics, persuasion, or power; it's found in goodness. Pure, simple goodness. As Marcus Aurelius wrote, "Waste no more time arguing what a good man should be. Be one" (Meditations).

Of course, it is so much easier to talk about goodness than to be good; so much more satisfying to insist on goodness from others than to be good ourselves; and so much more fun to grumble about people who are bad than to show them how to be good.

And that is the temptation we face when we are treated unjustly—to fight for justice rather than to behave justly.

When writing letters about situations involving conflict, disagreement, or misunderstanding, therefore, it is important to keep in mind these questions:

***Am I right?** Am I upholding what is truly right or only what is in my* *own best interest? "It must be a good thing to be good or ivrybody wudden't be pretendin' he was," wrote the American humorist Finley Peter Dunne in the voice of his Irish philosopher character Mr. Dooley ("Hypocrisy,"* Observances by Mr. Dooley*). Make sure your letter is written to uphold good, not just to uphold the pretense of goodness.*

Is my goal justice? *Am I using the word* justice *when my real goal is vengeance? Am I trying to punish the person/company/group for the injustice I believe I have suffered? "My judgment is just, for I seek not to please myself but him who sent me," said Jesus (John 5:30 NIV). The one true test of goodness is that it is done to please God the Father.*

Am I being fair? *Are my expectations reasonable or am I using the situation to get more than is rightfully mine? "It is very hard to be simple enough to be good," wrote Ralph Waldo Emerson in his* Journals. *The prevalent attitude today is that it is our right to get as much as we can whenever we can from whomever we can. It is very hard to settle for what is "rightfully mine" and it is even more difficult to be simple.*

How can I use this situation to achieve a higher good? *Will my letter make goodness attractive? What can I say (and how can I say it) that will make the receiver want to do what is good and right? "Jail doesn't teach anyone to do good, nor Siberia, but a man—yes! A man can teach another man to do good—believe me!" wrote Maxim Gorky in* The Lower Depths. *If a picture is worth a thousand words, then one life well-lived is worth a thousand lectures on justice.*

Fortunately, we believe in a God who is not only just, but who loves and rewards justice, and who provided guidelines for maintaining justice in society:

> *The proverbs of Solomon son of David, king of Israel: for attaining wisdom and discipline; for understanding words of insight; for acquiring a disciplined and prudent life, doing what is right and just and fair; for giving prudence to the simple, knowledge and discretion to the young—let the wise listen and add to their learning, and let the discerning get guidance—for understanding proverbs and parables, the*

sayings and riddles of the wise. The fear of the LORD is the beginning of knowledge, but fools despise wisdom and discipline (Proverbs 1:1–7 NIV).

And fortunately we live in a nation that values justice:

I pledge allegience to the flag of the United States of America, and to the Republic for which it stands, one nation, under God, indivisible, with liberty and justice for all.

Yes, we love justice. But one of our problems is the tendency to focus on "justice for me" rather than "justice for all." So when you write letters concerning problems related to services, products, or people, keep in mind one characteristic that should guide all Christian behavior. It is found in what Jesus says are the greatest commandments: "Love the Lord your God with all your heart and with all your soul and with all your strength. . . . Love your neighbor as yourself" (Mark 12:30–31 NIV).

If we use those criteria as guidelines for our letters, we will make the world better for others as well as for ourselves.

In many situations a letter, especially a certified letter, is better than a phone call or E-mail because it is evidence that you have acted as you say you have. Some people will deny having received a phone call or an E-mail, but they cannot reasonably deny having received your letter, especially if you send it by certified mail, which must be signed for when it is delivered.

CAR PROBLEMS

To manager of dealership

Rather than going "to the top" right at first, it is often advantageous to start at the bottom. Perhaps the complaint can be solved without too much work. It is a good idea to ask for a response within a reasonable length of time. Then, if nothing happens you can appeal to the next level of management.

Dear Mr. Olson,

I have enjoyed my new sports car, the Fantasy, which I purchased from your dealership this past summer. It handles very well and is, with one exception, a pleasure to drive. The one exception is a problem with the transmission that has, so far, required three visits to your service department and still has not been corrected. Although these visits have been covered under the warranty, repeated visits to correct the same problem are frustrating and time-consuming for your employees as well as for your customers, as I'm sure you know.

To eliminate this unnecessary annoyance, please decide on a plan for solving this problem and call me by the end of the week to let me know what it is. Thank you for your prompt attention.

Sincerely yours,

To manufacturer's district office

Dear District Manager,

In June of last year I purchased a new Fantasy from XYZ Motors. Within six months and 5,000 miles, a transmission problem developed. I was assured by Mr. Smith, the service department manager, that the problem would be corrected; however, I had to return the car twice for the same problem within one month after the initial visit. And despite repeated promises from Mr. Smith that my car would be completely repaired, the transmission still does not shift properly. A letter and phone call to Mr. Smith have failed to produce any response from the dealership. Please inform me by the end of this week what action you will take to fulfill the warranty on this vehicle.

Thank you.

Sincerely,

Certified letter to officer at corporate headquarters

Dear Mr. Jones,

Please read the enclosed copies of my letters to Mr. Smith of XYZ Motors and to your district office concerning the transmission problems with my Fantasy. As of this date, neither Mr. Smith nor your district representative has taken any action to repair this problem as provided for in my new car warranty.

I think you will agree that more than enough time and notice have been given for this problem to be resolved. Please inform me promptly as to what action will be taken by your office to correct this problem.

I expect to hear from you within five working days.

Sincerely,

Requesting arbitration through Better Business Bureau

Dear Mr. Olson,

The attached copies of my previous letters clearly show that the problem with the transmission in my Fantasy has not been corrected after repeated efforts on my part. I had hoped that this matter could be settled to our mutual satisfaction, but that has not been the case. I have, therefore, requested that this matter be resolved by arbitration provided by the Better Business Bureau. I have contacted them and sent them copies of my letters. They will be contacting you to discuss the situation.

I am determined to settle this matter fairly, but I am equally

The Art of Criticism

Kathie Kania

Those who oppose him he must gently instruct, in the hope that God will grant them repentance leading them to a knowledge of the truth.
— 2 TIMOTHY 2:25 NIV

CRITICISM. Sooner or later each of us will find ourselves on the giving or receiving end. I remember the end of a church service when a visitor walked up and began taking our pastor to task. We stood agape as he loudly criticized the sermon, the Scripture used, the people, and, finally, even a stained-glass Scripture lamp in the vestibule. Pastor stood quietly and listened until the fellow wound down. The man then turned and paraded himself out. We never saw him again, but his criticisms left a wake of bewilderment and pain.

By contrast, I've known some very talented criticizers. When my former boss Mr. Horsman disagreed with a method, his first words were, "Perhaps you could tell me your reason for this decision." He'd listen carefully. Sometimes he'd relent; sometimes he'd press on with his "druthers." But he never stripped away dignity.

Another supervisor, in the dietary department of a large hospital, took me aside about my leaving a butter wrapper on the cooler floor. When we were alone, he vociferated, "Someone could've slipped and fallen. Don't ever do that again."

When he was done, I thanked him. He was right. Plus he had disciplined me alone, away from curious co-workers' stares.

The best critics are those who truly want change—without alienation. Come to think of it, that's how Christ has always dealt with me, too.

Lord, if I give or take criticism today, may it be based on your "scriptural rules," and may it yield improvement and harmony.

determined to have it settled expeditiously, and my options in this regard seem to be shrinking.

If you have a suggestion for resolving this more quickly, I am open to hearing about it. But I am not interested in any stalling tactics that will further delay a resolution.

Sincerely,

Premature rusting and extended warranty

Dear Service Manager,

When I purchased my Fantasy, I paid for the 100,000-mile extended body and mechanical warranty. The manufacturer's warranty has now expired, and at 45,000 miles the rear fender panels are showing rust spots and bubbling of the paint. As specified on page 2 of the extended warranty agreement, this damage should be repaired.

I will call before the end of the week to set up an appointment.

Sincerely yours,

Certified letter to used car salesperson

Dear Mr. Burton,

The used car that I recently purchased from your dealership came with a 90-day, 3,000-mile warranty. Three weeks after purchasing the car, the transmission failed and I notified you by phone to send a tow truck to retrieve the vehicle.

It is now two weeks later and no action has been taken by you to repair the car as provided in the warranty. Failure to honor a warranty agreement is a serious breach of contract, so I expect prompt attention to this matter.

Thank you.

Sincerely,

Greedy dealer blows a sale

Dear Dealership Manager,

Last week I priced a new Fantasy at your dealership where I have purchased two other cars. After being assured that I had been offered the absolute lowest possible price, I decided to compare your offer with that of another dealership that had an identically equipped vehicle.

To my pleasant surprise, they priced the car almost six hundred dollars lower than your offer. I am disappointed that your salesman tried to take advantage of a loyal customer, but I am quite pleased with my new car and my new dealership.

I thought you would want to know why I will no longer be doing business with you.

Regretfully,

Reporting fraudulent sales tactics

Dear Consumer Advocate,

Last Saturday I called XYZ Motors to find out if the advertised price for a new Fantasy was indeed the actual selling price. After being assured that the ad was correct and complete, I visited the dealership only to find that the advertised price did not include a number of additional charges.

The dealer refused to sell the car at the advertised price without including the additional make-ready charges. Since I had specifically asked for the final price of the vehicle, it is clear to me that the dealership intentionally misrepresented the product and is guilty of deceptive advertising.

Please investigate this matter and call me at ___-___ to discuss your findings.

I look forward to hearing from you.

Sincerely yours,

A safety-related inquiry

Dear Dealership Manager,

It is my understanding that the air bag passive restraint system on my vehicle has been the subject of a recall by the manufacturer. I have not, however, received any notice that corrective repairs will be performed. I would appreciate your help in verifying if this repair should be done and if it will be covered by the manufacturer's recall program. You may reach me at ___-___.

Thank you for your help. I look forward to hearing from you.

Sincerely,

Can design flaw be corrected?

Dear Dealership Manager,

I read recently that numerous owners of Fantasies have, like myself, had a problem with water blowing through the upper door seal at highway speed. It is apparent that the seal does not fully engage due to an error in design. This is a considerable inconvenience during a rainstorm.

Can this design flaw be corrected by the dealership? Please let me know your plans for resolving this problem. You may contact me at ___-___.

I look forward to hearing from you.

Sincerely,

Good job spoiled by greasy fingers

Dear Dealership Manager,

Thank you for the prompt attention your service department gave to my car last Tuesday. I have had no further problems with the lights on the dash and was quite pleased by the courtesy and professionalism of the service manager.

I was dismayed, however, to find a glob of grease on the interior door handle of the car when I arrived home. Unfortunately, I did not find the grease until after I had smeared it all over an expensive business suit. I wish the mechanic had been as careful as were your other personnel.

I do not intend to let any other shop handle my repairs, but I do hope you will encourage your mechanics to pay greater attention to what they may consider small details. Take it from me, they are not.

Sincerely yours,

Service station complaint

Dear Mr. Floyd,

Last week I stopped at your station for gasoline. While I was filling the tank, I noticed that one of my tires needed air. When I located the air hose, the nozzle was missing. I asked the cashier at the counter if one was available. She replied that she didn't have time to look for it and suggested that I take care of my tire problems somewhere else.

I realize that you have limited services available, but my request deserved, at the least, common courtesy. I hope future visits to your business will find a more helpful attitude from your staff.

Sincerely,

Complaint to president of motor club

Dear Motor Club President,

As a member of your auto club for a number of years, I have appreciated the numerous times that courteous and professional personnel have helped me when I was stranded with a flat tire or dead battery.

My most recent experience, however, was not a pleasant one. Last week I called for help due to a dead battery. After an hour and a half wait, the tow truck arrived, and the driver proceeded to attach jumper cables to my car. In the process, he dropped one of the cables and put a deep scratch in the front left fender.

When I pointed this out, he rudely replied that it was my fault because it wouldn't have happened if I hadn't had a dead battery.

This kind of conduct is unacceptable in any situation, and it is certainly not why I pay membership dues.

I will call you this week to discuss the scratch in the fender.

Sincerely,

MEDICAL PROBLEMS

Request for insurance information

Dear Business Manager,

During my recent visit, I asked the nurse if procedures in the doctor's office were normally covered under my insurance. She was going to check for me, but was called away before I left. Would you please let me know if services of this type will be billed to my insurance or are to be paid directly to your office. I appreciate your assistance.

Thank you.

Sincerely,

Request for more information on insurance form

Dear Billing Department Manager,

I have enclosed a copy of my most recent statement showing the services and amounts that were covered under my policy for my surgery in your office. A number of items included on my statement, however, were not shown as paid. Would you please verify that you have sent the final doctor's statement. I realize that these things do take some time, but by now all charges should have been sent out. Please let me know if I can be of further help in clarifying this situation.

Thank you.

Sincerely,

Reminder that insurance form is long overdue

Dear Medical Claims Manager,

Two months ago I wrote requesting form A42 for filing miscellaneous medical claims. I have not yet received the form. Perhaps it has been lost in the mail. Please send a replacement form to me as soon as possible. Thank you for your assistance.

Sincerely,

To doctor at home when all else fails

Dear Dr. Russell,

I am sorry for writing to your home, but I don't know how else to get your attention.

For three months I have been attempting to obtain a corrected statement from your business office in order to complete my insurance filing. I realize that your office personnel have a multitude of tasks to complete, but more than sufficient time has passed for someone to fill my request. I would appreciate your immediate assistance in urging someone to complete this process without further delay.

Sincerely,

A way around that "pay now" sign

Dear Business Manager,

I realize that it is customary for you to receive payment at the time of services, but I would appreciate it if you would allow me to file a claim for my upcoming procedure with the insurance company and have them forward the payment directly to you. I will bring along the necessary form for your office to receive payment.

Thank you.

Sincerely,

Why I'm changing doctors

Dear Dr. Stone,

I have appreciated the number of times that you have assisted me with medical services. But there have been numerous times that your office staff has been unresponsive to my needs for assistance. I have experienced long delays in obtaining appointments as well as delays waiting for appointments in the office.

Recently I have found another physician who is more responsive to my needs, so I have decided not to return to your office. Please have your staff forward my medical records to . . .

Sincerely,

Explanation of partial payment

Dear Business Manager,

Please note that the enclosed check is in partial payment of your statement of April 1. I have not been able to obtain an itemized statement listing a complete record of the services that were provided. Until that list is forwarded to me, I will withhold the rest of the payment. I hope to hear from you soon regarding this matter.

Sincerely,

Complaints and compliments

Dear Business Manager,

During my recent office visit I was disappointed to learn that several items on my account have still not been billed correctly. Office paperwork must be a most difficult thing to handle with all the various companies and requirements involved, but this matter should have been resolved by now. Mrs. Simpson, however, was very helpful in looking into the matter, and I think she is an asset to your team.

Sincerely,

Complaint about rude nurse

Dear Dr. Brown,

I know that working in a clinic can be stressful and that everyone has bad days, but stress and fatigue are no excuse for unprofessional conduct.

The initial exam performed by your nurse last week was unnecessarily painful, and her questions and comments demonstrated a complete lack of sympathy for my problem and a lack of understanding of my difficulty in completing the exam.

I do not believe that you consider this kind of treatment acceptable, and I trust that it will not be tolerated. Please let me know what you have done to correct the problem before I return for my follow-up appointment next month.

Sincerely,

Compliments to hospital staff

Dear Personnel Director,

Being hospitalized is a stressful event, but the staff at Community Hospital did everything possible to make my recent stay as comfortable and painless as possible. The nurses, aides, and technicians were all so understanding and went out of their way to meet my needs. I can't tell you how comforting they were. I shall always be grateful for both their professionalism and their personal kindness. They were truly God's angels of mercy to me.

With much appreciation,

Thanks to surgeon

Dear Dr. Timmerman,

It was quite stressful to find out that I would need surgery, but I couldn't have asked for a more caring and competent doctor. Your medical skill was exceeded only by the personal concern you showed for both myself and my family before and following the surgery. I am so very grateful to you and thank the Lord for you.

With thankful regards,

Gratitude to staff of rehabilitation center

Dear Personnel Manager,

Recuperating from a difficult surgery was a long, long journey, but your staff walked each of those difficult miles with me, always encouraging me and maintaining a positive outlook. What a wonderful group of caring and kind professionals! I feel very blessed to have been served by you. My best wishes and thanks to all of you.

May God bless you with his kindness in return.

Sincerely,

Thanks to nursing home

Dear Mrs. Douglas,

Watching my mother go through the last days of a difficult illness has been painful and hard to accept, but the loving care provided by your staff has been a true source of comfort and encouragement to me. The many kind words and gentle care she received not only made her last days bearable, but helped me and our family through this difficult time as well. Thank you from all of us.

May God bless you all with an extra measure of his love.

Sincerely,

Refusing to pay bills

Dear Business Manager,

The treatment I received in your medical office resulted in complications for which I had to be hospitalized and that continue to affect my health. Due to these circumstances I am withholding payment. If you insist on trying to collect for these inadequate and damaging services, I will be forced to hire an attorney and protect myself legally.

Thank you.

Sincerely,

Complaint about bad doctor to state licensing agency

Dear Licensing Director,

I realize that no physician is perfect nor can a doctor always be one hundred percent correct in every decision. My recent treatment by Dr. Smith, however, resulted in a severe aggravation of my illness, hospitalization, and ultimately surgery. This condition could have been corrected without complications had the proper treatment been provided during my first visit to the doctor's office.

I want to file a formal complaint with your office regarding this matter. Please advise me how to proceed.

I will look forward to hearing from you.

Sincerely,

MOVING TO A NEW AREA, HOUSE, OR APARTMENT

Requesting information prior to move

Dear Chamber of Commerce,

I will be moving to your area in June and would like to know more about the services and businesses in the community. Do you have a booklet or other material available that lists services such as shopping centers, hospitals, churches, and businesses? I will appreciate whatever assistance you can offer.

Thank you.

Sincerely,

Missing item claim after move

Dear Claims Manager,

When we arrived at our new home, I did an inventory of boxes using the list provided by your driver. Almost everything is here and in good condition, but I cannot locate box 42, which contained towels and linens, and box 86, which contained dishes. According to the list, both are size D boxes. If these cannot be located, please have your claims agent call me to discuss the replacement value of these items.

Sincerely,

Damage claim

Dear Claims Manager,

When we arrived at our new home and began to unpack, we discovered that the fabric on both arms of the sofa had been torn. Since we purchased this sofa shortly before the move, I know its original value. I've attached a receipt showing the purchase price of $799. Since the damage cannot be repaired, I would like this item to be taken care of under the replacement value guarantee of our moving insurance.

I will look forward to hearing from you shortly.

Sincerely,

Inconvenience or delay claim

When stating your case, avoid using the word feel. In our culture we base too many things on the way we feel about things rather than on the way things are or ought to be. If it is necessary to express your personal opinion about the matter, use words like believe *and* think *when you are stating what ought to be done. Usually, however, your statement will be stronger if it is just that—a statement of fact—rather than just another biased opinion.*

Dear Claims Manager,

The contract for moving our furnishings called for the truck to arrive no later than June 15. The truck actually arrived on June 17, which meant that we had to stay in a motel for two days waiting for the arrival of our furniture and household items. Since this date was clearly stated in the contract, we believe it is reasonable to expect you to pay the cost of the motel stay. We have not included the cost of our meals. I hope you will agree that this is a fair way to handle the matter. I will look forward to receiving your check for the amount on the enclosed receipt.

Thank you.

Sincerely,

Seeking clarification of billing dispute

Dear Billing Manager,

In a phone conversation with Mr. Smith in your office, I notified you that the charge for special handling of the silver, china, and other valuables was to be deducted from our bill since these items were moved in the family car. Mr. Smith assured me that this charge would not be included, but I find that it has been added to the bill. Would you please verify this information with Mr. Smith and send us a corrected invoice.

Thank you.

Sincerely,

Dealing with unethical mover

Dear Mr. Gordon,

As you can see by the enclosed copies of my previous letters, we have attempted on several occasions to resolve a number of issues regarding our move last June. While I have been assured by your office that all of these matters would be taken care of, no settlement has been reached concerning the damage to our sofa, nor has a corrected bill been provided. We have been more than patient in waiting for this matter to be resolved, so we are now forwarding copies of our letters to our attorney, who will advise us as to the next step we should take.

Sincerely,

See you in court

Dear Mr. Gordon,

Since my letter of more than two weeks ago, I have had no response from your office. We have therefore instructed our attorney to proceed with a lawsuit. You will be hearing from him shortly.

We regret that this step is necessary, but your unwillingness to deal in good faith with our claims leaves us no alternative.

Sincerely,

Status report to regulatory agency

Dear State Regulator,

I have previously sent you copies of our letters to ABC Movers regarding unresolved damage claims and charges. They have refused to respond to our numerous requests to resolve the matters in dispute, and we have therefore turned the matter over to our attorney. Please let us know if we can be of further help in your investigation of this company.

Thank you.

Sincerely,

Engaging real estate agent

Dear Shirley,

Following our phone conversation of earlier this week, we have decided to use your services to locate a new home. We will be coming to Cincinnati on the eleventh of next month to look at homes. I will call to let you know what time we will arrive at your office.

Thank you for your helpful suggestions. We appreciate your service already.

Sincerely,

Thanks to real estate agent

Dear Shirley,

There were many stressful events in our move to Cincinnati, but the purchase of our home was the one oasis of calm and order in the whole process, thanks to you and your excellent staff at Home Finders. You went out of your way numerous times to find just the right house for us. We will always appreciate your friendliness, and we will recommend you to any friends who need a real estate agent.

Thanks again and best wishes!

Sincerely yours,

Notifying utility company of move

Dear Service Manager,

Please note that we will be moving from 3421A Mapleview on June 13. Please schedule the power and gas service to be discontinued on the morning of June 14. The final bill should be sent to our new address listed below.

Thank you.

Sincerely,

Notifying garbage collector of move

Dear Service Manager,

On June 13 we will be moving from 3421A Mapleview. Anything left for garbage pickup on June 15 will be placed at the curb in boxes. Please send our final bill to the address listed below.

Thank you.

Sincerely,

School records and transfers

Dear Ms. Allen,

On June 13 we will be moving to Cincinnati, Ohio, and are requesting that our children's school records be forwarded to the address below. If you need further information, please call me prior to the thirteenth.

Thank you.

Sincerely,

APARTMENT LIVING (from landlord)

Please pay rent on time

Dear Mr. DeYoung,

I realize that there are times when everyone encounters unexpected expenses that strain their budget, and I have accepted late payments in the past. But I can no longer allow you to be late with your payments.

Your rental agreement calls for payment no later than the fifth of each month. As of today, a late charge of ten dollars will be added on any payments received after the fifth of the month. Also, any payments received later than thirty days are cause for eviction.

I cannot meet the needs of all my tenants without everyone's cooperation, so I trust you will take care of this matter promptly each month.

Sincerely,

APARTMENT LIVING (from tenant)

Getting back security deposit

Dear Ms. Carder,

On June 13 we vacated the apartment at 3421A Mapleview. All items on our original move-in checklist have been completed. All areas of the apartment have been cleaned and the carpets have been vacuumed.

The rental agent and I have agreed on the amount of any deductions for damages and these have been noted on the checklist. Please forward the remainder of our deposit to the address below.

Thank you.

Sincerely,

Need an exterminator

Dear Mr. Riley,

Since moving into my apartment, I have found a number of roaches in the kitchen. Please schedule an exterminator to service this apartment as provided for in the lease agreement.

Thank you for your assistance.

Sincerely,

Trying to get things fixed

Dear Ms. Colson,

Attached is a list of items needing repair in my apartment. I've spoken with you over the phone regarding this, and I know you have a number of responsibilities to attend to. I would appreciate it, however, if these items would be taken care of as soon as possible. Some of them cause considerable inconvenience, and I look forward to having them corrected.

Thank you.

Sincerely,

Noisy tenants

Dear Ms. Roberts,

On two previous occasions I have called you regarding the excessive noise in the apartment below ours. We have tried to resolve this matter directly with the neighbors, but they have not changed their pattern of playing loud music until well past midnight several nights a week. This is a continuing violation of the lease agreement which all tenants have signed, and I hope that you will take prompt action to correct the situation.

Thank you.

Sincerely,

Noisy dog

Dear Ms. Peters,

I have spoken to the tenants down the hall regarding their dog, which they allow to run loose through the apartment complex and to bark for long periods of time every night.

I want to be as understanding as I can with my neighbors, but this is a violation of the lease agreement regarding pets, and it is a particular problem for those of us who cannot sleep at night due to this disturbance. Please discuss this matter with them as soon as possible and let me know the outcome.

Sincerely,

Emergency in rented house

Dear Mr. Joseph,

Last Friday I called to notify you that our furnace is not working. While we have had mild weather so far this fall, a change in the temperature will certainly necessitate our moving out of the house until repairs are made. In addition the water pipes will be in danger of freezing and creating considerably more damage.

Please let me know how and when you plan to resolve this problem.

Sincerely,

A way out of a lease

Dear Ms. Marvin,

Due to a change in my husband's job, we will be moving prior to the expiration of our lease. After hearing of our transfer, several people have asked if this house would be available. I have taken down their names and phone numbers as potential candidates to assume the remainder of our lease agreement.

I will call later this week to discuss these possibilities.

Sincerely,

HOME OWNERSHIP

Prodding a slow contractor into action

Dear Scott,

I realize that there are many unexpected factors that can slow down construction—bad weather, unavailability of materials, and so forth. None of these, however, seem to be a factor in the slow progress being made on our new home. Unless progress is made soon, it is probable that you will miss the completion date specified in the contract. This will cause considerable inconvenience to us.

I trust you will correct this situation so that work can move ahead promptly.

Sincerely,

Delays and poor workmanship

Dear Scott,

We are gratified to hear that you expect to complete construction by next month. This is, however, two months later than originally agreed upon in the contract. In looking at the recent work that has been done, we are not satisfied with the quality of installation in a number of areas that I have listed below. I will discuss these items with you during our next visit to the job site so we can arrive at a fair agreement to correct these items.

Sincerely,

No more money until job is done right

Dear Scott,

Since our last meeting regarding correction of problems in our new home, no repairs or modifications have been made to the numerous items listed on the "to be corrected" list. I have decided to withhold the final payment until these items have been corrected. Please note that paragraph 12 of the construction agreements calls for the "owner's approval of the completed repair list" before the final payment.

Sincerely,

Pickets will get a builder's attention

Dear Scott,

Since you have failed to reply to our previous requests for a meeting to discuss problems with construction on our project, we will do something to call your attention to the seriousness of our concerns. On Saturday we will place pickets along the public sidewalk at the entry to the job site. We hope that this public demonstration of our concern will prompt a serious discussion of the issues that need to be resolved.

Sincerely,

CONDOMINIUM LIVING

Working with the board

Dear Doug,

Although individual homeowners have some latitude regarding their property, residents of a condominium project, by necessity, must work together for the good of all concerned. Each of us has an investment at stake in this project, and it is very important that we work together to maintain both the appearance and the value of our residences.

Please meet with the board in the clubhouse at 7:30 next Friday as we make a final decision on last month's proposal. Your input is wanted and valued by the board.

Sincerely,

Clarification of rules and regulations

Dear Luke,

Since moving into Lakewood Condominiums, I have tried to follow the various rules and regulations outlined in the owner's agreement. I have noticed, however, that many of the rules are not being followed by other residents. Has there been a change in the regulations listed below?

I would appreciate it if you could clarify this situation for me.

Sincerely,

Monthly maintenance fee must be paid

Dear Michael,

As residents of a condominium community, it is necessary for all of us to contribute to the upkeep and repair of the property and recreation areas. When some members fail to pay the annual maintenance fee, important projects must be postponed or canceled. As a result, overall property values may decline.

Your payment is now overdue. Please take care of this obligation as soon as possible with the resident agent.

Sincerely,

Payment will be delayed

Dear Treasurer,

I apologize for not paying my maintenance fee sooner, but I have been unable to meet all of my obligations this month due to an extended illness and medical expenses. Please be assured that I will take care of this amount in full, plus whatever late charges are due. I trust you will understand and give me the necessary time to clear this debt.

Thank you.

Sincerely,

INSURANCE COMPANIES

New car

Dear Ken,

Next week I will take delivery on my new Fantasy from XYZ Motors. Please add this vehicle to my policy in place of the Pontiac Sunbird, which I am trading in. I have enclosed the dealer's sales order listing the VIN number and selling price.

If I can be of further help, please do not hesitate to call.

Sincerely,

Finding out options for changes in policy

Dear Ken,

It has been some time since I reviewed the provisions of my auto insurance policy. While we are transferring my coverage from my old car to the new one, perhaps we should also take time to make sure my coverage is complete. Would you send me information regarding the various optional coverages and amounts available through your company? Then we can make an appointment to discuss the options.

Thank you.

Sincerely,

Furnishing agent with claim information

Dear Dave,

Enclosed is a copy of the police report from my car accident of last week. I have also enclosed a copy of the other driver's insurance number and company as well as two estimates of repair costs from local body shops. I hope this is sufficient to settle my claim. If not, please call and I will furnish additional information.

Thank you.

Sincerely,

Substantiating a claim with photographic evidence

Dear Dave,

Please find enclosed a copy of the police report, the other driver's insurance information, and two estimates of repair for the damage to my car sustained in a collision on June 21. In addition I have enclosed four photographs of the front of the car, showing the damage. Please let me know if you need additional information to settle this claim.

Thank you.

Sincerely,

Inquiry to company requesting statement

Dear Dave,

The invoice for my policy normally arrives on the first of the month that the quarterly payment is due, but I have not received the statement. Since things do occasionally get lost in the mail, please forward a duplicate statement as soon as possible.

Thank you for your assistance.

Sincerely,

Name change notification

Dear Dave,

Earlier this month I was married, so the name listed on my auto insurance should be changed to reflect my new name as listed below.

Thank you for taking care of this detail for me.

Sincerely,

Requesting payment on life insurance policy

Dear Rob,

It has now been more than six months since my husband's death, and I have yet to receive the life insurance settlement due upon submission of the death certificate and settlement form. More than enough time has passed for this matter to have been resolved.

Please call me by the end of the week to let me know when I can expect the check.

Sincerely,

Changing beneficiary

Dear Ken,

Due to changes in my family status, I have decided to change the beneficiary listed on my life insurance policy. I have enclosed the "Change of Beneficiary" form that was included in my policy booklet, witnessed by two neutral parties as required on the form.

Sincerely,

Notification to company of intent to cash in policy

Dear Rob,

Due to changes in my family, I have decided to cash in my whole life insurance policy. I have signed the proper form and had it witnessed by two neutral parties, as required by the policy. Please send the check to the address listed below.

Thank you.

Sincerely,

Requesting change of agent

Dear Andrew,

Since my move to Cincinnati, Ohio, this month, I have not had my insurance information forwarded to an agent in this area. Please transfer my records to the nearest local office and have an agent contact me to review my coverage in the state of Ohio.

Thank you for your help.

Sincerely,

When more than one insurer pays on a claim

Dear Jeff,

Enclosed is a copy of my settlement from Interstate Insurance, Inc. for injuries sustained in an automobile collision in July.

According to my policy with your company, you will pay the balance of any amount due after my primary company pays. As I review the statement from Interstate, it appears that you will pay the amount listed in section 32.

Please send the check to the address listed below.

Thank you.

Sincerely,

Appealing nonrenewal notice

Dear Jeff,

I received notice that you will not renew my coverage for auto insurance when my present coverage expires in September.

Since I have had only one claim on this policy in the last five years, and since your portion of the liability coverage has not been settled in regard to the injuries suffered in a July collision, I request that you reconsider this decision.

I have an excellent record in paying premiums on time, and I expect you to fulfill all obligations regarding this policy during my time of need.

I look forward to hearing from you.

Sincerely,

Asking insurance commission to help speed up settlement

Dear Commissioner,

For several months I have been attempting to settle my claim for payments related to injuries that were covered under my policy with Interstate Insurance, Inc. As of this date the insurance company has refused to settle this claim and has threatened not to renew my coverage. I have enclosed copies of my policy statement and various other documents relating to this claim.

If you need more information, do not hesitate to call me at ___-___.

Sincerely,

Threatening suit if liability denied

Dear Jeff,

After several months of discussions your company has continued to refuse payment for my claims that are clearly covered under my automobile policy. Since you have refused my offer of arbitration in this matter, I see no other alternative but to refer this matter to my attorney for settlement through civil court. Please consider the additional expense that this will occasion for your company and for myself.

Let's see if this matter can be settled without further delay.

Sincerely,

Requesting arbitration from state

Dear Insurance Regulator,

As the enclosed documents clearly indicate, I have tried unsucessfully to resolve my claim with Interstate Insurance, Inc. Therefore, I am requesting your assistance in settling this matter. Please send me the necessary forms to begin the arbitration process.

Thank you.

Sincerely,

Will cancel if not treated fairly

Dear Sam,

I have never had a major claim against my automobile policy, but now find that you have not promptly settled my claim for $100 above my deductible for damage from vandalism to my car. Since this was not the result of any negligence on my part, I cannot understand your failure to promptly service a longtime customer. Unless this matter can be dealt with quickly, I will begin shopping for other policies.

I hope to hear from you soon.

Sincerely,

MISCELLANEOUS

Requesting deposit refund from store manager

Dear Store Manager,

While Christmas shopping in your store in November I put on layaway several items for myself, which I planned to pick up after Christmas.

Unexpectedly, I received three of the four items as Christmas gifts. When I explained this to your layaway clerk she told me that I was obligated to purchase all four items or lose my layaway deposit.

I apologize for the inconvenience to your store, but it seems as if it will be an added inconvenience for both of us if you require me to go through the motions of purchasing the items only to return them a few days later. Wouldn't it be more efficient and cost-effective for me to purchase only the one item I want?

Please let me know your decision soon so we can resolve this matter before I decide to avoid the hassle of shopping in your store.

Thank you very much.

Sincerely,

Never got my rebate check

Dear Rebate Manager,

I am inquiring about a rebate you offered on your video tapes. As I understood the agreement, the purchase of five (5) video tapes guarantees a rebate of three dollars ($3.00). I am enclosing a copy of the cash register receipt, the proof of purchase labels from the video tapes, and your coupon offer. As you can see, it was dated six weeks ago. I would appreciate it if you would check to see why I have not received my rebate check.

Thank you for your help.

Sincerely,

Asking newpaper's consumer column for help

Dear Consumer Helper,

In spring of this past year I hired a contractor to build a closet in my bedroom. I agreed to pay a deposit for the work to be done and he agreed to the have the project completed by May 1. Now May 1 has come and gone and he still hasn't begun the closet. Any time I try to contact him, I get a recording. Could you investigate this character? Is he a builder or just a con artist? I would like to have my closet built or my deposit returned.

Thank you for your help.

Sincerely,

Canceling door-to-door sales contract

Dear Customer Service Representative,

Last month I was contacted at my home by a salesperson from your company who wanted to sell me a year's worth of laundry detergent at a discounted price. Her demonstration of the product was very convincing, so I agreed.

After using the product for four weeks, however, I can tell you that she used either a concentrated formula or an entirely different product than the one she sold to me. The detergent I received does not get my clothes clean and it has a peculiar odor.

I am returning the unused portion of the product and requesting that my money be refunded, as promised in your "satisfaction guaranteed" policy.

Sincerely,

Home demonstration fiasco

Dear Customer Service Representative,

I was contacted by telephone for a home demonstration of your company's replacement windows. I have been considering such a purchase for some time, so I agreed to have a representative come to my home.

When he finally showed up two hours late, he smelled like alcohol, was unshaven, used foul language, and treated us rudely when we told him we were not interested.

As you probably have figured out, we did not buy the replacement windows, nor do we intend to buy them from anyone associated with your company. Please remove our name from your records and instruct your employees not to make a follow-up call.

I would also encourage you to insist that your sales representative be evaluated and treated for possible substance abuse.

Sincerely,

Poor landscaping job

Dear Sir,

Enclosed you will find two pictures: one of the breathtaking landscape you promised to create in my yard and the second of the catastrophe you actually produced. I can find no similarity. My concern now is how to correct this egregious mistake. I will expect a call from you in the near future to explain your proposal for how you might accomplish it.

Sincerely,

Protesting high utility rates

Dear Utility President,

I just received notice of your intention to raise the rates for electricity. Again! How can you even think about another rate increase so soon? What is happening to our money?

Naturally, I cannot be without electricity, so I am at your mercy, but I am not at all happy, and I want you to know it. I also intend to tell my state senator, representative, and the public utilities commission of my dissatisfaction with this decision.

Sincerely,

Dissatisfied with carpet-cleaning firm

Dear Customer Service Representative,

On January 4, I hired your company to clean my living room and dining room carpets. I specifically asked about a stain in the dining room carpet, which I was assured would come out. It did not. I want you to either come back and try again or give me a reduced price on the job. The decision is yours; I await your reply.

Sincerely,

Billing error on bank charge

Dear Bank Clerk,

I have been a customer with First Federal Bank & Trust for ten years. I have both checking and savings accounts with your bank and maintain balances that exempt me from monthly checking account charges. But on my last statement I was debitted eleven dollars ($11.00) for checking account charges. I'm sure this is a mistake.

I have enclosed a copy of my last statement, which has my account number on it. Would you look into this matter and make the appropriate adjustment?

If you have any questions, please contact me at home. The number is ___-____. Thank you.

Sincerely,

Dealing with Medicare

Dear Social Service Agent,

Thank you for providing me with the information I requested about Medicare coverage and for explaining the forms I'm to use.

Enclosed is a copy of a bill from my doctor that I thought would be covered. But it got kicked back to me for payment and I'm not sure why. Would you explain why it wasn't paid?

If you need further documentation, please contact me.

Thank you for your help.

Sincerely,

Charge account error

Dear Account Manager,

I just received my monthly invoice which showed that my $310.00 payment was applied to my Hudson's account instead of my Target account. Please transfer the entire $310.00 to the Target account, number ____-____-____, and remove any finance charges incurred by the mistake.

Thank you for taking care of this problem.

Sincerely,

Refusal to send payment on disputed invoice

Dear Customer Service Agent,

I have an invoice from your company indicating a charge for merchandise I returned. Enclosed is a copy of the cash register slip for the purchase as well as a debit slip issued to me when I returned the merchandise. Please correct your records to indicate the proper balance on my next statement and make sure that I am not charged interest on this erroneous balance.

Thank you for your cooperation.

Sincerely,

Package never delivered—delete charge

Dear Billing Clerk,

In May I ordered gardening shears from your company. Two weeks later I received a computerized postcard saying that the shears were out of stock. Now I have a bill from you for the shears I never received.

Thank you for deleting this charge from my account.

Sincerely,

21

The Caring Citizen

The church must be reminded that it is not the master or the servant of the state, but rather the conscience of the state. **MARTIN LUTHER KING, JR.**

In a public meeting I don't talk about God's will being done. Basically what I do is live out who I am, whether I'm in a public or a private setting. **BILL HARDIMAN**

Whatever makes men good Christians, makes them good citizens. **DANIEL WEBSTER**

Then Jesus said to them, "Give to Caesar what is Caesar's and to God what is God's." **MARK 12:17** NIV

*L*earning to be a responsible citizen of God's heavenly kingdom while still a citizen of this earthly kingdom is like learning to roller skate. The first time you lace up those skates and try to stand up, the left foot goes one direction and the right foot goes another and you wind up *in a contorted heap on the sidewalk. The goal of course is to get both feet working together in order to make smooth, forward progress, but it doesn't happen without practice. The same is true of the relationship between church and state. Though separate entities, they work best when they are working together, not independently; they serve society best when they complement one another rather than compete and conflict.*

There are, however, some people who consider the church to be a threat to government and, on the other side, some who consider government to be a threat to the church. The former use the phrase "separation of church and state" to prove that the U.S. Constitution requires everything religious to stay out of everything political.

The exact words of the First Amendment are:

> *Congress shall make no law respecting an establishment of religion, or prohibiting the free exercise thereof; or abridging the freedom of speech or of the press; or the right of the people peaceably to assemble, and to petition the Government for a redress of grievances.*

Sometimes our attempts to interpret information, whether the U.S. Constitution or the Bible, are indeed honest attempts to explain it. Many interpretations, however, lead to more confusion than clarification.

And certainly today the role of Christians in society is a subject that is surrounded by confusion and misunderstanding.

But the words of Scripture on this subject need little interpretation. They speak clearly and directly as to how we are to influence the moral culture of our earthly home while we await transport to our heavenly one. Knowing this will enable us to write effective letters that fulfill our responsibility and allow us to claim our rights as citizens of both kingdoms.

First, our job is not to outlaw all evil; it is to live righteously. *Jesus told us in the parable of the wheat and the weeds (tares) that the job of weeding out evil belongs to God, who will send his angels to do* *it—but not now; it will take place at the end of the age (Matthew 13:24–30; 36–43).*

Second, being right is not enough; we must be right in the right way.

> *Everyone must submit himself to the governing authorities, for there is no authority except that which God has established. The authorities that exist have been established by God. Consequently, he who rebels against the authority is rebelling against what God has instituted . . . (Romans 13:1–2 NIV).*

Sometimes we have the mistaken idea that being right entitles us to *"just a little bit"* of wrong behavior. Not true. There is never any excuse for failing to behave with kindness, love, and grace.

Third, prayer, not political activism alone, is necessary for maintaining an atmosphere of peace.

> *I urge, then, first of all, that requests, prayers, intercession and thanksgiving be made for everyone—for kings and all those in authority, that we may live peaceful and quiet lives in all godliness and holiness (1 Timothy 2:1–2 NIV).*

Our priority should be on creating and protecting a climate where godliness and holiness can grow.

Fourth, godly lives, not stricter laws or stronger arguments, will silence the ignorant, preserve morality, and win the lost.

> *Live such good lives among the pagans that, though they accuse you of doing wrong, they may see your good deeds and glorify God on the day he visits us. Submit yourselves for the Lord's sake to every authority instituted among men: whether to the king, as the supreme authority, or to governors, who are sent by him to punish those who do wrong and to commend those who do right. For it is God's will that by*

doing good you should silence the ignorant talk of foolish men. Live as free men, but do not use your freedom as a cover-up for evil; live as servants of God. Show proper respect to everyone: Love the brotherhood of believers, fear God, honor the king (1 Peter 2:12–17 NIV).

*"You **are** the salt of the earth," Jesus tells his followers; "you **are** the light of the world" (Matthew 5:13–14 NIV; emphasis added). He didn't tell us to **try to be** salt and light. We already are the preservatives of morality.*

Therefore, if the morality of a nation declines, it is because the morality of believers has declined. And if a nation moves toward darkness, it is because believers, perhaps out of fear, have moved from the visible but dangerous hilltop to a place of safety in the shadows (see Matthew 5:14–15).

Letters that shine a beam of goodness, gentleness, and love are a way to "let your light shine before men, that they may see your good deeds and praise your Father in heaven" (Matthew 5:16 NIV).

GOVERNMENT

Figuring out the correct form of address when writing to government officials can be confusing. The Appendix of this book contains a list of proper addresses and greetings.

Contacting House committee on pending bill

Dear Mr. Ehlers,

It is my understanding that you plan to hold hearings later this year to examine the needs of home-based businesses and to find ways to spur this type of entrepreneurship. One way to accomplish this, I believe, would be to stop penalizing interested parties with burdensome legislation, which drains our limited resources. I would like to volunteer my time for this important cause, either as a participant in the hearings or as a solicitor of information in my area.

Please contact me if I can be of assistance.

Sincerely,

An appeal to U.S. senator to change a law

Dear Senator Abraham,

I am contacting you in reference to the Homemaker IRA Equity Act (S. 287), which is slated for debate and vote in this year's session of Congress. Currently, a couple with a non-income-earning spouse may only contribute up to $2,250.00 per year to their individual retirement account. Dual-income couples may contribute up to $4,000.00 per year.

This is grossly unfair to those couples who choose to have one parent stay home with children or who have one partner who is unable to work outside the home for any number of reasons. These couples have the same retirement requirements as dual-earning couples.

The new bill will allow all couples, regardless of outside employment, to contribute $4,000 to a retirement fund. I encourage you to vote in favor of this legislation; please don't disappoint me.

Sincerely,

Protesting fund cutbacks to state representative

Dear Mr. Sikkema,

I am concerned about the perpetual draining of funds from our parks and recreational programs. The unsafe condition of the playgrounds and the decreased hours that our pools are open are two of my specific concerns. It's no wonder young people are roaming the streets looking for entertainment.

I would be very interested in hearing from you on this topic. What can a citizen like me do to change this situation? How can I support the Parks and Recreation Departments in my area?

Thank you for your attention.

Sincerely,

Complaint to mayor of neighboring city

Dear Mayor Wood,

I have a situation I hope you can help me with. I work in your community but I live nearby in Clinton.

My problem is this: I am required to pay city taxes in Ada since it is my place of employment, but I also pay taxes to support my own town of Clinton. I'm sure I do not use twice as many city services as other people, so I am hoping for some relief on the issue of city taxes. Are there exemptions available to citizens like me?

I will look forward to your response. Thank you for your help.

Sincerely,

Proposing new ordinance for village

Dear City Commissioners,

I own a small snowplowing business that services customers in your city, and I am concerned about the lack of odd/even parking ordinances in your community. Contractors for the city and business-men like myself are faced with randomly parked cars and trucks. It is tricky enough to navigate the narrow streets and alleyways on slip-pery surfaces, but without parking restrictions it is nearly impossible. Please don't let another season like this one come and go without addressing this problem.

Thank you for your consideration.

Sincerely,

The Privilege of Choice

Daniel Schantz

"Now look around among yourselves . . . and select seven men. . . ."
— ACTS 6:3 TLB

SOMETIMES I'm tempted not to vote, especially when my candidate seems to be the underdog. Then I remember the time my elder daughter, Teresa, ran for student council in the third grade and sent out this flyer:

> Dear Voters,
>
> I do not mean to brag about myself. I could be a good council member. I would try to solve your problems. I would work hard, and try to be fair, and I'd look over everyone's side to the problem. If you're nice to me, I'll be nice to you. I'll try to be kind. Please vote for me. I'll do my best.
>
> Teresa Schantz

She lost. And she was devastated for a while, until she began to put her loss into perspective. One day she said to me, "At least I gave my classmates a choice. That's important, isn't it, Dad?"

That started me wondering what it would be like if there were only one candidate on the slate when I went to vote. What if I had no choice?

So when I'm tempted to skip the polls, thinking, *My vote won't make any difference,* I remind myself that by voting—whether or not my candidate gets elected—I am voting for democracy.

Lord, thank you for the awesome privilege of choosing our leaders. Make me a good citizen of my present earthly home as well as my future heavenly home.

Alerting city hall to dangerous street conditions

Dear City Commissioners,

The Southeast corner of Wilson and Chambers Streets is visually blocked by an overgrown bush. Motorists cannot see past or around it once the leaves come out.

Please send a maintenance crew to trim it back or cut it down. At the very least, investigate the situation and form your own conclusions.

Thank you for rectifying this situation.

Sincerely,

Complaint to alderman clearing tree damage

Dear Alderman,

I am a resident of your ward which was hard hit by the windstorm of May 6. Many of the trees on the street side of the sidewalk were damaged and are now blocking pedestrian travel and inhibiting curbside parking.

Many freelance workers are willing to do your job of clearing the debris for a fee, but this raises a question of safety and city liability. I am requesting that you arrange to have this mess cleaned up before someone gets hurt.

Sincerely,

Requesting absentee ballot

Dear County Clerk,

I will be traveling out of state at the scheduled time of the November elections. Would you please send me an absentee ballot to use in lieu of a personal visit to the polls?

Thank you for your help.

Sincerely,

The Mother of Mother's Day

SHE was never a mother herself. She was a spinster schoolteacher. She was the daughter of a Methodist minister. At one point she was an advertising executive with a Philadelphia insurance firm. And for fifteen years she devoted her life to caring for her ailing mother.

After her mother's death in 1905, she yearned to find something to honor the memory of that good woman. And then she remembered the picnics that her mother had helped to organize back home in Grafton, West Virginia. They were called Mother's Friendship Day picnics, and mothers gathered at them in an effort to heal the hatred lingering after the Civil War. Then came the idea: Why not a national day to honor *all* mothers?

She wrote to the U.S. Patent Office and obtained a copyright for "Mother's Day." Then tirelessly she pressed her idea on governors, state legislators, congressmen, senators, clergymen, even the White House, to get "her" day recognized. At last, in 1914 President Woodrow Wilson signed a proclamation making Mother's Day a national observance.

For the rest of her life she campaigned to keep the holiday from becoming too commercialized. "Give your mother something useful," she once told a friend, "a pair of comfortable slippers, or shoes, new eyeglasses, an eiderdown if she isn't warm at night, or fix her stairs if they need fixing."

Upon her death in 1948, a wreath of forty-three carnations was placed on her grave, forty-three because that many countries celebrated Mother's Day due to her efforts. And why carnations? The carnation is the flower she suggested be worn on the holiday. It was her mother's favorite flower.

And it remains an enduring reminder of Anna M. Jarvis, the woman who gave birth to Mother's Day.

Asking U.S. representative for help

Dear Mr. Miller,

My son is graduating from Central High School in Madison, Wisconsin, next year and has expressed interest in attending the United States Military Academy. It is my understanding that he will need a recommendation from his U.S. Representative or Senator in order to apply. I have enclosed his school records, complete with courses of study, grades achieved, and extracurricular activities. Please review this material and let us know what additional information you need.

We appreciate all of your efforts on our behalf.

Sincerely,

Asking U.S. senator for help in securing a job

Dear Senator Abraham,

I am a casualty of government cutbacks. For the past twelve years I have worked in the County Clerk's office of Oakfield Township. Last December that office was closed and all employees were laid off. Since then, I have searched for appropriate employment without success.

I am asking you to help me find a job in one of the other County offices. I have enclosed my résumé and, of course, my files are open to you from my previous employment.

I look forward to hearing from you soon and thank you for your help.

Sincerely,

Requesting U.S. senator's intervention with VA

Dear Senator Abraham,

While serving as an army officer in the Korean War I sustained a back injury, which has given me trouble from time to time. In the past year, it has gotten increasingly worse. When I applied for help from the Veteran's Hospital, I was told that I am ineligible for benefits.

Clearly, this is a mistake, and so I am requesting your help to get it straightened out. Enclosed is a copy of my honorable discharge from the service. Please let me know what additional information you need. I look forward to hearing from you soon.

Sincerely,

Requesting scholarship information from state senator

Many states offer scholarships, grants, and loans to students on the basis of need and academic achievement. Your state representative or senator should be able to supply you with a list of funds available, the requirements for eligibility, and instructions for making application.

Dear Mr. Sikkema,

I am a student at Central High School with above average but not extraordinary grades. My father is dead and my mom is struggling to make ends meet at home. I want desperately to go to college, but there is no money for it. I am interested in information about scholarships, grants, or student loans available to me. Could you or someone in your office direct me as to where I might find my pathway to higher education? I will be very grateful for your assistance.

Sincerely,

Requesting home re-appraisal

Dear Assessor,

I am in the process of refinancing my home so I can invest in a rental property. I have made significant improvements on my house and would like to have it reappraised. I believe that a new appraisal will show increased equity in my home, giving me more collateral to borrow against for the rental property. Please let me know when you will be coming by.

Thank you.

Sincerely,

Assessed value of home is too high

Dear Assessor,

My home was assessed for tax purposes in May. I live in a subdivision built in the early 1960s, and many of the homes are similar in structure. Coincidentally, my next-door neighbor has a home with a floor plan identical to mine. What I do not understand is why my tax bill is six hundred dollars higher than his and five hundred dollars higher than anyone I have spoken to on my block. I believe that an error has been made on my assessment and am requesting that you check your records. Please contact me at your earliest convenience.

Thank you.

Sincerely,

Social Security—notice of retirement

Dear Sir,

This is to notify your office that I will be retiring as of April 4, 20__, and am interested in activating my Social Security benefits. I am enclosing the forms you sent me, which are dated and signed. I understand that my checks will be deposited directly into my checking account at Lakeside Trust. If you have any further questions or forms for me to complete, please contact me.

Thank you.

Sincerely,

Requesting education aid from the Veterans Administration

Dear Veterans Representative,

I served in Vietnam during the late 1960s and was honorably discharged after completing my tour of duty. I then went to work for my father and am now running the family business. Our company is in need of a technological facelift, and I am interested in financial aid to pay for education that will enable me to run the business efficiently and competitively.

Would you please send me the forms I need to apply for assistance? Thank you for your help.

Sincerely,

Requesting deferral from jury duty

Dear Jury Coordinator,

I received your letter concerning my availability for jury duty. Unfortunately, I have made vacation plans for the date specified in your letter and will be in the Bahamas. I have enclosed a copy of my ticket and itinerary for your review.

I am, of course, willing to accept another date in exchange for the one I have been assigned. Please contact me to confirm a replacement date.

Sincerely,

POLICE AND FIRE DEPARTMENTS

Requesting a stop sign

Dear Commissioners,

I live about halfway between the busy streets of Knapp and Leonard on the corner of Houser and Plymouth. At this time there is only a yield sign to control the traffic for this intersection and most motorists have quite a head of steam by this midpoint. Would you please consider upgrading the yield sign to a stop sign so that the speeders will be curtailed?

The neighborhood thanks you in advance for anything you can do.

Sincerely,

Offering to be a crossing guard

Dear Traffic Guard Coordinator,

I am a stay-at-home mother with elementary-aged children, and I am concerned about their walk to and from school as they must cross Monroe Avenue during a busy time. Would you be willing to hire me as a crossing guard at this busy intersection?

Sowing Seeds of Care and Concern

Susan Williams

Sow your seed in the morning, and at evening let not your hands be idle, for you do not know which will succeed, whether this or that, or whether both will do equally well. — ECCLESIASTES 11:6 NIV

ON the back page of our newspaper I read an article describing a bill pending in our state legislature. The ambiguous bill inadvertently could have allowed custodial parents to seek "child support" after the children had reached adulthood or even senior age. I was immediately struck by the long-term negative impact of this bill and the unreasonable financial burden it would place on the ex-spouses and their new families paying out child support. And I was astonished that it was about to become law without public discussion.

I called a number of friends about the bill. Most simply shrugged and said, "You're probably right, but what can one or two people do?" When I asked the Lord the same question, the answer he seemed to give me was this passage in Ecclesiastes.

So I immediately called my state representative's office and discovered that the vote was only forty-eight hours away. I decided to

Please contact me at home. My number is ___-____. Thank you for your consideration.

Sincerely,

Request a crossing guard for busy corner

Dear Traffic Guard Coordinator,
    I live on the northeast corner of Louis and Cleveland Streets, which

hand-deliver a letter to the committee, adding my voice to the democratic process. At least then I could say I had "sown my seed."

"You're against the bill?" an aide asked incredulously the next morning when I handed him my letter. "Why? Everybody is for it." I briefly outlined my objections. "You know, you have some valid points," the aide said. "I'll mention them to the senator."

Two days later, when I called the chairperson's office to find out how the vote had gone, I had a surprise coming. "The bill was set aside," the secretary told me. "The members decided it needed further study."

It never did make it through committee.

Although I cannot gauge how much impact I had on the process, I wonder what might have happened if I hadn't "sown my seeds" when I did. One thing is sure: The experience taught me never to hesitate to sow what I could—regardless of how small or how few my "seeds" might seem to be.

Father, show me how I can sow good seeds—in my world, my nation, my city, my neighborhood, my family—and trust you for the harvest.

is close to Bayview Elementary School. In early morning and at midafternoon the intersection is quite busy with parents dropping off and picking up their little ones. The steady parade of minivans and the speed at which the parents drive make this intersection hazardous to neighborhood children who must walk to and from school. Please consider assigning a crossing guard to assist these youngsters.

Thank you for your consideration.

Sincerely,

When help doesn't come in time

Dear Police Chief,

I am mortified by the ineffectiveness of the 911 system in our community. My urgent call for help fell on the bionic ear of an answering machine.

On September 30, I was across the alley visiting a neighbor when I saw figures moving about in my apartment. I had left a light on and could see three people ransacking my home. I immediately dialed 911, but was put on hold! By the time I actually connected with a human and explained the situation, the perpetrators had absconded with my jewelry, television, VCR, camera, and much more.

I was given no expectation of recovering any of my valuables and was advised to improve my home security. This is a sad commentary on the ability of our police force to protect its citizens.

A story like this is fascinating when it appears on a news program, but seeing it played out in my own home was frightening. Please let me know what you are doing to keep such a thing from happening again.

Sincerely,

Thanks to paramedics

Dear Paramedics Squad,

On September 20, 2003, I was struck squarely on the head by a falling forty-foot flagpole that was being relocated. Apparently, the crane operator simply lost control of it. Some kind person called 911, and the paramedics arrived within minutes. They immediately began CPR to jump start my paralyzed system, and their expert analysis of my condition saved me from severe brain damage, and quite likely extensive nerve damage to my neck and back.

I am an English professor at the University, and my mind is more valuable than any limb, but I am elated to tell you that I am expected to have a complete recovery.

Well done, and thank you.

Most sincerely,

Officer was great

Dear Police Chief,

You should know, if you don't already, what a splendid policeman you have in Officer Jones.

Two days ago I was involved in a fender bender; there was no serious damage done to either vehicle but Officer Jones made a thorough examination of the scene and spoke to each driver in a kind and professional manner. He made a special point of speaking to my young children who were in the back seat, allowing them to touch his badge and inspect his cap before he drove off in his squad car. My boys were delighted and have spoken of little else since the accident. Officer Jones's kindness did not go unnoticed by me and my family and I hope it does not go unnoticed by you.

Please give Officer Jones a salute for his exemplary handling of this situation.

Sincerely,

Officer was rude

Dear Police Chief,

On March 5, I was forcibly removed from my vehicle when I declined to undergo a roadside sobriety test. I was stopped for having a burned out tail light, but Officer Smith treated me as if I had Jimmy Hoffa in my trunk.

Ultimately, it was discovered that I was indeed sober and that Officer Smith had exercised poor judgment. I will settle for a formal apology from Officer Smith—one that includes an admission of poor judgment—and from the Police Department or I will file a grievance against both parties.

Let me know your decision. I will wait five days for your reply. If I do not have a satisfactory response by then I will register a formal complaint. We cannot expect to have law-abiding citizens if we don't have law-abiding officers.

Sincerely,

My side of the story

Dear Traffic Officer,

On February 17 I was cited for speeding. I believe, however, that the mitigating circumstances will persuade you to dismiss the citation. The driving snowstorm of the previous day had covered the speed signs, and, being unfamiliar with the area, I was unaware of the 30 mph speed limit. When the officer stopped me I was only driving 42 mph, a speed that was not excessive for the four-lane stretch of road between 36th and 44th Streets.

I would be very grateful if, after considering these circumstances, you would dismiss the violation. Please contact me with your decision.

Thank you.

Sincerely,

_____

The trend these days is to avoid the inconvenience of personal involvement. But if we are going to reclaim our communities and make them safe, caring citizens will have to find the courage to make themselves vulnerable.

Anonymous tip

Dear Detective,

I read about the vandalism at Parkside High School last Thursday night. I happened to see three boys leaving the school parking lot at 9:35 that night. They were driving a late model blue Geo, license number UKY897. I did not get a close look at the boys inside the car. I hope this information can help you.

A concerned citizen

Identifying suspect by name

Dear Detective,

I am an acquaintance of James Smith, who confided to me that he stole a car on January 23, which he then drove to Indiana and sold to a chop shop for parts. The car was a 1993 Ford Mustang, blue with gray interior.

I would prefer to stay out of court but will come forward if necessary. If you need to contact me, please do so at work. The number is ___-___.

Sincerely,

Witnessed hit-and-run accident

Dear Detective,

I was jogging on Clairmont Street Tuesday at about 6:30 A.M. when I saw a white Ford Country Squire station wagon, license number UKY654, back out of a driveway and into a parked car. After hitting the car (a green Buick Sedan, license number LKI549), the driver looked around and drove off. There was significant damage to the Buick, so I decided I should not keep this information to myself.

Please feel free to contact me concerning the accident.
Sincerely,

RADIO, TELEVISION, NEWSPAPER

The media are a frequent target of criticism for their contribution to the decline of morality in our culture. We can be "salt and light" through gentle reminders to various media sources of the importance of their commitment to uphold high moral and ethical standards.

Thanks for good music

Dear Station Manager,

I just had to write and thank you for bringing classical music to Grand Rapids. I enjoy the twenty-four-hour availability and appreciate your tasteful commercials. Rest assured that I will mention to as many of your sponsors as I frequent that I heard their advertisement on your station. Thank you again and keep up the fine work.
Sincerely,

Suggestion for talk show guest

Dear Mr. Lynch,

I have enjoyed your program for many years and admire your style and skill when you interview your guests. I would be very interested to hear a program featuring Raymond Rushing, author of the self-improvement book *You Can Do It If You Try*. Mr. Rushing cites many success stories that seem too good to be true. I would appreciate more information on this guru of self-made men, and I am confident that you, with your gift for asking insightful, probing questions, could get the real story for me and for your listeners.

Thank you for many enjoyable hours, and I hope to hear about an upcoming program with Mr. Rushing.
A faithful listener,

When your favorite DJ gets fired

Dear Station Manager,

I feel compelled to write to tell you how disappointed I am about your decision to fire Dave Kettle from the morning show on WLFT. I have enjoyed his good, clean humor and his thoughtful commentary for many years, and I will miss him immeasurably.

I plan to keep listening to WLFT in the morning, but I will have my hand on the dial to change stations if his replacement is any less gracious, less thought-provoking, or less concerned about the moral climate of our community.

Sincerely,

Criticism of listener-supported station

Dear WBLG Radio,

I have been a long time supporter of WBLG in Spring Lake. I enjoy the uninterrupted classical and jazz music, and I especially like the news broadcasts, *Morning Edition* and *All Things Considered*. But I think you have crossed the line with your acknowledgements from sponsors. You may still be a listener-supported station, but you are not commercial-free, as you are so fond of saying.

I am renewing my pledge this year but with reservations. I know money is difficult to raise, but the theatrics associated with your fund drives are wearing my patience thin. Please come up with ways to raise funds that do not contradict the professionalism and good taste of everything else you broadcast.

Sincerely,

TV soap opera is in poor taste

Dear Station Manager,

An injury I sustained recently is preventing me from returning to work for several weeks. While scanning my television options this afternoon, I was appalled by the soft pornography you are passing off as appropriate midday programming. I recognize that the twists of human behavior are intriguing to the curious viewer, but is nothing left to the imagination?

I do not condone this type of programming, and I believe it is my responsibility to do more than simply turn off the television. I hope that my written objection will make some impact on your future decisions regarding soap opera standards.

Sincerely,

Protesting poor taste in TV show

Dear Program Manager,

I am a television watcher; I enjoy relaxing in the evening in front of the tube. I tell you this so you won't think I'm an infrequent viewer with narrow opinions and low tolerance for today's programs.

Last night I watched the Monday night movie and was shocked by the nudity. It wasn't so long ago that those same scenes would have been steamy enough to qualify for an "R" rating at the movie theatre. Now they are on my home screen! I won't debate the issue of "rights" here, but what about responsibility? Soon none of us will have rights if so few of us are willing to take responsibility for the way we use them. Our young people's morals and standards have declined, and if the sex and violence on television continues they will become totally numb.

I am urging you to reconsider what you now accept as appropriate and look instead for what is good. We all need to work together to find ways to put higher morals into television programming.

Sincerely,

Criticizing children's TV program

Dear Program Manager,

My grandchild has just become interested in *Sesame Street* and I have watched it with her on many occasions. Today, the theme of the show revolved around a horrid green creature named Oscar. Oscar is rude, grumpy, and filthy, and my question is this: What is Oscar teaching impressionable two-year-olds? Do these darling children not come up with enough ideas on their own to get into trouble that we have to offer them recalcitrant role models?

You are doing a wonderful job on all other fronts, so I encourage you to reexamine Oscar's worth. If you do so honestly I believe you will want to put a lid on the trash can he calls home and keep it permanently closed.

Sincerely,

Complimenting children's TV program

Dear Program Manager,

I am a longtime supporter of public television. My older children enjoyed *Sesame Street* very much and now the baby is in love with *Barney*, the giant purple dinosaur. What a credit to you to add this program to your morning lineup. I often watch with the children, getting a refresher course on the songs and rhymes, but I like the craft ideas for children, too. I am particularly impressed with the interaction of the children with each other, and with Barney, considering the diversity in race and age.

Thank you for providing yet another quality program for my children.

Sincerely,

Request for rebuttal time

Dear Station Manager,

I was surprised by the unnecessarily sarcastic tone of your commentary against allowing a Bible club to meet in a classroom of our public high school. Your perception that "high school children would welcome any regulation that would keep them from having to humiliate themselves" was especially troubling. Many students, my own two teenagers among them, are not embarrassed or humiliated to have people know that they believe and study the Bible. Your misunderstanding of this issue needs to be addressed. Therefore I am requesting equal time on your program for a rebuttal. Please have someone contact me to schedule a time slot.

Sincerely,

To the sponsoring advertiser

Dear Advertiser,

I thoroughly enjoy the program *Homefront* and am congratulating you on your fine judgment in sponsoring this show. I am hopeful that this turn toward family entertainment catches on and we see more programs that entertain us without profanity, sex, and violence.

Please stand confident in your decision. I can speak only for myself, but I hope that I represent many when I promise to continue using your products and continue telling others about your company's civic-minded investment in moral values.

Sincerely,

TV commercial compliment

Dear Advertising Manager,

I saw your spot on *New Day* and was struck by the artistry and morality of the commercial. I even remembered the product, so I decided I should let you know how effective your ad was. I intend to buy your cola when I buy groceries next week. Keep up the good work!

Sincerely,

TV commercial complaint

Dear Program Manager,

I accept advertising as part of commercial television. But your station has more than other stations. I actually timed the advertising during *Just for Fun,* and there were nineteen minutes of programing and eleven minutes of advertising. Typically, viewers can expect a ratio of twenty-two minutes of programming and eight minutes of advertising. Is there some explanation for this other than greed? If so, I'd love to hear it.

Sincerely,

Reporting fraudulent advertising tactics

When filing a complaint against an advertiser, you may want to send a copy of your letter to the station or publication that aired or published the ad.

Dear Consumer Advocate,

This past week I visited the Vac Shack on Middle Avenue to look at the vacuum cleaner they had advertised on the radio and in the newspaper for one-half off the regular retail price. The vacuum was indeed one-half off, but the retail price was almost twice as much as the same item in a store across town. The promised "sale" was therefore not really a sale at all. This kind of deceptive advertising and sales practice warrants investigation. Please contact me if I can provide additional information. I appreciate your service to consumers in our community.

Thank you.

Sincerely,

22

Letters of Employment

Originality and the feeling of one's own dignity are achieved only through work and struggle.

FYODOR DOSTOEVSKY

Every man's task is his life-preserver.

RALPH WALDO EMERSON

Work is not the curse, but drudgery is.

HENRY WARD BEECHER

The LORD God took the man and put him in the Garden of Eden to work it and take care of it. GENESIS 2:15 NIV

Work is not a dirty word, but it has gotten a bad rap. Due to its unfortunate association with the fall of mankind, work has come to be thought of as part of the curse God placed on creation as punishment for Adam and Eve's disobedience. But that is not so. Work was part of God's original plan for creation. In fact, even before Eve was created, God gave Adam work to do in the Garden of Eden (see Genesis 2:15).

"Work," wrote Voltaire, "spares us from three great evils: boredom, vice, and need." If work did only these three things it would be of immense value. But it does much more.

First, work allows us to fulfill God's purpose for our existence. *Through work we discover the unique gifts and abilities God gives each one of us. "In work the greatest satisfaction lies—the satisfaction of stretching yourself, using your abilities and making them expand, and knowing that you have accomplished something that could have been done only by you using your unique apparatus. This is really the centre of life, and those who never orientate themselves in this direction are missing more than they ever know" (Kenneth Allsop,* Letters to His Daughter*).*

Second, work allows us to help others. *"Now to each one the manifestation of the Spirit is given for the common good" (1 Corinthians 12:7 NIV). Work that serves only one purpose (e.g., to bring home a paycheck) will be unsatisfying. Human beings need a sense that they are contributing to the good of the world. Without it, they begin asking, "Is this all there is?" To be fulfilling, work must be more than a means for self-indulgence.*

Third, work allows us to imitate God. *Contrary to popular opinion, God is not sitting in heaven twiddling his thumbs in boredom or wringing his hands in despair. He is at work, and he is at work on our behalf. "Come and see what God has done, how awesome his works in man's behalf! . . . He rules forever by his power, his eyes watch the nations. . . ." (Psalm 66:5–6 NIV). Our task, likewise, is to work on his behalf. "Whatever you do, work at it with all your heart, as working for the Lord, not for men. . . . It is the Lord Christ you are serving" (Colossians 3:23–24 NIV).*

Fourth, work helps us to understand what it means to be created in God's image (see Genesis 1:27). *When we work, and especially when we find satisfying work, we get to know God better because we get to see a part of ourselves that is like him. "A man's work* is rather the needful supplement to himself than the outcome of it" wrote Max Beerbohm in Mainly On the Air. *Much of the dissatisfaction and disillusionment in today's workplace comes from having people in positions that do not use their gifts and which, consequently, give them no sense of purpose or meaning.*

Therefore, whether you are writing letters in regard to finding work for yourself, hiring someone to work for you, or recommending a person to work for someone else, keep in mind the concept of giftedness. When a person's work is matched with his or her gifts and abilities, it is a dynamic combination. Also keep in mind the four things work accomplishes in our lives. The best types of work not only use our gifts; they also give us purpose.

LETTERS OF RECOMMENDATION

How to give one

There are four steps to providing a recommendation. First, establish your relationship with the individual you are recommending. Second, list his or her credentials, professional honors, achievements, educational and personal accomplishments. Third, describe the person's positive character traits. Finally, explain why you believe the person is a good candidate for the specific job.

To Whom it May Concern:

Mary Conner worked for me for twelve years at ABC Co. in Grand Rapids, Michigan. She does wonderful work, completes assignments ahead of deadlines, and is accurate and attentive to details. She works well with others and missed only four days of work in all the time she worked here. Mary genuinely cares about others but never loses her sense of professionalism.

I highly recommend her for the position you have open. I was sorry to lose her and would welcome her back anytime.

I wish her continued good luck in her chosen field.

Sincerely,

If you are asked for a recommendation as an employer about an employee, past or present, be aware of the legalities. You may provide the dates of employment, the title of the job the person held (but no job description), and whether or not the person would be considered for rehire in the same position. To avoid a lawsuit, do not state or infer anything negative.

Dear Mr. Hausman,

In response to your request for employment verification regarding Carla Front, I can confirm that Carla worked here as a customer service representative from June 3, 1981, until September 26, 1989. Carla would be eligible for rehire at our corporation. It is not our policy to release additional information about any present or former employees.

Sincerely,

How to get one

One way to get a good letter of recommendation is to make specific suggestions as to what the letter should include. Most people will welcome the help if you offer it tactfully. By reminding the person of your interests, abilities, and accomplishments you can almost write the letter yourself. Be as specific as you can about the job for which you are applying.

Dear Mr. Hillman,

As you know, I have been interested in the publishing profession ever since you started telling me stories about your adventures as an acquisitions editor. Now that I have finished my bachelor's degree in English, I am ready to begin pursuing my dream.

Alpha Publishing House is looking for a copy editor, and I see that as an opportunity to get my foot in the door. While in college I worked as a proofreader for a local typesetting company, so I am familiar with proofreading and copy editing symbols as well as with *The Chicago Manual of Style*. I know I can do the job well if I can just convince them to hire me. And that brings me to the point of this letter. I am wondering if you would be willing to write a letter of recommendation for me. You know me well enough and have worked with me long enough to know that books are my passion. You also know that I can pay close attention to details, am good at following through on assignments, get along well with people, have an insatiable appetite for learning, know how to compromise and show appreciation, and don't take it personally when I don't get my way. From what you've told me, these are all important qualities in the publishing profession.

You have been a great mentor and encourager for me, and I hope your belief in my abilities will cause you to say yes to my request.

Thanks for everything you've done for me over the years.

Sincerely,

Character references

Character references are required by many employers and especially by those in the helping professions such as social work, counseling, and ministry. When writing a character reference first establish your relationship with the applicant. Then illustrate or describe his or her values and morals. Close with a strong personal statement confirming your faith in the person's ability.

Dear Sir or Madam,

It is my good fortune to have John Osmer as my neighbor. He is cooperative and friendly, always ready with an extra pair of hands and a smile. He is comfortable with young and old alike—from the children across the street to the older folks down the block. I believe John will make an excellent counselor. He has always had a soft spot in his heart for those in need and an attentive ear for those who just need someone to listen.

Sincerely,

APPLYING FOR A JOB

Cover letter for a résumé

Dear Mr. Carr,

I am a recent graduate of Michigan University, with a B.A. in Sales and Management, and I am interested in securing employment in that field. I have enclosed my résumé for your examination, and I can be reached by telephone daily after 4:00 P.M. at ___-___-____. I look forward to hearing from you.

Sincerely,

Applying after being relocated

Dear Ms. Roberts,

I have recently moved to the Cleveland area and am seeking employment as a graphic designer. I held such a position for twelve years at ABC Advertising Agency in Toledo. My résumé and letters of recommendation are enclosed for your review. If you have any openings that fit my qualifications, please contact me at ___-___-____.

Sincerely,

Applying after being out of work

Dear Mr. DeVries,

I am seeking employment as a sales representative in the Western Michigan area. I have extensive experience in inside and outside sales, am known for my ability to develop leads, and have a good reputation for following up all prospects and new customers.

Due to budget cutbacks at Standard Furnishings, I have been

Weaving Threads of Love into Our Work

Marilyn Morgan Helleberg

Love covereth all. . . . — PROVERBS 10:12 KJV

WHEN my daughter was eleven years old, I became pregnant with our third child. Karen, not quite ready to give up dolls, was euphoric at the thought of having a real live baby in the house. Early in my pregnancy, she started knitting a baby blanket. Hours and hours and hours went into that green blanket. After school and on Saturdays, instead of playing with friends, Karen sat knitting, every stitch an act of love. Sometimes she got very frustrated and cried when she'd drop stitches or her yarn would unravel. But finally it was finished, and her grandmother crocheted around its edges. To tell you the truth, it was pretty awful—it had uneven stitches, big gaps here and there, and knots the size of peas—but to Karen it was beautiful because of the invisible yarn of love she'd knit into it.

Then my friends had a baby shower for me, and among the gifts were several lovely, soft, perfectly woven blankets. After we brought baby John home, I placed him in his crib with all his blankets. But there was one he wouldn't let go of—a very imperfect green one with uneven stitches, gaps, and knots. I believe that John chose Karen's blanket because the love with which it was made drew him in.

The lesson I learned from my daughter remains with me. Whenever I have work to do I try to remember to weave into it as much love as I can. It's the invisible yarn that makes the difference!

Creator God, may I weave your yarn of love into my work today.

"reorganized" out of my position after seventeen years of employment. As the enclosed résumé indicates, I have much to offer your company. Please contact me at ___-___-____ to set up an interview.

Thank you for your consideration.

Sincerely,

Answering ad for a teacher

Dear Mr. Lever,

I am responding to your advertisement in the classifieds on Sunday, June 4, for a teacher in elementary education. As the enclosed résumé indicates, I have many years of experience and have been recognized on several occasions for my innovative teaching skills. What my résumé does not reveal is my great love and concern for children. I have heard many glowing reports about your ability to inspire and motivate students and teachers alike, and I would be delighted to join your team.

To contact me for an interview, call me after 5:00 at ___-___-____.

Thank you for your consideration.

Sincerely,

Answering ad for a computer programmer

Dear Mr. Craig,

I am well aware that in the fast-changing world of computer technology it is essential to keep up with the latest innovations. I have done this through hands-on experience, additional classroom instruction beyond my degree program, and independent reading. I am comfortable with all forms of IBM hardware, PCs up to and including System 36, and the companion software. For more details about my qualifications and experience please review my enclosed résumé. I am very interested in speaking with you about this position and may be reached at ___-___-____ after 5:00 P.M. Thank you.

Sincerely,

Answering ad for a buyer trainee

Dear Mr. Peters,

I am writing to request an interview for the position of buyer trainee with your company. I have enclosed my résumé for your review. My qualifications seem to match exactly those you are hoping to find. Please contact me for an interview at the number listed above. I look forward to discussing the position with you.

Sincerely,

Cold call application for a secretary

Dear Sir or Madam,

I am interested in a position as a secretary with your company. It is well known that you are one of the area's best employers, and it has been my goal to work for you for as long as I can remember. As you can see by the enclosed résumé, I have worked hard to learn about your industry and to make myself valuable to your company. I would consider it a privilege to join your firm.

After reviewing my résumé, you may contact me for an interview by calling ___-___-___.

Thank you for your consideration.

Sincerely,

Cold call application for a retail manager

Dear Mr. Green,

I am an assistant manager at the Hillsdale Mall in Madison. I enjoy my employment there but see few opportunities for advancement. I believe, therefore, that it is time for me to move on, and I am interested in a management position with you. My two years of employment have allowed me to gain experience in all forms of management, decision making, scheduling, and displays. Please take the time to review the enclosed résumé. To contact me for an interview, you may call ___-___-____.

Thank you for your time.

Sincerely,

Cover letters for job applications

Dear Mr. Jackson,

Enclosed is an application for employment which Ms. Jones in your employment office instructed me to fill out and return to you. I believe my interest and enthusiasm for your type of work will more than compensate for what may appear to be my lack of experience. I am a reliable, hard worker and would appreciate the opportunity to prove it. I hope to hear from you soon.

Thank you very much.

Sincerely,

Interested in job suggested by a present employee

Dear Ms. Arnold,

It is my understanding that you have a position open at your Wyoming office to replace Carol Jones. Carol is an acquaintance of mine, and she encouraged me to inquire about it. I am enclosing my résumé for your review. To set up an interview you may reach me during the day at the office (___-___-____) or in the evening at home (___-___-____). I look forward to hearing from you.

Sincerely,

Accepting offer to be interviewed

Dear Ms. Arnold,

Thank you for the opportunity of interviewing for the position of customer service representative. I am looking forward to meeting with

So Simple That It's Profound

Penney Schwab

And whatever you do, whether in word or deed, do it all in the name of the Lord Jesus. . . .
— COLOSSIANS 3:17 NIV

IN a course on business ethics the instructor taught us the principles of the Four-Way Test, originated in the 1930s by Herbert J. Taylor. It consists of four simple questions:

1. Is it the truth?
2. Is it fair to all concerned?
3. Will it build goodwill and better friendships?
4. Will it be beneficial to all concerned?

The questions seemed too simple. Business today is sophisticated and complicated. I soon forgot about the Four-Way Test.

It wasn't long, however, before I started reading about big shake-ups on Wall Street. Tax fraud and embezzlement—is it the truth? Insider trading and illegal profits—is it fair to all concerned? Hostile takeovers leading to the bankruptcy of large companies—will it build goodwill and be beneficial to all concerned? The executives involved in these cases were skilled business people. But now they're paying penalties and putting hundreds of employees out of work—because they ignored a few simple, seemingly trite ethical guidelines.

I am no business tycoon, but I do work with others: in an office; at a church meeting; with my family at home. Today, and every day, I want to put in an honest day's work, one that supports the well-being of the group, that builds up the other members and compliments their abilities, that says to each, "You're important to me."

Heavenly Father, help me to put your principles of truth and love into action today.

you to discuss the responsibilities of the position and my qualifications for filling it. I will see you in your office at 8:30 A.M. on August 23.

Sincerely,

Thank you for recommendation

Dear Carol,

Thank you for suggesting that I contact Ms. Arnold about the job in customer service. I have an interview with her later this month. Also, thank you for the verbal recommendation you gave to her on my behalf. I owe you. Thanks again.

Your friend,

Thank you for interview

Dear Ms. Arnold,

Thank you for the opportunity to discuss with you my qualifications for the position of customer service representative. I enjoyed the interview and believe that I could perform the duties as you described them in an enthusiastic and efficient manner. Thank you for considering me for the position, and I hope to hear from you soon.

Sincerely,

Accepting job offer

Dear Ms. Arnold,

Thank you for offering me the position of customer service representative in your Wyoming office. I am delighted and excited to accept, and I look forward to proving that your confidence in me is not misplaced. I will report to work at 8:00 A.M. on Monday, September 15.

Sincerely,

Rejecting job offer

Dear Ms. Brown,

Thank you for the confidence you have expressed in me by offering me the position of Administrative Assistant. I am sorry to report that I am unable to accept your offer. Please accept my apology for the inconvenience this causes you.

Sincerely,

Resignation

Dear Mr. Hill,

Please accept my resignation as Quality Control Inspector effective July 24. I have decided to pursue other career opportunities. Thank you for the valuable experience I have gained during my years of employment with you.

Sincerely,

GETTING A BETTER JOB

Cover letter accompanying résumé

Dear Mr. Madison,

I am no stranger to work. In fact, it has been an important part of my life since high school. I worked my way through college as a retail sales clerk and am now proud to say that I have completed my coursework, received my B.A., and am ready to enter the professional work force. I am specifically interested in the field of Human Resources.

Please review my enclosed résumé and call me for an interview. I can be reached at ___-___-____ after 5:00 P.M. most evenings. Thank you for your consideration.

Sincerely,

Letter of application for sales position

Dear Sir or Madam,

I am responding to your classified advertisement for a sales representative. I have been a sales associate in an office supply store for two years and am familiar with most PCs, fax machines, and small copy machines. I believe I am now ready for a position in outside sales, and your need for someone to sell copy machines to businesses sounds like a perfect match. I can be contacted at ___-___-____ after 5:30 P.M. Thank you for your consideration.

Sincerely,

Homemaker's return to job market

Dear Sir or Madam,

I have decided to return to the work force after having been home with my children for fifteen years. In that time I have learned to manage my time and limited resources very well. I can work with difficult people and situations and I am very responsible.

Before taking on my full-time job as a mom, I was a copywriter for an ad agency and plan to pursue that line of work again. Although the technology has changed, the basics of writing and creating have not. I am computer literate and have learned several word processing programs. I believe, therefore, that I am now ready for full-time employment. I can be reached for an interview at ___-____ during the day. I look forward to hearing from you.

Sincerely,

Follow-up letter to employer

If you send a résumé to a potential employer and hear nothing for several weeks, write a gracious follow-up letter stating that you are still interested in the position. Avoid words or phrases that sound impatient, accusing, or condescending. A "you owe me something" letter probably will get you nothing except rejection.

Dear Mr. James,

I am writing to let you know that I am still interested in the position of marketing analyst and to ask if it is still open and if I am a viable candidate for the job.

I sent my application and résumé to you on February 5, so you should have it by now. If you have any questions about it (or if you have no record of receiving it), I can be reached at ___-___ after 6:00 P.M. most evenings.

Thank you for your consideration.

Sincerely,

Follow-up letter to interviewer

Dear Mr. Kole,

Thank you for the interview last Tuesday. I enjoyed meeting you and hearing about the position you have open. As we discussed during the interview, I am working in a related field and would be able to make the transition to this opportunity easily. I look forward to hearing from you soon.

Sincerely,

Using network of fraternity brothers

Dear Stan,

Can you believe it? My company is reorganizing again. This time I think there's a good chance that my position will be eliminated, so I'm trying to prepare for the inevitable. I'm contacting you to ask if you would keep your eyes and ears open for job opportunities in your area that might suit my skills. My degree is in industrial psychology, and I've been in various management positions for the past seven years. Naturally, I'd be willing to relocate for the right job. Call me collect with anything you find. It will be good to see you again if I land an interview in your area.

Thanks for anything you can do for me.

Please give my greetings to Sara and your two boys. I hope you are all well.

Your fraternity brother
Class of '74,

Using network of professional associates

Dear Jill,

I'm sure you're not surprised to find my résumé in your mail. I have been actively looking for a new job for a couple months. Even though the two of us are not in the same field I am hoping that you could contact me with a few leads I could follow up on. I am looking for a sales position and am willing to be flexible about salary as long as the health insurance benefits are good. Thanks a lot. I look forward to hearing from you.

Sincerely,

Using network of industry colleagues

Dear Ted,

You have been a good customer of mine for many years, and during that time I have observed your management style and seen your company grow with very little employee turnover. My own company seems to have lost sight of the value of its employees, and I'm beginning to realize that my days here may be numbered despite my many years of faithful, dependable service. You know my reputation and style; I'm loyal and trustworthy. I'm asking you to keep me in mind as opportunities become available in your company. I'm enclosing my résumé and references. Naturally, I'd appreciate it if you could keep this confidential. Thank you.

Sincerely,

Finding Joy in Work

Daniel Schantz

He should make his soul enjoy good in his labor. . . .

— ECCLESIASTES 2:24 KJV

THROUGHOUT Ecclesiastes, the writer moans about the futility of work, but he also admits to the great good in laboring. Sometimes I, too, have mixed feelings about the work I do.

"I'm going to quit teaching," I announced one day to my wife as I dropped my briefcase to the floor. "I hate it. I detest it. It's miserable, and I'm not going back."

My wife listened patiently to my dirge of complaints about students, staff, and procedures. Then in a sweet voice she said, "You do like some of your students, don't you?"

"Well, yes, some of them, but—"

"And you always seem to enjoy studying for your classes. I hear you whistling."

I nod. "But some of the people I have to work with!"

"But you like Richard, and Larry, and Patti, and Cheryl—"

I mumble my agreement.

"And you love eating in the cafeteria with students. You tell me all the funny things they do and say. And you have fun in the classroom, too. Remember that terrific discussion you had last week?" She pauses before driving in the final nail of her argument. "And I know one thing you like a lot—your paycheck!"

Lord, sometimes I'm awfully hard to please and it's hard to enjoy the good in my labor. Teach me to acknowledge the whole truth about my work—especially on those days when I'd rather be singing the blues.

Using network of former classmates

Dear Sarah,

Remember all the grumbling we did in college about unreasonable professors making impossible demands? Especially Dr. Griffith? Well, I don't know about you, but I'm finding out that life itself is more demanding than any college professor I had.

Right now I'm facing a particularly demanding problem, and I'm hoping you can help me. I have been trying for some time to make a career out of my freelance writing, but I am in a dry period now. Do you know of anyone who could take advantage of my creative writing or word processing skills? I'd appreciate any leads you could provide. I look forward to hearing from you soon.

Sincerely,

Special situations

Dear Elizabeth,

Before any more time passes, I want to let you know what a pleasure it has been to work with you on this project. I know that you took a big risk in hiring us for this assignment as we had never worked for you before. I also know that there were times along the way when you thought you had made a bad decision. But even in the middle of your most serious doubts and deepest fears you never allowed your personal concerns to crowd out your kindness. Your prodding was always gentle, your probing questions were always gracious, and you always managed to express yourself calmly, even when I had reasons to believe you were not feeling that way at all. In addition, your communication was always clear, your help always timely, and your suggestions always insightful.

As we near the end of the project I am sensing that your fears have been alleviated (at least somewhat) and that you are beginning to regain your initial enthusiasm. I hope that this momentum carries all the way to the end, that you and your colleagues are all pleased with the final result, and that you will soon be able to reap some rewards of your willingness to take a risk.

With respect and gratitude,

Thanks for help getting a job

Dear Susan,

A big thank you for telling me about the job posting at your office for a legal secretary. I met with Mr. Knowles and Mr. McKenna and they offered me the job! I started last week, and I love the people and the work. I can't thank you enough for your help.

Your friend,

Congratulations on promotion

Dear Shirley,

I just heard the great news. Congratulations on your promotion! I'm glad someone has recognized your talent and dedication. I can think of no one who deserves this more. Enjoy the new office, and let's get together soon.

Your friend,

Congratulations on retirement

Dear Ken,

Congratulations on your retirement. Have you decided yet whether to enjoy a few weeks of leisure or to launch right into all the projects you've had on hold? I hope this means that I'll see a bit more of you, too. Call me soon and let's make plans for lunch and a round or two of golf.

Your friend,

LETTERS WRITTEN BY EMPLOYERS

Requesting data from references

To Whom it May Concern:

Carla Front has listed you as her employer from June 1981 until September 1989. Please confirm the dates of her employment and add any information that will help us determine Carla's future employment with us. Thank you for your cooperation.

Sincerely,

Requesting data from applicants

Dear Mr. Stone,

I have reviewed your résumé and am impressed by what I see. Before proceeding, however, I need to verify the information you listed in the education section. Please submit a copy of your high school diploma and your college transcripts to my office. This will allow me to expedite the interviewing process.

Thank you for your cooperation.

Sincerely,

Tentatively accepting applicant

Dear Carla,

I am pleased to inform you that NJY, Inc. is prepared to offer you the position of data entry supervisor contingent on your willingness to supply income tax statements for the past two years. It is the policy of our company to review such documents before making permanent placement.

Please contact me at your earliest convenience. We are interested in getting you started as soon as possible.

Sincerely,

Invitation to interview

Dear Janet,

I am pleased to inform you that you have been selected as one of a number of candidates to interview for the position of secretary to our president, Don Deal. Your interview will be with Sandy Caldwell on Tuesday, August 5, at 9:15 A.M. Please call Sandy at ___-___-___ to confirm your appointment with her.

Sincerely,

Rejecting tentatively accepted applicant

Dear Ms. Thacher,

I am sorry to inform you that the position for which you interviewed has been put on hold due to budgeting constraints. Therefore, we are unable to offer you a position at this time. We will, however, keep your application on file and contact you if another position becomes available.

Sincerely,

Rejecting applicant who responded to newspaper ad

Dear Connie,

Thank you for responding to our advertisement for media relations director at ABC Co. That position has now been filled, but your résumé will be kept on file for future consideration. Should a suitable opportunity develop soon, we will contact you to determine your interest and availability. We wish you success in your search for meaningful employment.

Sincerely,

Rejecting applicant, position filled

Dear Susan,

Thank you for expressing your interest in working for our company as a direct mail supervisor. Unfortunately, that position has been filled. We will, however, retain your résumé for future consideration.

We wish you success as you continue your search for suitable employment.

Sincerely,

Rejecting unqualified applicant

Dear Martha,

Thank you for sending your résumé for my consideration. The variety revealed in your employment history is impressive; however, we have decided to concentrate on candidates whose qualifications more precisely meet the requirements of the position. We will keep your résumé on file and contact you if a more suitable opportunity becomes available.

We wish you success in your employment search.

Sincerely,

Accepting applicant

Dear Karen,

I am pleased to offer you the position as marketing director. Please report to Sam Black at corporate headquarters on Tuesday, August 8, at 8:00 A.M. for an orientation meeting followed by a tour of the facility.

We hope your tenure with our company will be professionally and personally rewarding.

Sincerely,

Welcome to new employee

Dear Susan,

Welcome aboard! We are happy to have you as part of our team, and we wish you success and enjoyment in your career. We believe that

A Change of Attitude to One of Gratitude

Mary Jane Clark

With gratitude in your hearts to God.   — COLOSSIANS 3:16 NIV

IT was one of South Carolina's sultry summer days, and the heat was oppressive even in the late afternoon as my husband, Harry, and I walked the few blocks from our home to church. After a frustrating day at the computer, I wasn't feeling very worshipful. I had struggled with some writing, grappling for the ideas and the right words to express them. Now I complained to Harry that my work had become drudgery. I was not in a good mood. We walked along slowly, exchanging brief greetings with the people we passed on the street.

"A long, hard day?" Harry remarked to a young man coming toward us. He was obviously tired and sweaty, his face and overalls paint-splattered and dirty.

In a surprising departure from the usual mumbled greetings between strangers, this man stopped, looked directly at us, and replied, "It's been a long, hot one. But I thank God for the work. Some people I know are goin' hungry—can't find work."

His words rang in my ears. I had spent the day working in our sunny, air-conditioned, office-at-home on the third floor of our charming Charleston house. I had muttered and complained my way through the day. Yes, I had talked to the Lord about my work that morning, but not with words of gratitude or thanksgiving. "Make it easy, Lord," I had prayed. But I'll not do that again. I will try instead to make this my prayer . . .

Lord, thank you for the work you give me to do each day.

your success as an employee is a key to our success as a company, so be assured that we will help you achieve your own goals and objectives as well as our own.

We hope your work here will be rewarding and that you will continue with us for a long time.

Sincerely,

Preparation of performance evaluation

MEMO TO: Lisa Wells
FROM: Sharon Cramer

The calendar has made another full cycle and it's time once again for your annual performance review. Please complete the two enclosed forms (use one to evaluate your own performance and one to evaluate mine) and bring them with you to my office next Tuesday at 9:15 A.M. I am filling out the same two forms. They will help us compare our assessments of each other, determine if there are areas that need improvement, and figure out a strategy for increased efficiency as well as personal satisfaction.

Thanks for taking the time to do this, Lisa. I believe this is a valuable exercise.

See you on Tuesday,

Job performance review

MEMO TO: Ron Nelson
FROM: Jim Thomas

Once again the calendar has rolled around and it is time for your annual performance review. As usual, I will meet with you to discuss your performance over the past twelve months. The review will cover the following areas: customer service; work habits; administrative abilities; and business development.

Plan to spend an hour with me on August 9 at 8:00 A.M.

See you on Wednesday,

Recommendation for promotion

TO: Richard Black, Human Resources
FROM: Kelly Homer, Shift Supervisor

I am writing to suggest that Suzanne Reynolds be promoted to the position left open by the retirement of George Waldorf. Suzanne has excellent interpersonal and communication skills; her work habits are used as a model for other employees; and her organizational skills are way above average. She is motivated and dedicated to our company's success. I'm sure you'll be pleased with her performance if you give her the oppportunity to fulfill her potential.

Congratulations on promotion

Dear Suzanne,

I am pleased to inform you that you have been chosen to replace George Waldorf as customer service supervisor. Your work history speaks for itself and you come highly recommended by previous department heads. I wish you much success in your new position.

Sincerely,

Notice of promotion

TO: Staff members of NBV, Inc.
FROM: Richard Black, Human Resources Vice President

Please join me in congratulating Suzanne Reynolds as she becomes our new customer service supervisor. Suzanne will replace George Waldorf as of January 1. She comes to the department with many years experience and a high level of enthusiasm for and commitment to customer service.

Please welcome her warmly and make her feel at home, as each of you does so well.

Sincerely,

Reprimand

Dear Melissa,

As a follow-up to our recent discussions, I am writing this formal letter of reprimand to address your ongoing tardiness and absenteeism. If you should receive three letters of reprimand in the course of one year, your employment will be terminated. As your supervisor, I would be sorry to lose you, so please make every effort to remedy this problem.

Sincerely,

Termination warning

Dear Steve,

A complaint filed against you by a co-worker accuses you of drinking while on duty as a crane operator. We will fully investigate this complaint before taking any action, but I must advise you that this is a serious infraction of company policy that is cause for immediate termination.

I am interested in hearing about this incident from you. Please contact my office for an appointment to explore this matter.

Sincerely,

Termination

Dear Ms. Jordon,

I regret to inform you that your position has been eliminated as of July 1. This is not a reflection of your work performance and you are welcome to reapply for other positions that become available. At this time, however, there are no others to offer you.

Please read carefully the information in the attached packet. It outlines the services and benefits we will continue to provide as you start your search for new employment.

We are sincerely sorry about the distress and inconvenience this causes you.

Best wishes,

Accepting resignation

Dear Nick,

I received your letter of resignation on June 5 and am confirming our acceptance of it as of June 14. We wish you well in your next venture. It has been good to have you on staff for the past five years.

Sincerely,

Notice of employee leaving

Dear Customer Service Department,

I regret to inform you that Cindy Jenkins will be leaving our company as of June 5 to accept a position with another employer. Even though we will miss Cindy's sense of humor and her genuine care and concern for all of her co-workers, I hope you will join me in wishing her continued success.

Sincerely,

Retirement congratulations

TO: All employees
FROM: Russ Ward

Please help me congratulate Harvey Jones as he completes thirty years as a valued employee of our company. Harvey started as a mail clerk and, through hard work and determination, eventually became operations manager, a position he has held for the past nine years. Harvey has been a fine example to all of us, and our memories of his sound thinking, fair-mindedness, and integrity will help us navigate our company safely into the uncertain waters of the future.

Congratulations, Harvey! Enjoy your retirement.

Best wishes,

LETTERS WRITTEN BY A THIRD PARTY

Recommending an applicant

Dear Karen,

I have a woman working in my department from one of the local temp agencies, and it is my understanding that she will be leaving as soon as she finds a permanent position somewhere. She is punctual, hard-working, efficient, and pleasant, so I believe it would be in our company's best interest to try to place her in a permanent position while we have the opportunity. Her name is Mary Homes, and she can be reached at extension 456 for the next two weeks.

Thanks for looking into this possibility.

Sincerely,

Rejecting an applicant recommended by a third party

Dear Mary,

Thank you for interviewing with me for a position on our clerical support staff. You came highly recommended by Judy Young, and your clerical skills are top notch. Unfortunately, we have no openings at this time. I will keep your application on file should an opening occur in the near future.

Sincerely,

Acknowledging a recommendation

Dear Judy,

Thank you for suggesting that I interview Mary Homes for a permanent position with our company. I have met with Mary, and she is indeed the kind of person we like to hire. Although I do not have a position for her at this time, I will keep her application on file and contact her when an appropriate opening occurs.

Sincerely,

Appendix

The Nuts and Bolts of Writing and Sending Letters

This appendix contains direction and information on some of the more mundane aspects of writing letters, like what your letters should look like on the page, what kind of closing phrases to use, how you should address important and not-so-important personages, and where you can find zip code information. We've also included the two-letter abbreviations for all fifty states plus dependencies, so you'll always be able to check whether MI means Mississippi or Michigan!

THE FORM OF LETTERS

Formal letters

There used to be just one acceptable way to type formal letters. The date was off to the right, under the letterhead, or, if you were using plain paper, under your own address. Then you skipped one or several lines, depending on how long the letter was going to be, typed the recipient's name and address flush left, skipped one line to the salutation, and then typed the letter single spaced, indenting each paragraph. The closing phrase, "Sincerely yours" or the equivalent, was then aligned on the right with the date. Four spaces under that you typed your name, and on the next line your position, if that information did not appear on the letterhead. (See Figure 1.)

Today, however, there are other equally valid formats. Sometimes the letterhead dictates the choice as to where, for instance, you place the date, your closing, and your signature. Other times your own preference is the determining factor in the placement of such elements.

You can write the letter with every element flush left, from date to signature, including the beginning of each paragraph. In that case, you would double space between paragraphs. (See Figure 2.)

Other writers like an extra spacious paragraph indentation, sometimes aligning it with the end of the salutation.

Dear Mr. Johnson,

            _____

_____

_____.

In this style, all following paragraphs should have the same beginning indentation.

The most important things are that your letter looks good on the page, is accurately and neatly typed, and is consistent in form from beginning to end.

If your letter is long enough to require a second page, type it on a piece of plain stationery and label it with the date, the page number, and the name of the person to whom you are writing. This not only is a courtesy to the recipient, but also a benefit to you if the pages of your copy become separated. Here are two samples:

Mr. Edward James   —Page 2—   June 22, 2003

or

Mr. Edward James — 2   June 22, 2003

The body of the second page should follow the same format you have established on your first page.

Punctuation, salutation, and closing

In the past, the salutation was followed by a colon in formal letters. While this is still common, the use of a comma is becoming more prevalent. In personal letters, a comma is fine. The salutation in a formal letter always uses the person's title—Mr., Mrs., Miss (or more often Ms.), Dr., Professor—followed by the last name. In the United States, a period always follows an abbreviated title. In Great Britain, however, the period is omitted. See pages 424–429 for the correct way to address members of the clergy and people in high office. If you are writing to someone you know personally, it is fine to use his or her first name.

Dr. Kenneth Earl

25 Whichever Street

Anyplace, NJ, 00055

Dear Ken,

The closing greeting is usually followed by a comma because it acts as a descriptive adjective for your name, telling the person your frame of mind in writing the letter. "Yours truly," "Sincerely yours," "Cordially yours," "With all best wishes," "Your friend in Christ," "In Christian love." These phrases are abbreviations of much longer closing greetings that were standard in the seventeenth and eighteenth centuries, when letter writing was a real art: "I remain your sincere and devoted admirer, _____." "I am your cordial and devoted friend in Christ, _____." "Your most affectionate Old Friend, and most humble Servant," wrote Isaak Walton at the end of a letter to the Bishop of Winchester. In other closings, letter writers summed up their situation: "Your poor friend, and Gods poor patient," was how John Donne closed one of his letters in the early 1600s! He closed a letter of 1607

Your address _____

_____

Date _____

(double space, or more)

Addressee _____
Title/position _____
Company _____
Address _____
_____
(double space)
Salutation _____,
(double space)

_____

_____

_____.

_____

_____

_____.

_____

_____.
(double space)

Sincerely yours,

(four spaces)

Name _____
Position _____

Figure 1

Date _____

Address _____
_____
_____
_____

Salutation _____,

_____
_____.

_____
_____
_____.

_____
_____
_____.

_____.

Sincerely yours,

Name _____
Position _____

Figure 2

with "Your Servant Extraordinary, And without Place." Today those kinds of phrases sound peculiar, so we choose a few simple words that best sum up the situation, our status, or our frame of mind.

Informal letters

There is no need to be so exacting about informal or handwritten letters. They still need to be readable, however, and to look inviting. In these days when practically everything we read is typewritten or typeset, not only have our handwriting skills deteriorated, but we are forgetting how to read handwriting! So your letters need to be clear and legible.

There are two important things to include when you write an informal letter or one by hand. The first is *the full date*: June 23, 1995, rather than just Friday, or even Friday, June 23. If your letter is important enough to write, and presumably to keep, the person on the other end will want to know in future years when exactly the letter was written. The second thing to include is *your full name* as well as *your address*. This last is especially necessary on Christmas letters (and cards). If someone knows several Julias, or perhaps hasn't heard from you in years, are they going to know which Julia you are if you don't include your last name? Or will they know how to get in touch with you if the letter has no return address and gets separated from the envelope?

If your letter runs to more than one page, be sure to number the pages so your correspondent can follow your train of thought.

FORMS OF ADDRESS

Whether you are writing to a public official, a government leader, or a member of the clergy, there is a way of addressing the person that is appropriate to his or her office. What follows is a list of such persons or offices, how they are to be addressed, and the correct salutation in a letter. For public officials, we have also included their office address. For clergy, even though the title may be given as The Reverend _____, the letter should begin "Dear Mr. _____" (or Dr. or Ms.). It is incorrect to begin even an informal letter with "Dear Rev. _____."

Person	*Letter Address*	*Letter Greeting*
President of the United States	The President The White House Washington, DC 20500	Dear Mr. President
former President	The Honorable James S. Smith Address	Dear Mr. Smith
Vice President	The Vice President Executive Office Building Washington, DC 20501	Dear Mr. Vice President
Cabinet members	The Honorable John (or Jane) Jones The Secretary of ____ or The Postmaster General or The Attorney General Address	Dear Mr. (or Madam) Secretary
Chief Justice	The Chief Justice The Supreme Court Washington, DC 20543	Dear Mr. Justice or Dear Mr. Chief Justice
Associate Justice	Mr. Justice Smith (or Madam Justice Smith) The Supreme Court Washington, DC 20543	Dear Mr. (or Madam) Justice
United States Senator	The Honorable John (or Jane) Jones United States Senate Washington, DC 20001	Dear Senator Jones

Person	Letter Address	Letter Greeting
Speaker of the House	The Honorable John (or Jane) Jones Speaker of the House of Representatives United States Capitol Washington, DC 20001	Dear Mr. (or Madam) Speaker
United States Representative	The Honorable John (or Jane) Jones United States House of Representatives Washington, DC 20001	Dear Mr. (or Mrs., Ms.) Jones
United Nations Representative	The Honorable John (or Jane) Jones U.S. Representative to the United Nations United Nations Plaza New York, NY 10017	Dear Mr. (or Madam) Ambassador
Ambassador	The Honorable John (or Jane) Jones Ambassador of the United States American Embassy Address	Dear Mr. (or Madam) Ambassador
Consul-General	The Honorable John (or Jane) Jones American Consul General Address	Dear Mr. (or Mrs., Ms.) Jones
Foreign Ambassador	His (or Her) Excellency Johan (or Jean) Jensen The Ambassador of ——————— Address	Excellency or Dear Mr. (or Madam) Ambassador

Person	Letter Address	Letter Greeting
Secretary-General of the United Nations	His (or Her) Excellency Ivan (or Ivina) Jones Secretary-General of the United Nations United Nations Plaza New York, NY 10017	Dear Mr. (or Madam) Secretary-General
Governor	The Honorable John (or Jane) Jones Governor of _____ State Capitol Address	Dear Governor Jones
State legislators	The Honorable John (or Jane) Jones Address	Dear Mr. (or Mrs., Ms.) Jones
Judges	The Honorable James S. Smith Justice, Appellate Division Supreme Court of the State of _____ Address	Dear Judge Smith
Mayor	The Honorable John (or Jane) Jones; His (or Her) Honor the Mayor City Hall Address	Dear Mayor Jones
The Pope	His Holiness, the Pope or His Holiness, Pope John XII Vatican City Rome, Italy	Your Holiness or Most Holy Father

Person	Letter Address	Letter Greeting
Cardinals	His Eminence, John Cardinal Jones, Archbishop of _____ Address	Your Eminence or Dear Cardinal Jones
Bishops	The Most Reverend John Jones, Bishop (or Archbishop) of _____ Address	Your Excellency or Dear Bishop (or Archbishop) Jones
Monsignor	The Right Reverend Monsignor Boling Address	Right Reverend Monsignor or Dear Monsignor Boling
Priest	The Reverend John Jones Address	Reverend Father or Dear Father Jones
Brother	Brother John or Brother John Jones Address	Dear Brother John or Dear Brother
Sister	Sister Mary Mark Address	Dear Sister Mary Mark or Dear Sister
Protestant Clergy	The Reverend John (or Jane) Jones*	Dear Dr. (or Mr., Ms.) Jones
Bishop (Episcopal)	The Right Reverend John Jones* Bishop of _____ Address	Dear Bishop Jones
Rabbi	Rabbi Nathan (or Naomi) Milstein* Address	Dear Rabbi (or Dr.) Milstein

* If the minister or rabbi holds a doctorate in divinity, one usually adds the abbreviation D.D. after his or her name in the address.

Person	Letter Address	Letter Greeting
King or Queen	His (Her) Majesty King (Queen) _____ Address (letters traditionally are sent to reigning monarchs not directly but via the private secretary)	

For commissioned officers in the United States armed services, the full rank is used as a title only in addressing letters and in formal introductions; one writes to Major General Ann Jones, U.S. Army, and introduces her as Major General Jones. In greetings the full rank is shortened to General: "Dear General Jones." Similar acceptable shortened greetings follow:

	Full Rank	Greeting
Army, Air Force, Marines	General of the Army	General
	Lieutenant General	General
	Brigadier General	General
	Lieutenant Colonel	Colonel
	First Lieutenant	Lieutenant
	Second Lieutenant	Lieutenant
Navy, Coast Guard	Fleet Admiral	Admiral
	Vice Admiral	Admiral
	Rear Admiral	Admiral
	Lieutenant Commander	Commander
	Lieutenant, Junior Grade	Lieutenant

For enlisted personnel, a similar principle applies. Sergeants—whether staff sergeants, gunnery sergeants, or first sergeants—are greeted simply as "Sergeant"; privates first class are referred to as "Private"; and, in the Navy and Coast Guard, chief petty officers are referred to as "Chief." Other noncommissioned officers are greeted by their ranks, although, informally, lower grades may be referred to generically as "Soldier" or "Sailor."

ENVELOPES

If an important letter has ever been delayed in reaching you due to an illegible or insufficient address, you already know the importance of envelopes that are neatly and accurately addressed. And anyone who has ever worked in a post office knows how much time (and therefore money) is spent trying to decipher illegible handwriting.

Today, if a machine can't read the address, the letter is automatically returned to the sender or sent to the dead letter office if the envelope has no return address.

The rules for addressing envelopes are simple, but it's easy to miss something.

1. Be sure you have the person's correct name and that you have it correctly spelled.

2. Be sure you have the right street name and number or the right post office box and/or route number. Sometimes the distinction between a street and an avenue is very important.

3. Be sure you have the right town and state. For the correct two-letter abbreviation for each state or U.S. dependency, which the post office asks us to use, see the next section.

4. Be sure you include the zip code. The post office will not deliver a letter without the zip code. The instructions on page 431 tell how to find the correct zip codes.

5. For letters going overseas, be sure you have included the country to which the letter is going, as well as the city and state or province. Many other countries also have zip codes, so make sure the address contains all the data needed for delivery.

6. Be sure to write your own name and address on the envelope—usually in the upper left-hand corner, or else on the back flap—and include your zip code, in case the letter has to be returned to you for some reason.

7. If you are using a manila envelope or one that is larger than the standard size, be sure to write "First Class Mail" on it, so it won't get put in with third and fourth class mail.

State abbreviations

Alabama	AL	Kentucky	KY	Oklahoma	OK
Alaska	AK	Louisiana	LA	Oregon	OR
Arizona	AZ	Maine	ME	Pennsylvania	PA
Arkansas	AR	Maryland	MD	Puerto Rico	PR
California	CA	Massachusetts	MA	Rhode Island	RI
Canal Zone	CZ	Michigan	MI	S. Carolina	SC
Colorado	CO	Minnesota	MN	S. Dakota	SD
Connecticut	CT	Mississippi	MS	Tennessee	TN
D. of Columbia	DC	Missouri	MO	Texas	TX
Delaware	DE	Montana	MT	Utah	UT
Florida	FL	N. Carolina	NC	Vermont	VT
Georgia	GA	N. Dakota	ND	Virgin Islands	VI
Guam	GU	Nebraska	NE	Virginia	VA
Hawaii	HI	Nevada	NV	Washington	WA
Idaho	ID	New Hampshire	NH	West Virginia	WV
Illinois	IL	New Mexico	NM	Wisconsin	WI
Indiana	IN	New Jersey	NJ	Wyoming	WY
Iowa	IA	New York	NY		
Kansas	KS	Ohio	OH		

Zip codes

In our computerized society, addresses need to include a zip code to guarantee delivery. You can buy a zip code directory from your local post office or you can look up zip codes in the directory at the post office. Larger post offices have a phone number you can call to get the correct zip code for a particular address. In addition, many libraries have a copy of the zip code directory on their reference shelves. One other place to look for local zip codes is in the phone book. In towns or cities with several zip codes, phone books often include a map showing the area covered by each zip code.

To All the Saints

Isabel Champ Wolseley

To all the saints in Christ Jesus . . . Grace be unto you, and peace, from God our Father, and from the Lord Jesus Christ.   — PHILIPPIANS 1:1–2 KJV

PERHAPS you have received letters from strangers beginning with "Dear Sister" or "Dear Brother" and signed "Your Christian Sister" (or "Brother")—terms that immediately acknowledge that you both belong to the family of God.

But if I were to be seriously addressed as "Saint Isabel," I would be dumbfounded.

I think of "Saint" as being reserved for such spiritual figures as Peter, Matthew, Mark, Luke, and John, whose exemplary lives seemingly have nothing to do with everyday people like me. Yet they were very human. And in biblical times, "saint" was simply another name for "believers." Ordinary people *just* like me.

So I will not only look up to the spiritual leaders around me with reverence; I will also take a long look at the vast community of Christian brothers and sisters who make up my family of everyday saints. And I'm going to give thanks for each of them this day.

Father, I'm going to treat my fellow believers with the respect they deserve—as saints. Thank you for placing each one of them in my life.

Postage

The post office won't deliver a letter or package without the correct postage. You can obtain from your local post office a pamphlet listing the current postage rates for all kinds of mail. If you need it, you can also get from them a booklet showing rates for various kinds of overseas letters, parcels, and packages. The post office also prints special commemorative stamps throughout the year. If you write regularly to someone overseas, it is particularly nice to use a different commemorative stamp on each letter, though be sure to add enough other stamps to make up the correct amount for postage to that country. The post office can give you a list of special stamps they expect to print each year.

Index

—A—

accepting resignation, 146
addressing
  envelopes, 416-17
  public officials, 410-15
adolescence, 104-5
advertising, fraudulent, 303-4, 321, 375
after Christmas letters, 40
aging, 63
airline services, 280-82
Allison, Myrel, devotional. 48-9
Allsop, Kenneth, 378
anger, 173-86
  dealing with, 165, 173-77, 180-81
  expressing in a letter, 174-75
  toward neighbors, 162-63
  See also complaints
announcements
  career change, 59
  divorce, 61
  engagement, 58-59
  new account representative, 59
  new baby, 59
  new business, 60
anonymous letters, 42-44
apartments, letters regarding, 334-37
apology, 152-53
  for behavior, 149-60
  for careless remark, 151-52
  for delayed answer, 156
  for delayed return of property, 154
  for delayed thanks, 152
  for indiscretion, 156
  for late report, 158
  to make amends, 154-55
  for missed appointment, 158
  overdue, 157
  for postponed dinner, 156

for project failure, 158-59
for schedule conflict, 155-56
why and how to, 149-50, 165
for wrong information, 159
See also forgiveness
applicant
  accepting, 396, 398
  rejecting, 397-98, 404
  verifying information, 396
appraisals, 361-62
appreciation, 65-78
  for advice, 70
  for anonymous kindness, 75-76
  to author, 76-77
  to church family, 71-72
  to coach, 248
  for companionship, 67
  for dinner invitation, 71
  for evening out, 74-75
  expressing, 73
  to faithful correspondent, 42
  to a family, 73-74
  for friendship, 67
  for gift, 68-69
  for going away party, 71
  how and why to express, 65-67
  for information, 70
  for job well done, 72
  for meeting attendance, 72-73
  to neighbors, 171-72
  for recognition, 71
  for recommendation, 70
  to scout leader, 250
  to sports coordinator, 248
  to spouse, 77-78
  to teacher, 94, 234, 245-46
  See also thank you letters
Aretino, Pietro, 25

Aristotle, 173, 313
Aurelius, Marcus, 314

—B—

baby
  announcement, 59
  birth defect, 145-46
  birth, recording, 98-101
  congratulations, 92-93
  dedication or baptism, 101-02
Bacon, Francis, 57, 205
Baldwin, James, 288
bank error, 348-49
Bauer, Fred, devotional, 275
Baumann, Ellyn, devotional, 180-81,
  240-41
Beecher, Henry Ward, 173, 271, 287, 377
Beerbohm, Max, 379
Better Business Bureau, 318-20
Bible, letters in, 45-46
billing error, 300-2, 326, 331, 348-49
bills, late payment, 289
  Medicare, dealing with, 349
  partial payment, 326
birth
  announcing, 59
  defect, 145-46
  recording, 98-101
birthday
  blessing, 100
  eightieth, 64
  letters for children, 102-5
Blake, William, 177
blessing, letters of, 95-116
  for baby's dedication, baptism, 101-2
  for birth and birthdays, 98-101, 102-5
  about death, 114-16
  for engagement, 106
  for entering adolescence, 104-5
  for high school graduation, 105-6
  for holidays, 108-9
  how to write, 95-98, 111-12
  for marriage, 106-8
  for parents, 109-12
  as spiritual testimony, 113-14
Boswell, James, 25
Bridgeman, Gina, devotional, 28, 107
builder, problems with, 337-38

business letters
  announce new business, 60
  appointment, clarify confusion, 312
  introduce new account representative, 59
  meeting memo, 125
  personnel matters, 396-403

—C—

cancellation
  credit card, 289
  travel, 282-83
car problems, 317-24
Carney, Mary Lou, devotional, 215
catching up, 27-29
chamber of commerce, 274-76
character references, 381-82
childcare
  requesting, 268-69
  See also school letters
children, 229-50
  birthday letters, 98-101
  commending honesty, 164-65
  how to write about, 229-31
  learning from, 247
  prejudice, and, 231-32
  scout letters, 249-50
  sports letters, 248-49
  See also school letters
Christmas letters, 36-41
  after Christmas letters, 40
  fresh ideas for, 36-37
  sample letters, 37, 41
church matters
  acknowledging good deeds, 189-90
  affirming pastor, 195-96, 198, 200-1
  disruptive children, 191
  expressing criticism, 187-89
  ineffective teacher, 198
  music, 192-93
  obtaining new pastor, 202-4
  seniors program, 194-95
  thank pastor's wife, 201
  thank youth pastor, 196
  thanks for help in illness, 71-72
  youth leadership, 196-97
  See also clergy
Churchill, Clemintine, 17

Churchill, Winston, 17
Clark, Mary Jane, devotional, 399
clergy, 187-204
  addressing, 190-91, 410-11, 413-14
  appreciation, 193, 195-96, 203
  compliments, 189-90, 195-96
  criticism, 187-89
  encouragement, 94, 189-90, 198
  invitation to speak, 197-98
  request for consultation, 202
  welcome new pastor, 204
  See also church matters
closing remarks, for letters, 407-9
college
  decline admission, 246
  request information, 246
Colton, Charles Caleb, 117
comfort, friends, 137
  See also death; supporting one
another; sympathy
complaints, 295-312
  advertising, 303-4, 321, 375
  car problems, 317-24
  carpet cleaning, 348
  church related, 187-89, 191-93, 198
  coach, 248-49
  competition, too much, 250
  delivery service, 178, 306, 308
  disruptive children, 166-68, 191, 235,
    237-39
  doctor's services, 328-29
  driver, 180-82
  handicapped parking, 186
  how to answer, 309-12
  how to express, 173-75, 295-97
  landscaping services, 347-48
  medical service, 326-27
  neighbor's eyesore, 169
  nurse, 327
  pets, 164
  post office, 175-76
  product packaging, 178
  repairman, 179
  restaurant, 182
  restrooms, 286
  salesperson, 184-85, 347
  services provided, 175-84
  taxes, 183

  teacher, 236-37
  tour, 183, 283-84
  umpire, 249
  zoning conflicts, 183-84
  See also consumer protection;
    criticism; E-mail
condolence, *See* sympathy
condominium living, 338-40
congratulations, 57-64
  baby, 92-93
  birthday, eightieth, 64
  engagement, 62
  graduation, 62, 105-6
  house, 92
  job, new, 92
  job well done, 93
  promotion, 395, 401
  retirement, 395, 403
  wedding, 62-64
Connolly, Cyril, 288
Connor, B. J., devotional, 139
consumer protection, 185-86, 285-86,
  332, 346
contractor problems, 337-38
controversial issues, addressing, 239
  See also criticism; complaints
cover letters, 382-86, 389-90
credit card, cancel, 289
credit matters, 287-94
  dealing with debt, 287-92
  letters regarding, 289, 292-94
criticism, 188-89
  sample letters, 175-86
  See also anger; complaints

—D—

day care, *See* school letters
death
  of beloved, 138
  of business associate, 134
  of child, 114-16, 133, 135-38
  of neighbor, 134
  of relative, 133
  of soldier, 135
  of spouse, 38, 133
  by suicide, 136
  See also sympathy; grief
debt, dealing with, 287-89

See also credit matters
declining an invitation, 125-28
delivery problems, 178, 306, 308
depression, 53-54
Dickinson, Emily, 15, 132, 175
difficult topics, bringing up, 32
disappointment, 32
dissatisfied customer, 310-12
  answering complaints, 310
divorce
  announcing, 61
  offering support, 142-43
doctor, 325-28
donations, 205-28
  alternatives to, 209
  decline request for, 209-10
  how to request, 205-8
  letters to accompany, 208-9
  thank you for, 69
  See also fundraising
Donne, John, 407
Dostoevsky, Fyodor, 16, 377
Dunne, Peter Finley, 315

—E—

E-mail, 18-20
  and letters of complaint, 18-19
  and fundraising requests, 18-19
Emerson, Ralph Waldo, 117, 295, 315, 377
employers, letters by, 396-403
employment
  applying for, 382-95
  letters of, 377-404
encouragement, letters of, 85-94
  academic challenges, 91
  accepting limitations, 32
  anonymous, 42-44
  baby, caring for new, 92
  bedridden, 88-89
  difficult times, 88
  emotional support, 88
  to friend, 137, 139, 141
  homesickness, 34-35
  how to write, 85-87
  injustice, 89
  job loss, 56
  job, new, 92

job stress, 34
job well done, 93
parent to child, 32, 34
pastor, 94
prayer letters, 43
teacher, 94
through thankfulness, 51
trust God's love and strength, 32
when God seems distant, 90
when relationship ends, 91
engagement
  announcement, 58-59
  letter of blessing, 106
envelopes, addressing, 416-17
error
  bank, 348
  billing, 300-2, 326, 331
  charge account, 349
  responding to, 302

—F—

fear, 56
Field, Faye, devotional, 100, 157
Fielding, Henry, 187
financial distress, 143-44
  See also debt, dealing with; credit matters
First Amendment, 352
forgiveness, 152-53, 156, 233, 240-41
  See also apology
format, formal letters, 408-9
France, Anatole, 79
friends
  encouraging, 137, 139, 141
  making, 123
  missing, 27
friendship
  in loneliness, 54-55
  thanks for, 67
fundraising, 205-28
  bequests, 227
  churches, 213-20
  library, 210-13, 221-22
  museum project, 227
  sample letters, 205-8
  schools, 220-26
  See also donations; E-mail

—G—

get well, 35-36, 144-45
getting back in touch, 27-29
Gide, André, 57
gift, unacknowledged, 78
giving, 206, 211, 215, 219
God, letters to, 45-56
  on depression, 53-54
  on fear, 56
  on gratitude, 47, 51
  on job loss, 56
  on loneliness, 54-55
  on pain, 51
  on praise, 48
  on repentance, 49
  on sorrow, 50-52
  why and how to write, 45-47
goodness, 314-15
Gordon, Arthur, devotional, 211
Gorky, Maxim, 315
government officials
  how to address, 410-15
  sample letters to, 183, 354-56, 358-61
Gracin, Baltasar, 65
graduation wishes
  announcement, 62
  high school, 105-6
gratitude, 47, 51
  See also appreciation; thank you
  letters
grief, 114-16, 129-32, 136

—H—

Hamlin, Rick, devotional, 33, 137
handicapped parking, 186
Hardiman, Bill, 351
Harter, Walter, 311
health, uncertain, 56
Helleberg, Marilyn Morgan, devotional,
  43, 63, 383
help
  asking for, 251-54, 261
  closing remarks, 270
  hurting friend, 137, 139, 141
high school reunion, 29
Hobe, Phyllis, devotional, 305
Holmes, Marjorie, devotional, 38, 167,
  199, 203

home ownership
  appraisals, 361-62
  building problems, 337-38
  declining to buy, 70
homesickness, 34-35
Horace, 161
hospital
  compliments and complaints, 327-29
hospitality, practicing, 120-21
hospitalized, 144-45
House committee, 354-55
house sitting, requesting, 170, 269-70
housing
  apartment concerns, 334-37
  condominium concerns, 338-40
  request repairs, 335-36
  request for sublet, 336-37
  See also home ownership
Hurst, Gerald, 287

—I—

information
  requesting, 254-55
  responding to request for, 255-58, 292
  wrong, 159
inquiries
  gift, unacknowledged, 78
  insurance information, 285
  vacation information, 273-86
  See also requests
insurance matters
  agent, changing, 342-43
  auto, 340-45
  beneficiary, changing, 342
  life, 342
  medical, 324-25
  settlements, 343-45
  travel, 285
interview
  accepting, 386-88
  follow up, 388, 391
  invitation to, 397
  refer someone for, 268
  requesting, 264
invitations, 117-28
  to bed & breakfast, 273
  to class reunion, 29-30, 124
  to church dinner, 122

declining, 125, 155-56
to dinner, boss, 124
to dinner, employees, 122-24
to dinner, friend, 119
to give invocation, 197
how to do it, 117-19
to join club, 121
to speak, 120
to visit, 30-31
See also refusal
Isenhower, Lisa, devotional, 151, 165

—J—

Jenks, William, devotional, 88-89
job
  accepting offer, 388
  follow up letters, 390-91
  loss, 56
  networking, 392-94
  performance review, 400
  pressures, 34
  referring a relative for, 268
  rejecting offer, 389
Johnson, Samuel, 85
jury duty, request to postpone, 363
justice, 313-16
Justice, Sam, devotional, 40

—K—

Kania, Kathie, devotional, 279, 319
keep in touch, 25-44
  with children, 32, 34
  with friends, 27-31
  haven't written, 27-29
  how to, 25-27
  with pen pal, 41-42
  with spouse, 33, 35
  See also Christmas letters
keepsakes, letters as, 95-98
Kennedy, John F., 45
Key, Ellen, 229
kindness, 65, 75, 153, 233
King, Jr., Martin Luther, 351
Knapp, Caroline, devotional, 52-55,
  60-61
Kuykendall, Carol, devotional, 110

—L—

La Fontaine, Jean de, 253
Labiche, Eugene, 251
Lawrence, D. H., 295
lease agreement
  request to sublet, 336-37
legal action
  letters stating intent of, 331-32, 344
letter writing
  basics of, 405-19
  enjoying, 26
letters
  closing remarks, 407-9
  formal, 405-6
  informal, 410
  as keepsakes, 95-98
  punctuation of, 407
  why write, 15-20
Lincoln, Abraham, 135
Lindstrom, Aletha Jane, devotional, 233
loan
  turned down, 289
  See also credit matters; debt, dealing
    with
loneliness, 54-55, 67
Lorenz, Patricia, devotional, 293
loss, catastrophic, 144
lost items
  at hotel, 280
  luggage, 280-81
  by movers, 330
love letters
  See spouse
Lukes, Bonnie, devotional, 154-55

—M—

marriage
  broken, 61, 143
  enhancing with love notes, 30-31
  name change notification, 341
  offering support, 143
  separation, 143
  See also spouse
media, letters to, 370-75
medical concerns
  sample letters, 324-29
Medicare, coverage inquiries, 349
memo, business meeting, 125
missing you, 27

money managing, 290
  See also credit matters; debt, dealing
  with
Mooneyham, Stan, 18
Moore, Thomas, 15, 16, 17, 81
moving, letters regarding, 329-34,
  342-43

—N—

neighbors, dealing with, 161-72
  blowing leaves, 171
  children, 164-68
  eyesores, 169
  fence repairs, 170-71
  house sitting, request, 170, 269-70
  how and why to write, 161-63
  neighborhood watch, 169
  parking problems, 304
  pets, 163-64, 170
Neukrug, Linda, devotional, 123, 301
newspaper
  delivery problems, 306
  requesting consumer help, 346
  sample letters to, 370-75

—P—

parents, blessing, 109-12
pastor, *See* church matters; clergy
Paul, the Apostle, 256-57
Peale, Norman Vincent, 45,
  devotional, 68-69
Peale, Ruth Stafford, devotional, 153
pen pal, 41-42
performance review, 400
permission to reprint, request, 263-64
pets, 163-64, 170, 269
Plutarch, 271
police
  compliments and complaints, 366-70
  reporting tips, 369
post office, complaint, 175-77
postage, 419
praise, 48, 165
prayer letters, 48-49, 54-55
prayer life, enriching, 45-47
prayers, written, 35-56
praying for you
  birth defect, 145-46

catastrophe, 144
discouragement, 32
financial distress, 143-44
homesickness, 34
illness, 36
job and family pressures, 34
marital discord, 143
mourning, 133, 135, 138
out of touch, 29
spouse, 35
sudden resignation, 146
unnamed tragedy, 146
price error, 185
pride, 251-52, 261
promotion, 395, 401
Proverbs, Danish and Moorish, 229
public officials, *See* government
  officials
public safety, 308-9, 358, 363-66
punctuation in letters, 407

—R—

radio station, sample letters, 370-75
real estate agent, 332-33, 342-43
rebate problems, 185, 346
recommendations, 379-81, 404
records, request transfer
  insurance, 342-43
  school, 334
referral, 268
refunds
  airline, 281-83
  hotel, 282
  layaway deposit, 345
  product, 185, 345-47
refusal
  to join club, 128
  to lead seminar, 127-28
  schedule conflict, 155-56
  See also apology
relationship, broken, 91
repairs, unsatisfactory, 179
repentance, 49-50
  See also forgiveness
reprimand employee, 402
reprint permission, 263-64
requests, 251-70
  for childcare, 268-69

closing remarks for, 270
for donations, 205-8
for forgiveness, 152-53
how and why to make, 251-54
for pet care, 170, 269
responses to, 255-58, 267
sample letters, 254-70
for time together, 30-31
See also inquiries
resignation, 146-47, 389, 403
retirement
  congratulations, 395, 403
  notify social security, 362
reunion
  college, 124-25
  high school, 29-30
Roberts, Faye, devotional, 290

—S—

salutations, 407
Santayana, George, 129
Schad, Vicki, devotional, 261
Schantz, Daniel, devotional, 126-27,
  176-77, 357, 393
Schantz, Teresa, devotional, 82
school letters, 231-50
  absences, 244-45
  abusive treatment of children, 239
  addressing controversial issues, 239
  athletics, 248-49
  building, request improvements, 242
  classroom, request use of, 243
  college, 246
  crossing guard, 364-66
  daycare, 231-32, 244
  disruptive behavior, 235, 237-39
  equipment, request improvements,
    243
  field trip suggestions, 238
  new club suggestions, 235
  notify bus driver of change, 243-44
  policy changes, request, 242
  preschool, 231-32, 244
  records transfer, request, 334
  teacher, appreciation, 234, 245-46
  teacher/parent relationship, 232, 234,
    237
  textbooks, concerns about, 239-41

  values, concerns about, 239-41, 248-50
  writing about children, 229-31
Schwab, Penney, devotional, 219, 387
secret pal, 42-43
self-acceptance, 52-53
Sledge, Linda Ching, devotional, 81,
  141, 277
social security, notice of retirement,
  362
Sortor, Toni, devotional, 21
spiritual testimonies, 112-16
spouse
  appreciation of, 77-78
  death of, 133
  love letters to, 30-31, 35
stamps, commemorative, 419
state abbreviations, 417
state regulatory agency, 332
Steele, Richard, 251
styles, for letters, 405-10
supporting one another,
  anonymously, 42-44
  by bearing burdens, 139
  in disappointments, 141
  in loss, 129-32, 142-44
  with prayer letters, 54-55
  in tragedy, 144, 146
surgery, 144-45
sympathy, 129-47
  belated, 138
  expressing thanks for, 67, 140-42
  from business firm, 136
  sentences expressing grief, 138-40
  See also death; grief

—T—

taxes, protesting, 183
television station
  sample comments to, 370-75
terminate employee, 402
thank you letters, 65-78
  for advice, 70
  for anonymous kindness, 75
  for attending meeting, 72
  to author, 76-77
  belated, 152
  birthday gift, 68
  for companionship, 67

for dinner invitation, 71
for evening out, 74-75
to a family, 73-74
for financial support, 69
for friendship, 67
to God, 51
for going away party, 71
for help during illness, 71-72, 172
for help getting job, 395
for help with new baby, 172
how to write, 65-67
for information received, 70
for interview, 388, 391
for job well done, 72
for medical help, 327-28
for paramedics, 366-67
to real estate agent, 333
for recognition, 71
for recommendation, 70, 388
for referral, 72
to surgeon, 327-28
for sympathy, 140-42
to vacation resort, 278
See also appreciation
Thatcher, Margaret, 205
Thurber, James, 17
tithe, 202, 206, 211, 215, 293
tourist information
sample letters, 273-86
tragedy, 144, 146
travel
insurance, 285
See also airline services; tourist
information

—U—
utility rates, protesting, 348

—V—
vacation, 271-86
letters about trips, 273-86
planning, 271-72
vandalism, neighborhood prevention,
169-70
veterans administration, 360-63, 447
Voltaire, 378

—W—
Walton, Isaak, 407
weakness, 32, 36, 48-49
Weary, Dolphus, devotional, 247, 307
Webster, Daniel, 351
wedding
congratulations, 62-63
parental advice, 106-8
welcome, letters of, 79-84
to church visitors, 82-84
to new member, 84
to new resident, 80
West, Marion Bond, devotional, 30-31,
120-1, 176
Wheeler, Bonnie, devotional, 51
Williams, Susan, devotional, 364-65
Wolseley, Isabel Champ, devotional,
432
work, *See* employment

—Z—
zip codes, obtaining, 417